MALTA

A Childhood Under Siege

Linda Peek

Woodlands
PUBLISHING

First published in Australia in 2023.

By Woodlands Publishing
woodlandspublishing.au

© Linda Peek 2023

The right of Linda Peek to be identified as the author of this book has been asserted by her in accordance with the Copyright Amendment (Moral Rights) Act 2000.

A catalogue record for this book is available from The National Library of Australia.

ISBN paperback: 978-0-6458761-0-9
ISBN e-book: 978-0-6458761-1-6
ISBN audiobook: 978-0-6458761-1-6

Cover designed by James Peek, Margaret's grandson, shows the Staples family on the steps of their house "Carmen" in Dragonara on 24 January 1939, the day they arrived in Malta. Back row: Hilda Mary, Margaret, Sam. Front row: Ed, the twins, Joan & Daphne, Pat.

Margaret (in red in the middle) and her two brothers are all wearing roller skates which they received a month earlier for Christmas, but had not been allowed to wear on board the ship sailing to Malta.

The black and white photos in the book are the property of Linda Peek or have been reproduced with the permission of David Clarke or The Boy Scouts Association of Malta.

Design: Urška Charney

To my mother Margaret.
This is the book she wanted to write.

TABLE OF CONTENTS

Map of the Mediterranean showing the location of Malta

1   Fort St Elmo
2   Maison Notre Dame
3   St John's Co-Cathedral
4   Lascaris War Rooms
5   St Georges
6   Grandmasters Palace
7   Manoel Theatre
8   St Andrews
9   Sa Maison Gardens
10 Auberge de Castille
11 Is-Suq tal-Belt (Valletta food market)
12 Royal Opera House
    (demolished during the war; now an open-air theatre)
13 Chiswick House, Windsor Terrace Sliema (now a hotel)
14 Scouts' HQ
15 Verdala Palace
16 The Salina Salt Pans

Close up map of Valletta and Floriana where the story takes place

NOTE FROM THE AUTHOR

We grew up listening to my mother Margaret's stories about Malta, where she lived during the Second World War.

My grandfather was posted to this British colony with the Royal Engineers, accompanied by my grandmother and their five children, aged between seven and eleven.

Margaret was the middle child and just nine years old when they arrived in Malta at the beginning of 1939. With its Mediterranean climate and friendly people, at first it seemed like heaven on Earth. But then the Second World War started and everything changed. Margaret was a young woman of 15 when the family sailed back home to England six years later. She was lucky to have survived and very nearly didn't.

After my mother died in 2018, a month short of her 89th birthday, I helped my sister to sort the photographs and personal papers in her house. We found lots of half-written stories about Malta, some repeated several times, most unfinished.

There was also a note which said:

Malta—The Island that Wouldn't Die
An Eyewitness Account
By Margaret Staples Hutchinson

I would like to dedicate this story to my daughter, Linda Peek, without whose encouragement I would not have completed it.

She obviously intended to write a book, but far from completing it, she never started it.

A few years earlier, when she first mentioned writing a book about her experiences in Malta, my mother sent me a couple of cassette tapes. I had every intention of transcribing them, but never got around to it.

The experience of living in a war zone had a huge impact on her. Clearly, she wanted her story to be told and she wanted my help.

I have used my mother Margaret's voice and set her stories into the realities of war-torn Malta. Most of these stories are in my head and I can still hear my mother telling them.

I have tried to keep things in chronological order, as far as possible, and to get the facts right, but this is not a traditional history book. For a detailed history of the Second World War in Malta I suggest you read *Fortress Malta* by James Holland.

My grandfather kept a diary, which has helped me to fill in many of the details, especially about his life before Malta. This has been augmented with chapters and sections that explore the history, culture, military and other contexts of the story, providing a macro- and microscopic view of this remarkable, tragic and ultimately heroic time in the life of this island nation.

Between them the Staples Five produced 11 offspring—Pat had two, Daphne had six and Margaret had three. Ed and Joan never married. Pat's son Shaun is the only one with the Staples surname amongst the 11 first cousins. There are 20 years between the eldest (me) and the youngest. But we remain a close-knit family. Despite living on three different continents, we are in regular contact.

We have all inherited the Staples love of singing, dancing, telling stories, laughing—especially at anything ridiculous—and globe-trotting. We have all received a good education and we are all financially secure. We have a lot to be thankful for.

If you have never been to Malta, I hope this book encourages you to do so. It's a gem.

Linda Peek
Canberra 2023

PART 1

BEFORE MALTA

MY FATHER

Maybe he wasn't quite as tall and handsome as I thought he was, but when my father walked into a room in his uniform people took notice.

I adored him and, until I married, he was the love of my life—and he loved me too. Of course, I wasn't the only one he loved—he also loved my mother and my four siblings. But I always felt we had a special bond.

Knowing how much my father loved us, it's hard to comprehend how, when I was 12 years old, and we were living in Malta, he had a plan to kill the whole family.

THE GUN

My parents were whispering again and glancing over their shoulders to see if any of us were within earshot. Children have ways of encroaching on whispers, and we were constantly trying to hear what they were saying.

We caught only bits here and there, but we knew something was wrong. Stressed, short-tempered and irritable, our parents were not their normal selves.

We may have been short of food, but my father was always able to get cigarettes from the NAAFI shop. He smoked his whole life, but the frequency and intensity with which he smoked indicated his mood.

He was chain-smoking.

There was an invisible atmosphere of fear in the house, like we were waiting for something unpleasant to happen.

The weather didn't help. The summer of 1942 was stinking hot. Day after day, from a cloudless azure sky, the sun came blazing down. At the beginning of August, the hot Sirocco winds started blowing sand over the island from North Africa. There was dust and sand everywhere—in your hair, in your eyes and in your food. It made us all grumpy.

It was customary in that era to believe that, by keeping children in the dark, they were protected.

This much we knew from what we overheard: Hitler wouldn't give up on his goal of taking Malta or wiping it off the map. The island's dependence on getting food and other supplies sent in by sea was our weak point. If we had been more self-sufficient, things would have been different. Hitler was trying to starve us into submission.

My parents didn't whisper so quietly in front of my brother Pat. He was 15 and nearly a man. They told him things they didn't tell us. Pat didn't pass everything on to us, but he became the link between the adults and the children. One day he told us that there was a target date of 31 August, beyond which we could no longer survive and would have to surrender. He said that an invasion or surrender were both distinct possibilities. I was too young to understand the implications.

My father said that my brothers needed to learn how to shoot a gun. It seemed like something all boys should do, particularly in a military family, so I didn't give it much thought. Dad arranged for Pat and Ed to have lessons twice a week at a firing range at St George's Barracks, using service rifles. Ed's shoulder was bruised black and blue from the practice lessons, until he learnt how to handle the recoil.

One morning I was helping Carrie to change the sheets on our beds when she asked me to go and get clean ones from the linen cupboard. I had to use a stepladder to reach the top shelf and even then, I stood on tiptoes. As I reached in for some pillowcases, I felt something cold and hard.

It was a gun.

As I took it out, I was surprised how much heavier it was than I'd imagined a gun would be. I was fascinated and turned it over in my hands, feeling the textured grip on the handle. I didn't know it at the time, but it was my father's service revolver—an Enfield No 2 Mk 1.

I looked down the barrel but couldn't see a bullet. I supposed it was empty. I carefully put it back under the pillowcases.

Pat came home from school, and I waited until we were alone.

"I found a gun," I said, somewhat proudly, uncertain as to whether or not he would be cross and want to tell on me.

"Where?"

"In the top of the linen cupboard, under the pillowcases," I replied. "I was helping Carrie change the sheets."

I thought he'd be intrigued and want to see it for himself, that we'd be co-conspirators, in on a big secret. Not so.

"I know all about it," said Pat, trying to act nonchalant.

"Why didn't you tell me about it?" I asked.

"Not allowed. Can't say any more," he replied.

This was not the co-conspiracy I had expected. Pat was clearly leaving me out of something, and I didn't like it.

"What's it for?" I insisted. "What's it doing in the linen cupboard?"

"Never you mind," said Pat. "Don't touch it. It's loaded."

Loaded? I hadn't seen a bullet, but I had looked straight down the barrel. Thinking that it might have gone off made my legs go to jelly.

"Tell me. I want to know," I said.

Pat sighed, looked around to make sure we were alone.

"If there's an invasion, or we have to surrender, Dad's going to use it to shoot us all."

The blood ran down to my toes, draining me pale.

"If he's not here," Pat continued, "Mum has to do it. And if neither of them is here, it's my job."

Mum and Dad were going to kill us? I had so many questions, but they stuck in my throat. I was mute.

"Dad says the alternative doesn't bear thinking about," Pat went on, doing his best to sound like a grownup. "He doesn't want us to be captured by the enemy. Terrible things happen, especially to girls."

I was horrified. I couldn't conceive of anything more terrible than a family deciding to kill each other.

SAM FROM BRIGG

Before we reach that desperate time, I will go back and follow the path of my father, Herbert William Staples, as he made his way from a small town in the north of England to the island of Malta, where he played an important role as an officer of the British Royal Engineers during the Second World War.

My father, for some reason known as Sam, was born on 29 November 1900 at 11 Warneford Terrace, off Stanley Street, a poor area of Hull in the north-east of England. He never talked about his early life, because he was illegitimate, which was a big deal back then.

The back of Warneford Terrace in Hull, where Sam was born, now demolished.

Sam's mother, Annie Lizzie Staples, worked as a domestic servant. When she turned 22, she had two little boys, but no husband. Both sons took her surname. If Annie Lizzie ever told Sam who his biological father was, he kept it to himself. When writing in his diary, he glossed over the subject of his paternity:

My father died while I was in my mother's womb and so, after a week or so of life, I was taken to my grandfather's house in South Killingholme and remained there for a time.[1]

After Sam was born, Annie Lizzie went to work at number 16 Engine Street in Glanford Brigg, now known as Brigg. She was employed as a housekeeper for a widower, William Kennington, who was 14 years her senior. William's wife had died in childbirth, leaving him with four small children. He worked at the Yarborough oil mill in Brigg where, amongst other things, they made linseeds into cow cake for feeding the cattle in winter.

In 1904, Annie Lizzie married William and brought four-year-old Sam to live in the Kennington household. Her other son, John, who was three years older than Sam, stayed in South Killingholme to be raised by her parents.

Brigg is a market town in North Lincolnshire on the river Ancholme, about 140 miles north of London. It started out as a small fishing hamlet—prehistoric dugout boats have been found in the town dating to around 900 BC. But when Sam was growing up it was a thriving town, with a population of just over 3,000 and well-paved streets lit with gas.

Annie Lizzie and William had six children. William was a kind man, and it wasn't until Sam was eight years old that he realised that he wasn't his biological father. William never treated him any differently from the other children living under his roof.

Three months before his fifth birthday, in 1905, Sam started at the Church of England public boys' school on Albert Street, a short walk from home. That same year, the political party Sinn Fein was formed to campaign for the independence of Ireland, and Emmeline Pankhurst led the first public protest by suffragettes at Westminster.

Every Sunday morning the Kennington family went by horse and buggy to the Primitive Methodist Chapel, followed by Sunday school for the children in the afternoon. Sam also attended evening classes once a week held by the Salvation Army. Reflecting on his childhood some years later, Sam wrote:

The church seemed to have a stranglehold on everyone, so much so that in a town of 3,000 inhabitants there were seven places of worship:

The Church of England Church
The Immaculate Heart of Mary Roman Catholic Church
The Primitive Methodist Chapel
The Wesleyan Chapel
The Congregational Chapel
The Methodist Free Chapel
The Salvation Army

Sam became an avid reader, devouring everything that came within his grasp, including all the newspapers: he was one of the top students in his class. Sam loved watching football, although he didn't like to play. He developed an encyclopaedic knowledge of the rules of the game, which earned him the nickname "Fesh," short for Professional, from his Kennington siblings and friends.

He saw his first motion picture when he was about six, in a marquee at the Brigg Fair. By the time he was nine, a cinema had opened in Brigg. It screened a Saturday afternoon show for children and a show for adults on Saturday and Wednesday evenings. Sam saw all the early Charlie Chaplin films and loved them. They were silent, with the occasional accompaniment of a piano to add to the atmosphere.

Teeth were only cleaned on high days and holidays and many people didn't bother at all. As a small boy, Sam had an excruciating toothache and, after crying for hours, was taken to Dr Goodman—a medical doctor, because there were no dentists in Brigg. As Sam wrote:

> He took out a pair of pliers, gave my back teeth a hard tap and said, "Is that the one?"
> I said, "Yes!"
> With a yank that seemed to pull my jaw off he took it out.
> I said, "You've got the wrong one!" so he took the next tooth out, too.

Guy Fawkes Day, or Bonfire Night, celebrated on the fifth of November, was a great occasion in Brigg. Sam learnt the danger of explosives when one of his friends had his hand blown off while messing around with fireworks.

But corporal punishment wasn't just self-inflicted. It was the norm back then, both at school and at home:

My mother bought me a lovely brown suit, which I wore the following Sunday to church. Afterwards, I went with several other boys down Mill Lane, not far from where we lived. There was a small stream infested with frogs, known as Denton's Ditch. I was pretty agile and had jumped it cleanly on many occasions. Showing off to my pals, I took a flying leap, landed in a hole on the other side and fell back into a mass of reddish-brown mud which smelled awful. I hurried home and can still see the look on my mother's face. She got out the hairbrush and I got well and truly thrashed—so much so that I have never forgotten it.

In 1910, nine years after the death of Queen Victoria, her son and successor Edward VII died of pneumonia. Mr William Pawley, Headmaster of Sam's school, made the announcement, got them all to sing "God Save the King," then gave the 180 students the rest of the day off. It was the year that Sam turned 10.

The same year there was a terrible fire at the Yarborough oil mill where William worked. It was the first great fire attended by the Scunthorpe Fire Brigade, who fought the blaze from early Saturday morning until the arrival of the Grimsby Brigade on Monday morning. The factory was completely destroyed but was rebuilt in 1912.

The following year, on 22 June 1911, the people of Brigg celebrated the Coronation of King George V with parties in the streets. Buildings in Brigg were lit specially with electric lights and coloured lamps. Having only known gas lighting until then, this was quite an event for the people. The Lincolnshire Show was held in Brigg over three days in July that year. This celebration of the arts, crafts, industry, food and traditions of Lincolnshire began in 1885 and has been held annually ever since. That year, special excursion trains brought spectators from as far away as Rotherham, Sheffield and Worksop. This would have been a great highlight of the year.

In his teens, Sam joined the Wesleyan Methodist Band of Hope Temperance Society, a meeting place for young people which was held each Thursday in Brigg. Founded in 1885, its goal was to teach children the dangers of alcohol and the importance of leading a teetotal life. It encouraged young people to sign a pledge to abstain. Periodically concerts were held, and Sam participated in them: it was the start of a lifelong love of music. Abstinence was another matter, though: he refrained from signing the pledge.

The winters in the north of England at that time were severe. The children made slides on the ice-covered streets and had great fun flying along. Older people, fearing they might slip, often carried a handful of salt with them. When this was sprinkled on one of the slides, the ice melted, and the children had to find another spot. The older people did this in the name of safety, but there may have been some curmudgeonly fun-spoiling involved.

During Sam's early years many momentous events occurred, and inventions were realised. He listed some of them in his diary:

- The Wright Brothers got the first aeroplane in the air
- Guglielmo Marconi's wireless radio spread through the world
- The telephone was perfected
- Moving pictures were invented
- The automobile became part of our lives

With so many mouths to feed, money was tight in the Kennington household. When Sam turned 13, he left school and got a job in Mr Edwin Bell's grocery shop. He had been working there after school and on weekends for the past year. It was hard work, lugging baskets of groceries and pushing heavy hand carts. He earned two shillings and sixpence per week.

Mr William Bramley, master painter and decorator, was a neighbour and friend who lived nearby at Westfield House. He was about 55 at the time and had a significant influence on Sam's life. Knowing that Sam was a top student, he offered to pay for him to attend Brigg Grammar School, a private school for boys, where he had sent his own son. Alas, Sam's parents were too proud to accept.

Sam had been working at Bell's grocery shop for about a year when Mr Bramley spoke to his parents again. He suggested that an apprenticeship in his successful house decorating and signage business would serve Sam much better than his working in a grocery shop. To this they agreed.

Sam was glad to get away from the grocer's shop and never looked back. He loved the work, particularly the higher forms of decorating, such as lettering, gilding, marbling and graining. He also enjoyed Mr Bramley's company as he was a well-educated man. On the way to visit a carpenter or joiner—anywhere up to 15 miles from Brigg—he would chat to Sam about all kinds of topics, as they went down the country lanes in the pony and trap.

William invited Sam to use his extensive library at Westfield House. It had a huge collection of children's books and in due course Sam had read them all. He then moved on to history and other subjects of interest. Before long, Sam was earning more than £5 a week and wrote in his diary:

> I was fiercely interested in the work and will say that, in my opinion, the training I received in this job was largely responsible for my future success. I learned and learned and worked each evening to perfect myself.

At about that time, Sam became addicted to dancing and spent many evenings at dances held in the Brigg Town Hall. He also had singing lessons with Mr Charles William Cray, a reputable local teacher who played the organ at the Methodist Church. Sam walked to his home, Point House, which was on Albert Street.

In 1914, the First World War started. Posters of moustachioed Lord Kitchener, British Secretary of State for War, pointing a finger, with the caption "Britain Needs You," were prominently displayed at the Town Hall and elsewhere.

Two of Sam's half-brothers, John and William Wallace Kennington (always known as Wallace, because his father was William) were amongst the many young men who volunteered from Brigg. As they marched to the railway station, crowds of people, including 14-year-old Sam, lined the streets. Everyone cheered and waved as their fathers, sons and brothers headed off to the Western Front in France, though the enthusiasm of the moment eclipsed the knowledge that many would never return. It was a moment of optimism and nationalist solidarity. No one could imagine that this war would slog on for four long, bloody years and would claim so many lives.

At the start of the War, British author H G Wells first coined the term "The war that will end war." He believed that, by crushing the militarism of Germany under the Kaiser and its allies, the Austro-Hungarian and Ottoman empires, the conflict would create a new world order that would make future conflict impossible. He was often quoted.

Two years later, in March 1916, conscription started. All single men between the ages of 18 and 41 were liable to be called up, unless they were widowed with children or were ministers of religion.

With most Brigg breadwinners off fighting the enemy, many families struggled. Some ended up in the Workhouse—a place for the completely destitute. Workhouses were not abolished in England until 1930. A soup kitchen opened in the Town Hall. The soup was provided by Brigg Urban District Council at cost price and served by volunteers. People of all classes queued up to take pint-sized servings home to their families.[2]

Every week John and Wallace sent letters home to their parents. Annie Lizzie would read them out over breakfast. Sometimes they went for weeks without hearing anything, then 10 letters would arrive, all at once. They were heavily censored, due to concerns that valuable information might fall into enemy hands if the soldiers were captured. There were often large pieces that had been crossed out. Sometimes whole pages were missing, or half a page had been torn off.

Just after Christmas, Wallace wrote saying how much he had enjoyed receiving a Christmas pudding, especially when he learned that it had come from his hometown. Spring's Jam Factory in Brigg had sent Christmas puddings to all the servicemen fighting abroad, to cheer them up.[3]

John and Wallace made their letters as cheerful as possible. They didn't want to upset their mother. They didn't talk about the grim realities of living for months on end in narrow, rat-infested, muddy trenches, with constant heavy gunfire from the nearby German trenches. It was some years before they opened up to Sam about their experiences. The things they had done and seen could not be forgotten and would stay with them forever. They had lived in appalling conditions, including overflowing toilets and trench foot—where a soldier's feet started to rot because of being constantly wet. Outbreaks of typhus, malaria, typhoid, diarrhoea, yellow fever, pneumonia and influenza were common.

Tobacco and alcohol were their only pleasures. Pipe smoking was the most common form of smoking, with soldiers receiving packets of loose tobacco and matches as part of their rations. As the war continued, cigarette smoking increased in popularity. The muddy trench conditions in northern France made it difficult to keep loose tobacco dry.[4]

In 1916, a Royal Air Force airfield was established at Elsham Wolds, four miles north-east of Brigg. It was part of Britain's Home Defence, to combat German Zeppelin bombers' night raids. One of the many pilots stationed at Elsham during its operations was Lieutenant Leefe Robinson. He was awarded the Victoria Cross as the first pilot to shoot down a Zeppelin. When he visited the marketplace in Brigg, the Kenningtons were all there, cheering and clapping. Sergeant Frederick Hobson, a native of Brigg, was also awarded the Victoria Cross for gallantry. Brigg was very proud of its war heroes.

Many in Britain had thought that the war would be a short one, with the Allies quickly triumphing over Germany. They were wrong.

Sam turned 18 in November 1918, the month the war at last ended, after four long years.

More than three quarters of a million servicemen from Britain and the colonies had lost their lives in the conflict. It was a stroke of great fortune that Sam's two half-brothers both survived so devastating an era. Their survival likely helped fuel Sam's enthusiasm for becoming a soldier himself.

Peace celebrations were held in Brigg, including a lunch for local heroes who had survived the war, held at the smart Angel Hotel. John and Wallace Kennington both attended the event. A few months later, the whole family attended the unveiling of a war memorial which listed the names of 105 young men from Brigg who had lost their lives.[5]

But war was only one of the mortal dangers of the time. Many of the brave soldiers who had survived the war were struck down by the Spanish Flu and died thereafter. Some brought it back with them from the trenches and gave it to other members of their families. Many more people died from the Spanish Flu pandemic (estimated to have taken anywhere from 50-100 million lives) than had died during the First World War, which claimed some 18 million.

Quite amazingly, there were no deaths in the Kennington household during the pandemic.

SAM THE SAPPER

In January 1919 Sam decided to join the Army and travelled to Lincoln to sign up. He wasn't planning on joining the Royal Engineers (REs)—he had never even heard of them. As he wrote of the event:

> "I want to be in the cavalry," I said.
>
> "Sorry, there are no vacancies." said the Recruiting Sergeant. "Do you have a trade?"
>
> "Yes, I am a painter," I replied proudly.
>
> "Well, why not get trade pay by joining the Royal Engineers?" he said.
>
> "If you can recommend that I will try it," I said.

He gave me papers to sign which said, "To serve in any part of the world." I had, in my innocence, thought that since the war had ended, I would always be in England.

Sam signed up for six years as a Sapper, the rank equivalent to a Private in the Army. Over the years the term "Sapper" has evolved. Nowadays it is used with pride by Royal Engineers of all ranks, to identify themselves. To be able to say "I am a Sapper" places an individual into a unique fraternity.

When Sam became a Sapper in 1919, the British Empire was at its height. With colonies and territories all over the world, each with a military base, the REs provided engineering and technical support to the Armed Forces in those British outposts. This included building and maintaining railways, roads, water supplies, bridges and transport. They were also responsible for building the infrastructure for communication by wireless, telephone and signals.

After an uncomfortable night in the Lincoln Barracks, with a straw-stuffed mattress and two rough blankets, he travelled south by train to London. He was going to miss his family but decided that, with his first pay packet, he would treat his mother to a telephone to be installed in Brigg, so he could ring her every week. She said that she didn't need one, because she didn't have anyone to call up. Sam felt sure that would change. The telephone company in Brigg had 20 subscribers at that time and phone numbers only included a couple of digits.

The REs Headquarters was in Chatham, Kent, some 120 miles south. The furthest Sam had travelled before was to Cleethorpes, about 20 miles from Brigg, on the coast. The train journey from Lincoln to London King's Cross Station took three hours:

London completely took my breath away. I was astounded at its size compared to Brigg and dawdled as I made my way across London, from King's Cross to Victoria Station—about two miles or so—to get the train to Chatham which took about an hour.

Sam stayed at the Brompton Barracks and completed a 10-week basic training course at Regimental Headquarters in Chatham. He wrote:

It was the hardest time of my life. This method of training young men who were quite unused to such things was more like prison life. It's a very good job it has gone forever. I incurred the wrath of one Sergeant "Nobbler" Noakes who made my life almost unbearable. I became the butt of his wit without any means of retaliation.

But all things come to an end and Sam's platoon successfully passed out in front of Lieutenant Colonel Weekes. An engineering course at the Royal School of Military Engineering (RSME) followed the basic training course. Sam learnt about knots and lashings, bridging, demolition, mining, drilling, wiring and a host of other things too numerous to mention.

Sports was an important part of life at RSME, with an open-air swimming pool, football and hockey grounds and three tennis courts. Sam got involved in all the available activities, including football, billiards and boxing.

My friend at this time was called Hoad—we all went by our surnames or nicknames. He was the son of wealthy parents and a really nice fellow. Amongst other things he was a brilliant artist who produced life-like sketches of various personalities in the barracks. Hoad used to take me to a restaurant in Chatham at the weekends for tea and I began to realise how crude my Brigg manners were. But I was learning fast. I shared my billet with an old Scottish miner which was just what I needed—a real friend and almost a father.

By this time, Sam had finished growing. At just under five foot nine, he was of average height, broad-chested and stocky. He wore his straight, dark brown hair slicked back over his high forehead. His clear blue eyes always looked directly at whoever he was speaking to. Outgoing, confident and well-liked, he was also ambitious. He had started to work on losing his northern accent, quickly realising that it highlighted his working-class background.

The men in his platoon generally lacked education. Encouraged by his Scottish roommate, Sam decided to educate himself by studying at night. He found the Second-Class Certificate of Education easy, passed it in a matter of weeks and started to study for the First-Class Certificate.

LIMERICK

After finishing the engineering course, Sam was posted to Limerick in Ireland with the 12th Company, REs, in December 1919.

The War of Independence was a guerilla war fought in Ireland from 1919 to 1921 between the Irish Republican Army (IRA) and British forces. It actually began earlier, as a result of the 1916 Easter Rising, and went on beyond 1921. The Irish wanted independence and for Britain to move its army out. Sinn Fein was the largest party of the IRA.

In Limerick, Sam was promoted to Corporal and put in charge of running the Sergeants' Mess, which involved ordering all the supplies and keeping the accounts.

Soon after I arrived, whilst carrying a basin up some greasy concrete steps, I slipped, my elbow hit the step and was broken. I spent Christmas 1919 in the military hospital at the Victoria Barracks in Cork, with my arm in a sling, where it remained for some weeks. Plastering was used on broken bones during the Great War, but they didn't seem to have heard of it in Ireland.

Due to his strict Methodist upbringing, Sam had never been in a public house before he arrived in Limerick. One Sunday lunchtime, he was invited to join his men in a pub. It was a long weekend, and the following day was a public holiday. "Come on Corporal, have a stout," they said. Then, "have a whisky." Sam walked back to the barracks and went to bed at 1:30 pm. The next thing he knew it was Tuesday morning. He had slept for more than 41 hours without waking.

One evening, the men decided to put on a concert to entertain themselves. To the complete astonishment of the other soldiers, Sam sang an old song called "Mary, Sae Kind and Gentle is She," earning him a standing ovation.

The man who slept in the bunk next to him was Sapper Speight. He was addicted to dancing, a pastime which Sam loved, too. They soon discovered that the girls of Limerick were "smashers at dancing," so they danced their feet off. One night, Speight set Sam up for a blind date with a young lady called Miss Hilda Mary Hastings.

> She was of superior appearance, extremely modest, and a good dancer. I saw her home and said good night. That was the first of many meetings, and she was my girl, without a doubt, for dancing, at any rate.

Sam and Hilda Mary met regularly with a group of friends to dance and walked out together whenever he was off duty. It wasn't easy for a Catholic Irish girl to be seen with a Protestant British soldier, so they had to be careful, and he wasn't introduced to her parents.

One evening, a girl came up to Sam at a dance and said she had seen Hilda Mary walking out with an old Irish boyfriend.

> We met a day or so later and I told her she could have her Valentino and said goodbye. I then went out with a girl called Madgie O'Shea. She was a dull egg compared with Hilda Mary, but I had to make do.

By the middle of 1920, Sam had been moved to Tralee in County Kerry where, amongst other things, he learnt how to blow up buildings. Sinn Fein were very active and one night they blew a hole in the barrack wall. Sam had a narrow escape.

He was ordered to blow up a building in Listowel, in retaliation for the capture of an English general called Lucas.

These large-scale reprisals, for acts committed by the IRA against the British Army, were often more vicious than the incidents which provoked them. I remember having lunch in a cafeteria, on my way to blow up the building. In my pocket was a box of detonators and around both shoulders two bandoliers of gun cotton slabs. At my rear a huge open fire was burning, but I could not remove my overcoat for obvious reasons. So, I sat and boiled.

A good thing that he only "boiled" and didn't explode, considering the proximity of open flame and explosives strapped to him. Sam spent over two years in Ireland and got back to England on 22 February 1922. He was posted to the Aldershot Barracks, where he became Pay Clerk, also in charge of Army rations.

Sam continued to study at night and passed his First-Class Certificate with top marks.

TURKEY

In September 1922, Sam's unit, the 12th Field Company, was posted to Chanak (Çanakkale), a city on the Anatolian side of the Dardanelles Strait, to help guard the Dardanelles from Mustafa Kemal Ataturk—always referred to by the British soldiers, rather politically incorrectly, as *Mustapha Camel*. The Chanak Crisis was the name given to this flare up in September 1922 between Britain and Turkey.

Sam's unit sailed from Glasgow on RMS Empress of India and disembarked seven days later in The Narrows—the narrowest part of the Dardanelles. These straits, which connect the Sea of Marmara with the Aegean Sea and the Mediterranean, are also known as the Strait of Gallipoli. It is a very narrow stretch of water, ranging from about three quarters of a mile to four and a half miles wide.

On arrival in Chanak, Sam was put in charge of building lean-to cookhouses for the troops, using Turkish carpenters.

They were hard-working, courteous and likeable chaps. A

great friend was Husseindi, who owned a boat and offered to row me over to Gallipoli.

"Ay! Ay! Husseindi!" I would yell on seeing him.

Out would come his cigarettes, which were absolutely appalling. The upshot was that, after trying his brand once, it was I who always provided Dame Nicotine.

On his first day off, Sam took up Husseindi's offer to visit the old battle beaches on the Gallipoli Peninsula, as well as the poetically named Lone Pine Cemetery, where the casualties of the First World War's Battle of Gallipoli were buried. Sam climbed into the old Turkish trenches overlooking the beaches and wondered how any man who had landed on them had lived to tell the tale.

Husseindi invited Sam to join him for dinner one evening. He suggested meeting in a part of the town which was out of bounds officially for British soldiers. Sam took a chance and went.

Husseindi took me to a small café, and we had a wonderful meal which appeared to be principally of chicken and tomatoes, but the delicious taste defies my pen to describe. We then went to another café next door and had very small cups of sweet strong coffee. Afterwards we smoked a hubble-bubble pipe.

These interactions are indicative of my father's welcoming attitude to striking up friendships with locals. This was not the norm—British soldiers and officers tended to keep to themselves, and to socialise within their rank—officers with officers, and so on. It is an approach that would be vital to our time in Malta, where everyone relied on each other, foreigners and locals, privates and officers, alike.

Sam missed Hilda Mary. He didn't know if she missed him, and he was too nervous to write and ask. One of his close friends, Tom, had also been stationed in Limerick and was part of the group that used to go dancing together. Tom was in regular correspondence with an Irish girl he had met in Limerick and was planning to marry. One day he told Sam that Hilda Mary Hastings had told his fiancée that she missed Sam and would like to hear from him. Sam was thrilled and immediately sent her a letter. He soon realised that she was the one for him.

Winter in Chanak was extremely cold, while summer was extremely hot. When Sam arrived, it was early September and the sea was still warm, so the men spent their free time swimming. Sam quickly improved and decided to enter the quarter mile race in the Company Sports Competition. A strong swimmer, he won by 15 seconds.

Swimming was not the only sport in which he stood out. He had always loved recreational boxing and put together a team which he took by boat to Constantinople (now Istanbul)—a journey of some 150 miles—to take part in the Army championships:

> My memories of this trip are of a very uncomfortable and cold journey on a small steamer and of seeing the dawn, a brilliant dawn, across the Golden Horn as we sailed into Constantinople. The beauty of the minarets catching the first golden rays of dawn was a sight never to be forgotten. We were quartered in the old Turkish Officers' barracks at the bottom of a magnificent boulevard known as the Rue de Pera. The shops, mosques and buildings were a sight for sore eyes, and I revelled in them.

The Russian Army had recently been defeated by Lenin's Red Army in the Russian Civil War, which had started in 1917 and had just ended, in October 1922.

> In Constantinople, we saw hundreds of White Russian refugees who had fled their homeland during the war, without any means of a livelihood. Their condition was pitiful. We had three Russian princesses serving us tea and cake in the canteen. They were quite obviously young ladies of the first quality.

Walking along the street in Constantinople, Sam was approached by a young Russian man who said he was starving. He took out a wad of Russian banknotes which he wanted to sell. Sam felt sorry for him and bought the notes for three shillings and sixpence (about 5 GBP in todays' money). They would have been worth a considerable sum of money in the old Russian currency but had become of no value.

The boxing team didn't do very well, but it was a pleasant break before they headed back to Chanak. At that time, October 1922, there was a threat of war between the United Kingdom and Turkey. The crisis was caused by Turkish efforts to push the Greek armies out of Turkey and restore Turkish rule in the Allied-occupied territories. Turkish troops marched against British and French positions in the Dardanelles neutral zone.

For a time, war between Britain and Turkey seemed possible. But after the thousands of dead and wounded during the First World War, which had ended only three years earlier, the British public had no appetite for more deaths on foreign soil, and neither did the British military. The crisis ended when Turkey agreed to a negotiated settlement that gave them the territory they wanted.

Sam had been trained and, in a way, indoctrinated, to fight Britain's enemies; and no doubt he expected to have to do this. But the prospect of an actual war left him torn between a feeling of patriotism and pride in his skills on the one hand and fear—of what war might bring for him and his fellow soldiers—on the other. Many of them had seen the horrors of combat. They were all glad that war had been avoided and celebrated in the canteen.

A little later, Sam was sent to join his section at Soganli Dere, located on a small inlet, towards the bottom end of the Gallipoli peninsula. The word *dere* in Turkish means "stream."

One of my men took me across the Narrows in a rowing boat, then went back. I had to walk the 15 miles to Soganli Dere. Transport was extremely short in those days and Soganli Dere was isolated. My job was to supervise the building of a pier on the river. One night a terrific storm broke out and the half-finished pier and stones were all washed away. So we built another, this time of sandbags filled with concrete. We stood in the water to set the bags in position.

Sam returned to Chanak, where he was given the job of cleaning out some wells which had not been in use since the time of Christ. They were located about four miles along the coast, north of Chanak.

When we got back to Chanak, I was hot and sticky. I went down to the pier we used for diving and stripped off, only to be told by the boys that no further bathing in the nude was allowed, as two ladies had arrived and were living in a house nearby. So I waited for a friend to finish and borrowed his swimming shorts and belt. We were not allowed to go beyond 50 yards from shore, but I got my head down and went way out, by means of what we called the American Crawl. Suddenly I saw something large swimming towards me. I felt it graze my thigh and swam back to shore quicker than I have ever swum before. When I clambered out, I found my shorts had disappeared, but the belt was still around my waist. I bought my friend a new pair of shorts.

Several species of shark have been spotted in these waters, although they are quite rare. It may be that Sam encountered one of them and was lucky to escape with all limbs intact, and merely the loss of a borrowed pair of shorts.

Nearby was a large vineyard with delicious grapes and the soldiers ate their fill.

We felt so very small when the Turkish farmers came up to us with a large basket full of even better grapes than the ones we had stolen and gave them to us as a gift.

On one of their days off, Sam assembled a party and visited the old, ruined city of Troy, about 20 miles south of Chanak. It was slightly inland, about 300 yards from the beach, opposite the top of the Gallipoli Peninsula. For many years, it was believed that Troy only existed in stories, until its ruins were found by a German archaeologist who started excavating in about 1871.

Below the Roman walls is the wall of the old Greek city. The stones had been so well dressed and fitted by the masons of the time that you couldn't get a knife between the joints, which were built without any mortar. We saw the ramp up which the wooden horse, according to Greek mythology, was allegedly dragged. The remains of a Roman Theatre and pieces of exquisitely carved marble were lying all around.

At the end of September 1923, Sam and his section sailed back to Southampton on HMS Neuralia.

HILDA MARY

Let's go back and learn the story of Hilda Mary, Sam's dance partner in Ireland, who in due course became my mother.

On 22 November 1894, Hilda Mary Hastings was born in Limerick, Ireland. Her Mam (as she called her) already had two little boys and Hilda Mary would be followed by three more girls and two more boys. In the space of 17 years, from 1891 to 1908, her mother gave birth to 11 babies. Only nine survived. Large families were not unusual for the time and place, nor was the survival rate.

Hilda Mary's two older brothers were Christopher and William. Then after Hilda Mary came Mary, Catherine, Bridget, Joseph, Annie and John. That made the tribe of nine children, who were known as Sonny, Willy, Hilda Mary, Molly, Kitty, Birdie, Joe, Annie and Jack. Hilda Mary was always called by her full name. She was of medium height and slender, with long wavy dark hair, porcelain skin and blue eyes.

Her father, Patrick Hastings, was a carpenter. Her mother Margaret, née Brosnahan, was a housewife. They lived in a small, two up, two down, terraced house at 2 James Street, near the People's Park in Limerick City, four blocks from the River Shannon.

The Brosnahan grandparents lived next door, at 3 James Street, with a couple of unmarried children in their 20s. Hilda Mary's family continued to grow, so her eldest brother Sonny moved in with their grandparents next door. In the 1901 census, there were also two boarders living at number three. How they all fitted into those two little houses is a good question.

Tuberculosis was the single most critical health issue in all the major towns and cities in Ireland at that time. Overcrowded housing and poor sanitation aided the spread of contagious diseases, leading to increased mortality rates and decreased life expectancy. Infant mortality was high, as was death in childbirth. In 1912, there was an epidemic of measles in Limerick which claimed the lives of many children. Most deaths occurred in the poorer areas of the city.

The Irish branch of the Catholic Truth Society, founded in 1899, published and distributed books, pamphlets and magazines until well into the second half of the twentieth century. These publications were against abortion, contraception and homosexuality and told their Catholic readers what to think about such issues. The Catholic Church played a central role in the social and cultural life of Limerick.

The Brosnahans were Church of Ireland Protestants, and the Hastings were Catholics. The Catholic Church insisted that children of such mixed marriages be brought up "in the true faith." Every Sunday the Hastings children attended Mass at St Joseph's Catholic Church, with their father. As time went on, almost all the Brosnahans converted to Catholicism. Children attended Catechism classes to prepare for their First Holy Communion when they were about seven and Confirmation when they were about ten.

The girls went to the Presentation Convent School for Girls and the boys to the Christian Brothers School, both within walking distance of James Street. As the eldest girl, Hilda Mary stayed home from school one day a week, to help her mother with the washing and other household chores. Getting the clothes dry in winter or when it rained, which it often did, was not easy.

When her mother was sick, or had a baby, Hilda Mary stayed home from school for at least a week. She learnt to make "goody," stale bread soaked in warm milk and sweetened with lots of sugar, to feed to anyone who was unwell. Nobody in the Brosnahan/Hastings family died of tuberculosis. This made them fortunate, given how tuberculosis was the scourge of the era. However, bronchial pneumonia was a common ailment, complicated by the fact that most of the men were smokers.

Hilda Mary missed a lot of school, one way and another. The school leaving age was 13 and she got a job at the Cleeves Toffee factory, wrapping toffees and packing them into boxes. It was on O'Callaghan's Strand, a short walk from home, on the other side of the river.

Workers were paid by the number of boxes they filled each day. Unfortunately, Hilda Mary was easily persuaded to hand over some of her wrapped toffees when the girls stopped for a tea break or lunch: "Hilda Mary, I only need six toffees to fill my box, won't ye give me some of yours?" And like a proper eejit (to use her words) she would hand them over.

She didn't fill many boxes.

In 1908, a year after she started work, her Mam gave birth to her last surviving baby. Jack was a sweet child and Hilda Mary loved taking him to the park and pretending he was her baby. They couldn't afford to buy a baby's bottle, so they used an old lemonade bottle fitted with a teat. Her Mam told her to wrap it in a tea towel when she was feeding Jack in the park, so no one would see that it wasn't a proper baby's bottle. They were poor but proud.

Life wasn't easy in Ireland when Hilda Mary was growing up. Poor families lived from hand to mouth and unemployment levels were high. The unemployed went to the Labour Exchange to sign on for the dole. When things were really bad, poor people could go to the St Vincent de Paul Society and ask for a docket, similar to food stamps, to exchange at the grocer's for food.

The Irish diet at the time was not varied. Potatoes, bread and porridge were the staples, as they were cheap and filling. Cabbage, carrots, turnips and parsnips made regular appearances for the same reason. Sugar consumption was high—as sugar was relatively cheap —and dental care was poor. Ham, sausages, tomatoes, jam and steak were considered luxuries by the poorer families. Takeaway fish and chips were a special treat. Smoking and alcohol helped many to forget their problems.

One day Hilda Mary was darning socks when her mother asked her to take Jack to the park. He'd been bawling his head off all day and was driving everyone up the wall, she said. Hilda Mary stuck the darning needle into the top of her dress, picked up Jack and walked to the park. When they arrived, she sat on a park bench with the baby on her lap. He was red in the face and crying even more loudly than before. She was about to give him his bottle, to see if that would help, when she saw the very end of the darning needle sticking out of his chest. It must have come out of her dress and gone into him as she walked to the park. She laid him down on the bench and just managed to remove it with her teeth before it disappeared altogether. Jack stopped crying, drank his milk and was none the worse for the experience. Hilda Mary decided it was best not to tell her mother what had happened.

A year after Jack was born, her mother was pregnant again. The delivery was difficult, the baby died, and her Mam took months to recover. Hilda Mary, then barely a teenager, took on more of the household chores.

The downward economic spiral in Ireland had begun with the potato famine in 1845. Also known as the Great Hunger, it had lasted about seven years. It had been brought on by the introduction of a mould, *Phytophthora infestans*, which ruined roughly half the potato crop in the first year and up to three-quarters over the next seven. Potatoes were the staple food of the working class.

By the time the Great Hunger ended in 1852, an estimated one-million Irish had starved and another million had left the country as hunger refugees, settling abroad in places like America, Australia and New Zealand. The Irish blamed the famine on the British government who hadn't handled the situation very well. This was the beginning of strained relations between the Irish and the British which got worse as time went on. The population of County Limerick dropped by more than 20% during the 1840s and continued to decline until 1900, because of emigration.[6]

The Hastings and the Brosnahans had several friends and relations who left Ireland to start a new life overseas. They had nothing to lose. Hilda Mary's family still talked about the famine over sixty years later, especially her grandparents, who had lived through it.

Dancing played an important role in the working-class culture of Ireland and was what kept Hilda Mary and her friends sane. Moving pictures were in their infancy, so dance halls were where the young met to socialise. They didn't have much else to look forward to each week.

Traditional Irish dancing called Ceili dancing, like line dancing, was very popular. Instead of paying for a group of musicians with a fiddle, an accordion or a flute, some dance halls would organise "gob music." This was the local name for what is also known as lilting, diddling or mouth music. A man, or often two who would take it in turns, would sing a never-ending song, with nonsensical words, to the rhythm of an Irish jig. They provided music for the dancers for the whole evening.

There were several dance halls in Limerick and Hilda Mary frequented them all. One night in January 1912, when she was 17, she went to a dance at the Rink Palace with a couple of girlfriends. There she met a young man called Patrick Lane. He was 16 and lived in Clare Street, just around the corner from James Street. They danced together a few times and he bought her a drink. Patrick told Hilda Mary that he was emigrating to America. He had saved up the fare of £7.15 (about 500 GBP today, or nearly a month's wages at the time) for a third-class ticket and was looking forward to making his fortune and coming back to Limerick as a millionaire. The ship he was sailing on was called *The Titanic* and it would be calling in to Queenstown near Cork on 11 April to pick up all the Irish emigrants. He was very excited.

Three months later, a friend at the toffee factory told Hilda Mary that there had been a terrible disaster and a big ship called the Titanic had sunk. It was 15 April 1912, one day after the "unsinkable" ship smashed into an iceberg and sank. During her lunch break, Hilda Mary rushed out to buy a newspaper. There, in the list of those who had drowned was his name: Patrick Lane.

Quite a few people from Limerick lost their lives on that fateful voyage. Hilda Mary was in shock for weeks.

When the First World War started in 1914, Hilda Mary's two older brothers, Sonny and Willy went to England and joined the Army as volunteers. They both survived the war, but Sonny suffered from mustard gas poisoning, and said that, as a result, his hair had turned white overnight. While recuperating in a hospital, he met a nurse called Doris. They married after the war and Sonny stayed in London. Willy went back to Limerick.

The Spanish Flu struck Ireland between the spring of 1918 and the spring of 1919, brought back by soldiers returning from the First World War. This pandemic claimed about 23,000 lives in Ireland in just over a year. In the month of November 1918 alone, over 200 people were buried in Limerick which had a population of less than 150,000.[7]

Hilda Mary's brother Willy was almost 25 and engaged to be married when he died suddenly of the Flu. Then Uncle John Brosnahan, who lived next door, caught it, and died. His sister, Aunt Roseanne Brosnahan, who also lived next door, said that two deaths in the family was enough. She made masks for everyone and insisted they wore them. She was convinced that smoking made things worse, so she banned it inside the house. These measures had a good effect. No one else in the two houses in James Street contracted the deadly disease from that point on, despite the crowded conditions.

As we saw in an earlier chapter about Sam in Limerick, British forces were sent there to fight in the Irish War of Independence which started in 1919 and lasted about three years. It was a complicated and bitter conflict ending with the creation of the Irish Free State on 6 December 1922.

You would have thought that things couldn't become any worse for the Hastings family, but they did. They were not just poor, fresh from surviving the Spanish Flu, they were now living in a war zone, with fighting between the IRA and the British disrupting their lives.

Large numbers of British soldiers started arriving and Molly and Hilda Mary got to know a few of them at the local dances. At a popular venue called Todsies, at St Mary's Dance Hall, Hilda Mary met a British soldier called Sam. He was also a good dancer and people admired them as a couple on the dance floor. She went out with him a few times but didn't tell her parents. They were more relaxed than some parents, but officially they wouldn't have approved. Dating a British soldier wasn't as bad as dating a Black and Tan, but it was nonetheless frowned upon. In some ways it was more about what the neighbours would think. Hilda Mary took the view that what they didn't know could do them no harm.

The Black and Tans were recruited into the Royal Irish Constabulary (RIC) from Britain during the War of Independence. The nickname "Black and Tan" came from the colour of their uniforms. The majority were unemployed former British soldiers who had fought in the First World War. Their job was to help the overstretched RIC maintain control and suppress the Irish Republican Army (IRA). Everybody hated them.

One of Hilda Mary's so-called friends told Sam that she already had an Irish boyfriend. It wasn't true but Sam broke off the relationship. It was only after it was all over that Hilda Mary realised that she was deeply in love with Sam. She was devastated, but there was no point in crying over spilt milk. She continued to work at the toffee factory, joined by her sister Molly. Working as a team, they were able to wrap more toffees than working alone, but they were still earning a pittance relative to the hours they were putting in. They gave their mother as much money as they could each week.

Hilda Mary and Molly attended all the local dances together. Hilda Mary had a few boyfriends and a couple of marriage proposals. Everyone said she was "knocking on 30" and couldn't afford to be so fussy. If she wasn't careful, they said, she would be left on the shelf. While there was a shortage of young men of marriageable age after the casualties of the First World War, Hilda Mary was determined not to end up like her mother, with a house full of children, no money and constantly feeling exhausted. None of the young men she met in Limerick could offer her the life she wanted.

Hilda Mary in Limerick 1920 aged 26.

Hilda Mary's father died suddenly in 1923 of a heart attack, aged just 60. Having lost the main breadwinner, her Mam struggled. Of the nine children, only Molly, Hilda Mary, Annie and Jack were still living at home. Kitty had married and moved out. Sonny had stayed in London and married Doris after the war, Willy had died in the Spanish Flu epidemic and Birdie and Joe had both emigrated to New York. They regularly sent letters home, encouraging Hilda Mary and Molly to join them, but they didn't want to move to America. It was too far away.

At the end of 1923, when she was 29 years old, Hilda Mary decided to move to London. A few weeks before she left, she was thrilled to receive a letter from Sam. She wrote back and told him her plans. He said he was finishing up in Turkey and would be back home soon.

Hilda Mary caught the overnight ferry from Dublin to Liverpool with a girl called Nelly Phelan, who had just broken up with her childhood sweetheart and was also keen to get away from Ireland and start a new life. Nelly was of a nervous disposition, with fingernails chewed down to the quick. She started feeling homesick the minute they boarded the vessel. Hilda Mary shared a cabin with Nelly and listened as she sobbed her way through the night. When Hilda Mary awoke next morning, it looked as if there had been a massacre during the night. There was blood everywhere—all over Nelly's bunk bed, the sheets and the pillow. In her anguish Nelly had gnawed her way through two of her fingers, right down to the bone. Hilda Mary took her to the ship's doctor who bandaged her up before handing her over to the doctor who would be on board the ferry when it sailed back to Dublin, later that day. Nelly, who was still sobbing, was glad to be going home to her Mam. Within less than a year she had married her childhood sweetheart and given birth to twins.

Hilda Mary caught the train from Liverpool to London where she soon found a job as a waitress and rented a small bedroom in a lodging house. She wrote to Molly, begging her to join her and Molly arrived a week later. The girls shared a bed, but it wasn't the first time they had done so. Each week they sent money to their Mam by telegraphic money order from the post office. It was double what they had given her when they'd worked at the toffee factory.

With their first pay packet, the sisters went to Oxford Street and bought some smart new clothes.

Every weekend they "dressed to kill" and headed off to a tea dance at the Palm Court of the Waldorf Hilton Hotel. Tea dances took place from 4 to 7pm and were popular all over Britain. After sandwiches, cakes and champagne, new dances were taught to the guests. Hilda Mary and Molly were good dancers and never short of partners. They soon learnt the Charleston, which was all the rage at the time, and several other new dances they hadn't seen in Ireland.

At such a classy venue, a girl could meet a nice young man, get married and move up in the world.

ROMANCE

Sam returned home from Turkey towards the end of 1923 and was stationed in Aldershot, where he worked as an instructor. It was just an hour from London by train, where Hilda Mary was now living. He wrote and asked her to meet him in Trafalgar Square.

At the appointed time, there she was, in a smashing brown outfit. She used to dress to kill at that time. We shook hands and were quickly in Lyons Tea Room enjoying tea.

The romance blossomed. Once a fortnight, Sam met Hilda Mary in London, where she was working at a hotel in Earls Court. They walked everywhere and visited museums and art galleries, watched silent films (Cecil B DeMille's epic *The Ten Commandments* was the talk of film circles, as was Harold Lloyd's slapstick masterpiece, *Safety Last*) and attended football matches. They also went to tea dances and any other dances they could find. They made an attractive couple.

Sam and Hilda Mary saw all the great performers of the 1920s, including Peggy O'Neil, an Irish American vaudeville actress, Harry Lauder, a Scottish singer and comedian who always wore a kilt and sporran and was the first UK singer to sell a million records, and the amazing Diaghilev's Russian Ballet.

Sam stayed at the Union Jack Club in Waterloo, where members of the armed services could get a room for one shilling and ninepence.

Unfortunately, bad women haunted the area and many good men have been ruined by these wretches. They would take a soldier or sailor to a private house where he was robbed. Many got a severe beating from the toughs these women were hand-in-hand with.

One of Sam's friends called Reggie invited him and Hilda Mary to join him and his fiancée Primrose for dinner at the Cavendish Hotel, a much-loved haunt of London high society. It was run by a woman called Rosa Lewis who had worked her way up from chambermaid to owning the hotel. Reggie warned Sam that Rosa was well-known for asking anyone she didn't like the look of to leave. Fortunately, they passed muster. The food was solid British fare. Sam refrained from telling their hostess that the beef pie was not a patch on Annie Lizzie's when she came to their table to ask if they had enjoyed their meal.

Sam decided to "pop the question" and Hilda Mary, who was also head over heels in love, said yes. Her sister-in-law Doris, who was married to her brother Sonny and lived in London, had noticed a nice diamond ring in a shop in Edgware Road. In due course the "gager," as Hilda Mary called it, was on her finger and admired by everyone who saw it.

In Aldershot, Sam carried out a succession of jobs, including Mess Corporal, Company Clerk, Education Instructor and Regimental Police Corporal. He loved amateur boxing and was beaten twice in the finals of the RE Aldershot Middleweight Championship by a Corporal Fox. Both times he had to see Hilda Mary while sporting a big black eye. For two years, he represented the Corps in the 440 yards swimming championship, as well as in billiards. On occasion, when the team was one man down, he joined the water polo team.

In January 1925, having completed the six years he had signed up for when he enlisted with the REs in 1919, Sam signed up for another six.

A few months later, the Hastings sisters were devastated when their Mam died. She was just 56 and the death certificate gave the cause of death as "exhaustion." By this time, Jack had moved to England and joined the Army. Out of the nine children, only Kitty and Annie stayed in Limerick.

Sam and Hilda Mary were married on 14 April 1926, coinciding with Sam moving back to the Brompton Barracks in Chatham. He was 26 and she was 32. Hilda Mary was so embarrassed by her age that she lied on the marriage certificate which shows her as 29. Social norms indicated that a woman should be younger than her husband. She obviously didn't have to show her birth certificate to prove her age and got away with it!

We had a superb wedding breakfast with speeches but having spent all our money on the "splash," we stayed at home for the honeymoon.

Sam and Hilda Mary, wedding day
14 April 1926, aged 26 and 32.

FIVE UNDER FIVE

The newlyweds rented a room in a house in Chatham. On 5 May 1927, my brother Patrick was born at the Army hospital near the Kitchener Barracks in Chatham. Living conditions were cramped, but Sam was thrilled to bits with his little family.

In the middle of 1928, he was promoted to Staff Sergeant and posted back to the Deepcut Barracks near Aldershot, about 20 miles from London. Sam and Hilda Mary moved into married quarters at number 6, B Block with baby Patrick.

My salary was now four pounds 10 shillings per week with a free house, coal and light, rations of bread and meat twice a week and about 15 shillings a month extra for rations. We had not a lot to spare, as we had no spare clothes, but we had all we needed. We were in our first home—really ours and not renting from other people.

On 4 August that year, my brother Edwin was born at the Louise Margaret Hospital in Aldershot. Just a year later, on 23 September 1929, I arrived.

Margaret Annette Staples, that's me. I was called Margaret after my maternal grandmother and Annette after my paternal grandmother, Annie Lizzie. My father called me Liz, my mother called me Margaret, while my siblings called me Liz or Mags.

My father always made me feel special. He wrote in his diary that he remembered my first year with the greatest of pleasure. After two boys, he'd been hoping for a girl. He loved to take me out in my pram and say to anyone who looked in "This is my daughter."

I was so pleased when she arrived. She looked so nice, I could have kissed her and kissed her, but was not allowed to do so. I had a ukulele which I used to strum and sing "My Bonnie Lies over the Ocean," with little Patrick, who quickly learnt the words.

A month after I was born, on 28 October 1929, the stock market crashed. Fortunately, my parents had no shares or investments, and the Army provided a security blanket for our family. At a time when many businesses were going bankrupt, unemployment was at an all-time high and suicide was a not uncommon escape from financial ruin, my father felt relieved to be in a secure job.

On Christmas Day 1931, when I was two and a quarter, another baby was due to arrive. Sam dropped Hilda Mary at the Louise Margaret Hospital early that morning.

At about 3 pm I left Pat, Ed and Margaret with friends and returned to the hospital. No one was in the maternity ward. I rang the bell, but they were all at a Christmas concert, which I could hear going on at the other end of the hospital. I sat and read a book, then paced up and down. At about 4pm Matron appeared. When I enquired about my wife, she told me that she was "as well as could be expected," then disappeared.

A while later she returned to tell me I was the father of a beautiful daughter, and my wife was "as well as could be expected." Four young children, and my wife was only "as well as could be expected?" What if something has happened to my love? Preparing myself for the worst, I continued to pace up and down. Twenty minutes later Matron was back to tell me that I was the father of another beautiful daughter. My wife continued to be as well as could be expected. I wasn't allowed to see Hilda Mary until the next day and went home in a daze. Five children under the age of five!

My mother spent a week at the Louise Margaret Hospital. When she came home with my twin sisters, Joan and Daphne, my four-year-old brother Pat enquired: "How is it you have two babies Mummy, when other people only have one?"

Like a flash my mother said, "Well, I was in the corner of the ward next to the door. Father Christmas came in and said, 'Who will take two little girls?' and I just got my hand up in time."

"Good Mum!" Pat replied and trotted off.[8]

With five small children, my mother didn't have time to give us individual attention. I was sometimes jealous of the twins, but my father would give me a cuddle and dry my tears.

Mid-morning, he would ride home on his bicycle to look after three toddlers, while my mother fed and bathed two babies. He would then rush back to work and do without a lunch break. It was a busy, noisy household. Domestic help was not available for servicemen of my father's rank. There were no grandparents to help out. Both our Irish grandparents had died before we were born. Dad's stepfather, William Kennington, died when I was about one. We didn't see Granny Kenny very often because Brigg was a long way from where we lived.

My mother was never a good cook, but we knew no different. We always ate ravenously. We were growing kids and always hungry. Mum's unmarried sister, Annie, came over from Limerick to help out for a week when my twin sisters were born. She couldn't cook, either.

My father agreed that my mother would bring up the children as

Catholics. We were all christened at the Catholic Church in Deepcut and attended Mass there every Sunday. Dad attended a nearby Church of England service.

There were a lot of things that people could die from back then which can now be cured with medication. Penicillin was invented in 1928, but it wasn't widely available until after the Second World War ended in 1945.

On Good Friday 1932, Dad's legs suddenly became very stiff. By Saturday, his knees were locked. He hobbled to his car and drove to the doctor who sent him straight to the Cambridge Hospital in Aldershot. A few minutes after he arrived, he passed out, and when he came to, he found himself in a hospital bed. He stayed there for two months and was on the dangerously ill list. There were seven men in his ward and five of them died. The doctors did not know what was wrong with my father and said he was very lucky to recover.

It seems likely that he had rheumatic fever, which today is treated with antibiotics. If there's any damage to the heart the patient often stays on medication for several years. Lack of proper treatment could have left Sam with a weak heart and contributed to the heart attack he suffered some 40 years later.

After this experience, my mother said they should save £100 and keep it in the bank as an insurance against anything happening to my father. It was the first money my father had ever saved. They would use it as a deposit when they bought a house, some 20 years later.

When I turned three, in September 1932, I started at a local nursery school. By the time I was four, I was reading like a ten-year-old, devouring books such as Alice in Wonderland, Winnie the Pooh and all the books by Beatrix Potter. My father also read to us when he had time. He loved having precocious children. We each had a different song he would ask us to sing when we had visitors. Even my two baby sisters had a party piece.

On Christmas day 1933, when the twins turned two and I was four, my father announced that we were moving to Hong Kong. We really had no clue what it would be like, living in a country so different to England, not even my parents. Anyway, we had little time to think about it as we had to leave in early January. I helped Mum to pack our belongings into trunks and tea chests.

ON OUR WAY TO HONG KONG

On a cold wet morning in early January 1934, we left England on the Peninsula and Oriental Steam Navigation Company (P&O) luxury steamship SS Naldera.

During the First World War, the Naldera and her sister Narkunda were requisitioned by the British government as Armed Merchant Cruisers. They were returned to P&O in 1919 to be refitted and sail as luxury passenger liners.

Naldera carried 426 First Class passengers and 247 Second Class passengers. She had two masts and three big black chimneys which belched out thick black smoke as we sailed out of Tilbury dock.

We were travelling Second Class, but for us it was the lap of luxury, and we were very excited. There was a three-berth cabin for my father and the two boys on one side of a small corridor, while Mum, Joan, Daphne, and I had a four-berth cabin opposite. The cabins were above the waterline, so we could see out of the port holes. We had electric lights and fans and a washbasin with running water—details that many a permanent home was without. We shared a bathroom with two other families.

The spectacular timber-panelled dining room was the full width of the ship. It had a ceiling four decks high covered with hand-painted frescoes. There was a huge main lounge with a bar, a ballroom where they held dances at night, a library where I spent many hours devouring all the books I could find by Enid Blyton, a writing room where Mum went to write letters to her sisters and a smoking room, where Dad met his military friends. There was also a music room with a piano but none of us played at that stage.

The meals were wonderful and served buffet-style, so you could help yourself to whatever you fancied. A typical lunch consisted of a hot section, with soup, steak and kidney pudding, a curry, roast beef or lamb and several different kinds of potatoes and other vegetables.

The cold section had ham and other cold meats and salads. The dessert table always had my favourite tinned fruit salad and cream, as well as rice pudding, custard, several large cakes and a huge platter of cheeses and fresh fruit.

We loved going up and down in the lift between the different decks. Hide-and-seek was a pastime which kept us amused for hours. We weren't allowed to run on the decks, in case we knocked someone over, but we learnt to walk very quickly to cover the vast decks of the ship. We spent hours in the indoor swimming pool, playing with new friends we had met on board. As we headed south and the weather improved, an outdoor pool was erected on the deck. We preferred being out in the sunshine, a natural phenomenon in relatively short supply back in the north of England.[9]

My parents returned rather late from dinner one night to find me in the cabin washbasin, sound asleep. I had fallen out of the top bunk. Fortunately, I had landed in a sitting position and escaped with a small cut above one eyebrow, which left me with a small scar. My father said that the Staples luck had protected me. It would not be the last time that my family found good fortune amidst potential disaster.

My parents also enjoyed the balmy weather, sitting for hours in deckchairs, sipping cocktails and chatting to the other passengers— Mum under a huge hat, because she always burnt easily. The women loved strolling around the spacious Promenade Deck, showing off their new dresses. My father was amazed to see one woman wearing trousers. This was almost unheard of back then and I never saw my mother wearing them. Even the men had bought new clothes to wear on board this luxury liner. Gone were the drab brown and grey suits of London. They all wore cream and white.

Everyone was seasick as we crossed the Bay of Biscay, but by the time we had sailed down past Portugal, we all had our sea legs. Our first stop was Gibraltar, opposite the northern tip of the African continent. Dad went ashore alone to meet up with an old chum who was posted there. Once in the Mediterranean, we headed to Marseilles and from there to the island of Malta, where vendors came on board selling tablecloths and other items made of lace. Then we stopped in

Port Said in Egypt before we went through the Suez Canal.

Sailing into Port Said early one morning was different to the other ports where we had stopped. Instead of an ordinary harbour there was about a mile of break-water rocks before we finally anchored. On the shore, at the entrance to the canal, we saw a big statue of a man. Dad said it was Ferdinand Marie, Comte de Lesseps, a French diplomat who had founded the canal. We didn't go ashore, but as we were looking through the portholes, we saw some little boats pulling alongside our ship, bobbing and jostling for position, with traders selling all sorts of things. We asked Dad for some money and bought peanuts and Turkish delight. Dad bought a leather wallet.

The canal is only about 120 miles long and by the following day we had passed a place called Suez, which was at the other end, sailed through the Red Sea and were on our way across the Arabian Sea to Bombay in India. From there we sailed to Colombo in Ceylon, Penang in Malaya and finally to Singapore, our last stop before Hong Kong. Dad explained that all these places, except Marseilles which belonged to the French, were British colonies. He said there was a saying that the sun never sets on the British Empire.

There were lots of parties on board for the children and the adults, including fancy dress and talent competitions—where the Staples Five won lots of prizes—and the weeks passed quickly.

PENANG

We didn't leave the ship every time it stopped in a port, but when we got to George Town in Penang, we went ashore to have lunch at the Eastern and Oriental, a very smart hotel on the waterfront. After the opening of the Suez Canal in 1869, which meant travellers could avoid sailing around the Cape of Good Hope to get to Asia, and the arrival of the steamship, travel to Asia became possible to enjoy in luxury. Before the canal opened, ships had to sail more than 6000 miles around Africa, whereas the Suez Canal cut that down to just 100 miles. Writers, actors, playwrights and others who could afford it became globetrotters, seeking adventure beyond Europe. It was the start of world travel and the biggest step forward for tourists until the advent of commercial flight.

The Armenian Sarkies brothers, Martin and Tigran, built the Eastern Hotel in Penang in 1884 on a piece of land facing the sea. Encouraged by its success, they opened another hotel, the Oriental, in 1885, on an adjacent piece of land. Combined, these two hotels became the largest in Penang. Every guest room had an English-style long bath with running hot and cold water, two large beds and a telephone. These were remarkable luxuries at the time.

In 1891, Arshak Sarkies, a younger and more flamboyant brother, joined the business and added a large ballroom. The E&O became the centre of social life in Penang and its surroundings. Famous guests included Noel Coward, Rudyard Kipling and Somerset Maugham.

Martin and Tigran both died in 1912 and Arshak Sarkies took over. When the Great Depression hit the world in 1929, he found himself in serious financial trouble. He had borrowed a lot of money and allowed too many friends and acquaintances to stay at the hotel for nothing. Arshak died in 1931 and in 1938 the hotel was sold for a song to the owners of the nearby Runnymede Hotel.[10]

We had afternoon tea on the lawns. When the waiter pulled out my chair for me to sit down, arranged a white linen napkin on my lap and poured my tea, I felt like a princess. I dreamt about it for weeks and decided to marry a prince, so I could live in places like that when older.

SINGAPORE

We stopped in Singapore for a whole day, so almost all the passengers left the ship. I had my first ride in a rickshaw. We needed three to fit everyone in. I was surprised to see that there was no horse to pull the little buggy along. Just a man with a conical hat and bare feet. It had just stopped raining and there were huge muddy puddles everywhere. It looked like very hard work.

Our destination was Raffles—another luxury hotel built by the Sarkies brothers in 1887. Mum and Dad had a cocktail called a Gin Sling while we shelled and ate peanuts, washed down with freshly squeezed lemonade. The friendly barman said there were peanut plantations nearby.

"Go on," he said. "Just throw the shells on the floor. Everybody does."

We looked around and, sure enough, everybody was throwing their peanut shells on the floor. So we did, too.

After a light lunch of sandwiches in the bar, we went to a shop which seemed to sell everything. Dad bought a new Kodak camera he had been wanting for some time.

A colleague he knew from his time in Turkey had moved to Singapore with his family. We had afternoon tea with them at the Tanglin Barracks. Before returning to the ship, we managed to fit in an early dinner at one of the hawker cafés. Old tables and chairs were set up on the pavement and they cooked the food right there in big black pans—which Dad said were called woks—on portable burners. I don't remember what we ate—all sorts of things I had never eaten before—but it was delicious.

HONG KONG

Britain had acquired Hong Kong Island under the Treaty of Nanking in 1842, at the end of its first war with China. Friction between China and Britain increased in 1850 when a new emperor assumed the Chinese throne. A second war, fought between 1856 and 1860, resulted in Britain obtaining the tip of the Kowloon Peninsula and Stonecutters Island.

In the late 1800s, colonialism was in full swing and Hong Kong became a popular destination for western travellers to Asia. Imports of tea into Britain, shipped by the British East India Company, amounted to more than 13,000 tons a year and China was their main supplier. During the British occupation, when we were there, Hong Kong was of great strategic importance, allowing Britain to maintain military and commercial control of the region.

Hong Kong isn't large, measuring roughly 30 miles north to south and 45 miles east to west. The principal city and port of Victoria is on a deep harbour. Hong Kong was occupied by the Japanese during the Second World War from 1941-1945. It would remain a British colony until 1997, when it reverted to being part of mainland China.

Our ship finally docked in Hong Kong at Victoria Harbour.

There were hundreds of vessels of all shapes and sizes, jostling for position in the choppy water. Our ship was the biggest. Hundreds of dock workers communicated by yelling at each other in a strange language. The big ships joined the conversation with their booming sirens. Having been on board Naldera for five weeks, we were all familiar with her distinctive voice. The small boats, called junks, had sails and some had a man at the back with a very long oar.

We stood on the wharf, which was teeming with people, waiting for our luggage. A salty breeze carried whiffs of tantalising food being cooked and less appealing odours of rotting rubbish. It was noisy, hot and humid. Most of the people looked very different to us, like the people we had seen in Singapore. Some of them stared at our pasty English complexions. Dozens of rickshaws queued up patiently, waiting to give people a ride.

The Chinese workers wore what looked to me like baggy pyjamas which came to just below their knees, and wide-brimmed hats with a pointy bit on top, like we had seen in Singapore. They were unloading vessels by passing things from one man to another, down a long human chain. Others were working in pairs or foursomes, carrying heavier items. It was a time before shipping containers, when cargo was sent in wooden crates, pallets, boxes, barrels, or trunks. Hundreds of crates were stacked on the wharf. The suitcases and trunks of those who were leaving the ship were hoisted ashore in big nets.

Rickshaw pullers had a number on their hat which matched the number on their rickshaw. Men carried heavy loads suspended on each end of a wooden pole which went across the back of their shoulders. They were all barefoot.

The buildings along the seafront were four or five stories high, with a covered walkway at ground level and open balconies on the levels above. They appeared to be made of concrete which had once been white but was now rather dirty. European men wore smart cream or white business suits and fedora hats, stepping carefully to avoid the muddy puddles. Some of the women carried parasols.

Someone from the barracks was there to meet us. We piled into two Army vehicles to drive the short distance to what was described as a Second-Class apartment in a block called the President Apartments, on Nathan Road, the main street in the district of Kowloon. It wasn't far but we made slow progress through the congested streets.

There were double-decker buses and a few cars, but most people travelled by bicycle or rickshaw, or they walked. Many of the buildings on each side of the road had a shop or restaurant on the ground floor. Goods were displayed on the walls and on the pavement: all kinds of food, pots and pans, spices and clothes. People shouted and cars honked.

Dilapidated, shoddily constructed shacks made of corrugated iron and bits of wood provided a primitive home for some. This abject poverty contrasted starkly with the luxury cars and immaculate clothes of the expatriates and wealthy Chinese.

There were a lot of beggars. Adults and children. Some of the Chinese women had babies tied onto their backs. The children were dirty and barefoot, with tangled hair and ragged clothes. I was shocked to see one teenage boy pulling himself along on a little trolley with wheels. He had no legs.

There were signs everywhere, but I couldn't read them because they were all in Chinese. By the side of the road people cooked food in huge black woks which they heated on portable stoves, like we'd seen in Singapore. There were lots of new smells, some pleasant and some not, and strange music blared out from the restaurants. People squatted on the ground to eat, shovelling food into their mouths with two sticks from a small bowl held against their chin. It was the first time I had seen chopsticks.

I soon discovered that it didn't matter what time of day it was. There were always people eating on the streets of Hong Kong.

18 HANKOW ROAD

The apartment on Nathan Road was too small for the seven of us, so a few days later we moved to a larger apartment at 18 Hankow Road in Tsim Sha Tsui, near the end of the Kowloon peninsula and just a short walk from the harbour. Dad said the Army called it a First-Class Apartment and indeed it was much bigger and more modern than the previous one. I had my own bedroom, while the two boys and the twins each shared. My father started work at the nearby Whitfield Barracks as Quartermaster Sergeant, in charge of Army supplies and their storage, as well as some building projects. He wrote in his diary:

> We had seen pictures of Chinese people, but it is quite different when one sees them in the flesh. I found it most confusing and brain tiring to try and distinguish their features. This continued for some months until suddenly I could pick people out with ease. One of my Chinese colleagues told me that they had the same problem telling us apart. My experiences with the Chinese builders were often quite amusing, but generally one had to keep a careful watch that the specifications were properly adhered to.

Our apartment block had been built by the British Department of Public Works and completed in 1929. There were shops and restaurants on the ground floor and three floors of apartments above—30 apartments altogether. Ours was on the top floor. A covered walkway at ground level went all the way along the street, providing protection from the hot sun. Pillars every few feet supported the floors above. These concrete buildings had no architectural merit. They were just functional.

On our first Sunday, after attending Mass at the nearby Rosary Church, we caught the Star Ferry from the Victoria wharf across to Hong Kong Island, where we went on the Peak Tram to the top of the big hill we had seen in the distance when we arrived. It was called Victoria Peak. More than 1800 feet above sea level, the peak was an exclusive residential area for non-Chinese and we saw some very expensive mansions as the tram approached the top. When we got off the panoramic view of the harbour took my breath away. The ships looked so small, like my brothers' toy ships in the bathtub.

We engaged a nanny, known as an amah, to help my mother. Amahs in Hong Kong all dressed the same: loose, full-length black trousers and a white short-sleeved top with a mandarin collar. A week later she left, having learnt that the amah who had worked in the apartment before we arrived had died there. Word got around that our apartment was full of bad spirits. Two weeks later, we were still without an amah. When the next prospective employee turned up, she had a quick look around then said sorry, she couldn't take the job after all, because of the bad spirits. She had been told about them but had to come and check for herself. Her name was Ah How, which we thought was very funny. But she was about to leave, which my mother did not find funny at all.

With five small children, she was desperate. Drastic measures were called for. Mum rolled up several newspapers into a kind of sword, lit one end and ran around the apartment, waving it in every corner, leaving a trail of smoke and screaming like a banshee. When she had finished, she threw the burning newspapers out of the window and clapped her hands. Ah How was impressed. We all were. Ah How, her jet-black hair in a plait which reached down almost to her waist, nodded sagely and said "Bad spirits all gone now. I stay."

Pat, Ed and I started at the Maryknoll Convent School, founded by the American Maryknoll Sisters in 1925. I was four and the boys were five and six. The twins joined us at the kindergarten early the following year when they turned three. All the lessons were in English, but we learnt the Chinese language called Cantonese well enough that I have never forgotten how to count to ten.

Our school uniforms were white, and we all had the same short haircut with a fringe, what you would describe as a Pudding Basin Haircut. Girls wore a white skirt and blouse and boys wore white shorts and shirt. There were children from all over the world, including a few wealthy Chinese, but we all looked the same. My mother was relieved now that we had Ah How to wash the school uniforms and my father's uniforms. Electrical goods were much cheaper than in England and Dad bought a steam iron. Ah How burnt holes in all our clothes until she got used to it.

Ed, Pat, Margaret, Joan and Daphne, Hong Kong, circa 1935.

Ed, Joan, Sam, Margaret, Hilda Mary, Daphne, Pat, Hong Kong circa 1935.

During our lunch break, an old man wearing a conical straw hat tied under his chin and traditional Chinese clothes, which always looked to us like pyjamas, sold delicious sweets through the school railings. He rode an old bicycle with a basket on the front containing his wares. He didn't wear shoes and his feet were filthy. He had very long, dirty fingernails. We all loved his sweets and, whenever I had some money, I joined the queue to buy some.

It took me just under half an hour to walk home from school. The boys said they could do it in fifteen minutes, but I liked to stop and look at things. One day, when I was about halfway, I felt a compelling need to find a toilet, but there wasn't one nearby. I climbed through a hole in the fence and found a place to squat in a vacant block. To my horror, out came what looked like a white snake. It was several feet long and I was horrified to think it had been inside me. When I got home, I told my mother, who said it was a tapeworm. We were all taken to see the Army doctor who gave us some foul-tasting medication. Most of the children who had bought sweets from the old man got infected, so the headmistress, Sister Mary Paul McKenna, made it a punishable offence to buy his sweets and he eventually stopped coming.

One day, Ah How said to my father: "Master owe me four dollars."

My father asked why.

"Number one son, he want go see pictures and not got any dollars, so I give."

In Chinese culture, the eldest male in a household is the boss. So when my father wasn't there Ah How thought that Pat was in charge. When he asked her for money, she couldn't refuse. My father had difficulty explaining that, in Western culture, it didn't work that way. If he wasn't there then my mother, not my eldest brother, was in charge.

My father gave Ah How the money, told her not to do it again and gave Pat a good telling off.

Ah How turned up one day with a teenage girl trotting behind her. The girl's name was Ali and she was a trainee amah. She couldn't speak English, but she was a hard worker and a quick learner and Ah How said we didn't have to pay her because she would give her some of her wages. Ah How enjoyed bossing the trainee around and doing very little herself. About a month later, Ali disappeared and was never seen again. Ah How said she had "gone walkie to Canton," which we were told meant that she had got herself a better job. Or a better deal.

The expatriate women loved to go shopping in Hong Kong because there were lots of bargains. Dad bought a portable, wind-up record player made by His Master's Voice and started collecting vinyl records. He loved the music of George Gershwin, Cole Porter, the Glenn Miller Orchestra and the comic operas of Gilbert and Sullivan. Dad would sing along as the music blared out in our apartment.

Mum found a dressmaker and had some cotton dresses made for herself, my sisters and me and some shirts for Dad and my brothers. I found a photograph in a magazine of Princess Elizabeth, who was three years older than me, wearing a lovely dress with lots of little buttons down the bodice and capped sleeves. We bought some similar floral fabric and the dressmaker copied the design. I called it my princess dress.

A few months after we moved to Hong Kong, my mother was gravely ill and spent about three weeks in Kowloon hospital. In her absence, Army friends brought food and took it in turns to babysit. There was a lot of whispering. Many years later, Mum told me she had lost a baby which was almost full-term. She also lost a lot of blood, so they had to do an immediate hysterectomy. An infection, at a time when there were no antibiotics, was an added complication. It was touch and go. Children were always kept in the dark back then. Sometime later I put two and two together and worked out it had something to do with the bump. Mum didn't have it when she came home, looking dreadfully pale and thin. There was no more talk of the imminent new addition to the family. Mum had enough to do, with five small children, and it was a relief to know that there would be no more.

THE WET MARKETS

Even though I was quite young when we lived in Hong Kong, I have vivid memories. Everything was so different, especially the noises, the colours and the smells. Life back in England was mundane, black-and-white by comparison.

Mum would sometimes take me with her to the wet markets in Kowloon. There was no refrigeration back then, so fresh food was bought daily. If you wanted to buy a chicken, they would cut its head off right in front of you. All sorts of weird things were for sale, such as rice wine with a whole snake inside the bottle and bats, for making bat soup.

A huge amount of seafood was consumed in Hong Kong, including things I had never seen before, such as sea cucumbers and sea slugs. My mother couldn't take Daphne and Joan to the markets, especially Daphne, who would faint at the slightest provocation. They stayed at home with Ah How. My brothers didn't go because they weren't interested. It was a pretty smelly place—a combination of fish, blood, cooking oil and sweaty bodies—but I was fascinated.

When we were all at school, Mum went to the market with Ah How, who helped her choose the freshest fish and introduced her to some vegetables we had never seen before. She also taught Mum how to cook rice and serve it with fried fish covered in a delicious spicy sauce. The twins didn't like spicy food but the rest of us loved Ah How's recipes.

A SOCIAL WHIRL

The 1920s and 1930s saw an unprecedented pursuit of pleasure, with excesses of partying and drinking too much. It was thought to be a reaction to the austerities of the First World War, when a generation of young men were wiped out.

My parents enjoyed a hectic social life in Hong Kong, with dances, sing-along soirées—where they all gathered around a piano—and dinners. We were often invited to children's parties and went frequently to the cinema. The Alhambra Theatre in Nathan Road was the first luxurious cinema in Hong Kong. It opened a week or two before we arrived and the first movie they showed was a musical called *Gold Diggers of 1933*.

We loved musicals. After seeing the films *Rags to Riches* and *On the Good Ship Lollipop,* I learnt all the songs sung by Shirley Temple, a child actress who was one year older than me. Just five years old and already an international star! I was in awe.

It was at about this time that we started to put together our first Staples Five Show. Pat and I were in charge, while Ed, Joan and Daphne did as they were told. Ah How clapped enthusiastically as we rehearsed.

Dad was appointed Secretary of the Royal Engineers Old Comrades Association, in charge of organising a weekly dinner-dance with a live orchestra in the Rose Room, on the 6th floor of the Peninsula Hotel. With seven floors and 168 rooms and suites, this five-star hotel was only a few years old, having opened in 1928. It was built in the Baroque style by two brothers, Ellis and Elly Kadoorie, a wealthy family from Baghdad.

Located opposite the quays where passengers disembarked from the ocean liners, the Peninsula was the tallest building in Hong Kong at that time. It quickly became synonymous with white-glove service and Old-World grandeur, advertised as "the finest hotel east of the Suez." It was just a five-minute walk from where we lived, and we walked past whenever we went to catch the Star Ferry across the harbour.

When guests arrived at the hotel, a pageboy wearing a starched white uniform and a pillbox hat opened the door with a flourish and ushered them inside with a bow. All the rich and famous stayed there. When Dad came home and said he had seen Charlie Chaplin eating breakfast, we were very impressed. We went to see all his films. Dad talked to everybody and one day he met a very likeable young man from America who was a playwright. His name was Tennessee Williams. We remembered his unusual name and followed his career with great interest.

The Peninsula, or the Pen as it was affectionately known by the regulars, was *the* place to be in Hong Kong. There were dinner-dances, balls and buffet dinners in the Rose Room or on the Roof-Top Terrace to celebrate every possible event in the calendar: Christmas, New Year, Chinese New Year, St Patrick's, St George's and St Andrew's day. One year, Mum took part in the Easter Bonnet Parade and won a prize. We loved to see my parents in their finery, heading off to a function at the Peninsula. Sometimes they would bring back balloons or fancy masks for us.

My father described a typical Chinese banquet at the Pen in his diary:

Turtle soup
Bird's nest soup
Shark's fin soup
Crispy skin of duck
Chopped chicken
Curried prawns
Bamboo shoots
Shellfish of all kinds
Fried rice with ham and egg

Duck was very popular and the Chinese ate every part of the bird, even the feet. Dad said the only part they didn't eat was the quack.

Every afternoon, a tea dance was held in the lobby, with a live jazz band. It was always packed, with almost as many Chinese as expatriate couples. The locals had taken to Western dancing in a big way. Darjeeling and Ceylon tea were served in bone China teapots, with dainty crustless sandwiches, tiny cakes and scones with strawberry jam and clotted cream, all balanced on tiered silver platters. There was an unwritten protocol whereby the attached ladies sat on the right-hand side of the lobby and the unattached ladies sat on the left-hand side.

When King George V celebrated his Silver Jubilee in May 1935, the Peninsula was covered in fairy lights, all the way around the edge of the H-shaped building. We went to see it one evening after dark. It looked like a huge Christmas tree.

I dreamt of dancing at the Peninsula when I grew up.

THE TYPHOON

One of my most vivid memories was when there was a typhoon on 17 August 1936. Typhoons are common in the China seas. They can travel great distances across land and water, leaving a wake of destruction behind them. The wind velocity at the height of the storm reaches extraordinary levels. In its journey, the typhoon often banks up tidal waves which are disastrous to seafront towns in the path of the storm.

The warning signals were up on the Harbour Tower, the ferries had ceased to operate, and everyone sought shelter. The harbour was devoid of the innumerable junks which normally covered its surface. They had all moved to the typhoon anchorage. Just after lunch, the sky darkened. My father raced around closing all the windows and doors.

We remained shut in for three days. The only damage we suffered was that the window in the kitchen was blown in, so we were unable to cook, except on a little charcoal stove which Ah How used to cook rice. We lived mainly on tinned food, of which we had quite a stock. The wind blew at 147 miles per hour and it was certain death for anyone who remained outside. If you weren't picked up by the wind, flying objects would quickly finish you off.

After three days of imprisonment, the wind moderated and I went downstairs to look around. The street was 8 to 10 feet high in fallen branches and fish lay here and there, even though we were about 350 yards from the harbour. There was a great deal of broken glass, as well as doors, windows, corrugated iron bent into fantastic shapes and all sorts of other miscellaneous objects. Most of the trees had been uprooted. My father knew there would also be a number of drowned bodies, so he made me come inside and close the door before I saw any.

When he came home from work the next day, he told us that a 6,000-ton steamship called the Sunning had been lifted from the harbour onto Stonecutters Island. It was carrying British officers and Chinese passengers. Another had pulled her moorings and been smashed against the rocks and broken in two. Altogether over a hundred people had died. These typhoons originated in the Sea of Formosa, which is now called the Strait of Taiwan. My father said they were a terrible warning from Mother Nature of man's smallness and helplessness.

SUNDAYS AT THE BEACH

A more pleasant memory is of the Sunday afternoon picnics. A group of families would rent a boat to sail out of the harbour and up the coast to Clear Water Bay. It was a beautiful spot. Near the beach was a Chinese temple we used to visit. The main feature of this brick structure was that it had circular doorways about eight feet in diameter. My father told me that the Chinese had built them like that because they believe that the Devil cannot enter through a circular door opening.

One Sunday, we went across to the beach on Stonecutters Island. In the 1990s, the piece of sea that separated it from the Kowloon Peninsula was filled in and reclaimed, but back then it was an island.

Pat, who was about six at the time, threw off his clothes and ran off as soon as we arrived. A few minutes later, someone came running up to tell my parents that something had happened to him. My father ran to find Pat lying behind the Pavilion with two men resuscitating him. It had all happened so quickly. He had dashed into the water, where a huge wave had pulled him out to sea. Luckily, he was seen by a man standing on the beach, who swam out and brought him back, more dead than alive. Pat survived that dreadful experience, but within a week my father had organised swimming lessons for the five of us.

Parasols for the hot sun, Hong Kong, early 1937:
Joan (5), Margaret (7), Daphne (5).

George V died of smoking-related lung disease in January 1936 and was succeeded by his elder son, Edward VIII. He reigned for less than a year, deciding to abdicate and marry a divorced American socialite, Wallis Simpson. George V's second son took the throne: King George VI was crowned on 12 May 1937.

That same month, in May 1937, my father's posting came to an end.

We were all so happy in Hong Kong, we asked my father if we could stay. He said unfortunately that wasn't possible. Another family was already on their way from England, and they would live in our apartment. Dad started to talk about being back in England and all the fun we would have seeing Granny Kenny and meeting our cousins. We were still sad to leave.

We sailed home on SS Rajputana, another P&O luxury liner. We were travelling First Class and again there were lots of parties for the children and fancy dinners for the adults. We stopped at all the places we had visited on the way to Hong Kong, in reverse order.

DARLINGTON

The journey home was uneventful, and we arrived at Tilbury Docks on 4 June 1937, three months before my 8th birthday. After a few days in London, where we caught the end of the coronation celebrations for George VI, we travelled north by train to Darlington and moved into comfortable Army quarters in the barracks.

Based in Darlington, my father's new title was Clerk of Works, covering Richmond, Bishop Auckland, Hartlepool, Redcar and Darlington. The work involved producing high-level engineering designs for military buildings and supervising their construction. Pat went to St Mary's Grammar, a fee-paying Catholic school for boys, while the rest of us went to a local primary school.

Dad travelled quite a bit in his new job, and he had to provide his own means of transport. He bought an old Wolseley Hornet for £45. It was a complete dud, continually letting him down. Fortunately, he managed to sell it for the same price. He then bought a Morris 10 which was only a couple of years old for £10. Every Saturday, he took my brothers to watch either Darlington or Middlesbrough play football.

Many of the parks we went to in Darlington displayed an old tank from the First World War which we loved to play in. Early in 1938, they all disappeared. When I asked my father what had happened to them, he said that they were being melted down, in case there was a war. The metal would be used for new munitions. Then the iron railings in front of many houses also disappeared. They all went into the melting pot. We saw men filling sandbags and were told they would be needed if there was a war.

THE IDEAL HOME EXHIBITION

Whenever we were living in England, my father went to the Ideal Home Exhibition in London, every year, without fail. He loved to see the innovations in home equipment and find time-saving devices for his large family. Sometimes he went with my mother, but more often he went on his own.

In April 1938, he took me with him. We drove from Darlington to London, stopping in Brigg to spend a night with Granny Kenny. I had only met her once or twice before, so I never really got to know her. Dad rang the doorbell, and she must have been waiting because she opened it almost immediately, beaming with delight. She was wearing a cotton floral pinafore over her clothes. It had a front and a back and ties at the sides, to keep her clothes clean while she was cooking or cleaning. She never took it off. Granny Kenny was in her late fifties at the time, short and stocky, with snow white hair pulled into a bun, pale skin and florid cheeks.

The red brick house was quite large which was not surprising since at one time there had been 13 people living there. The living-cum-dining room ran the entire length of the house and when we arrived there was a roaring fire burning at one end. The room had five big windows and was filled with pictures and indoor plants.

Granny served a lamb hot pot for dinner, or supper as she called it. Dad rubbed his hands together with glee when he saw that his favourite steamed treacle pudding, smothered with creamy custard, was for dessert. My mother had tried to make it once, but it had been a disaster. I met some of my Kennington half-cousins. They all had strong northern accents and said I sounded posh. After dinner, Dad and I sang a duet which he normally sang with Mum. I loved it when my parents sang a duet together. They always looked into each other's eyes, and you could feel the love.

An early night was in order and Dad set his alarm clock for five the next morning. We arrived at the Exhibition in Olympia just as the doors were opening. Dad showed me where I had to come back to if I got lost, then we set off, in a logical fashion, to visit every single stand. My father planned all activities with military precision.

The Exhibition Centre was huge, with ceilings so high they had built several complete houses inside! There were even swimming pools and gardens. We walked our feet off, looking at all the new gadgets, collecting all the brochures and tasting all the food samples. There were hundreds of people, but I managed not to lose sight of my father, who chatted with everyone.

Dad ordered a Bendix washing machine, a Hoover vacuum cleaner, a General Electric toaster and a new steam iron, to replace the one we had bought in Hong Kong which wasn't working very well. Mum had just received a small inheritance from one of her Irish aunties, which funded Dad's shopping spree. We even saw some machines for doing the washing up. Dad said we might get one next year. A stand selling John Line & Co wallpaper gave Dad a free set of farmyard designs which he stuck on the wall of the boys' bedroom when we got home.

It was late afternoon when we left, and I was exhausted. We stayed overnight in London with Auntie Molly, Mum's sister and her husband, Uncle Will. They lived in Hackney and had two boys, Don who was nine like me and Billy, who had just turned one and was starting to walk.

We left for Darlington after breakfast the next morning and stopped for fish and chips for lunch. I slept some of the way and we sang lots of songs—a Staples tradition when travelling anywhere by car. We got home just as it was getting dark.

POSTED TO MALTA

In the summer of 1938, I was confirmed at the local Catholic church on the same day as both my brothers. I chose St Theresa as my confirmation saint.

In September of that year my father was promoted to Warrant Officer—the most senior of the non-commissioned ranks. Warrant officers had responsibilities that included training soldiers, as well as engineering tasks, such as supervising military buildings and giving technical advice on new installations.

Within a few days of receiving his promotion, Dad was informed that he had been posted to Malta. He told us all about it over dinner. I'd heard of Malta but didn't know much about it. Dad filled us in.

Malta was a small island near Italy. Within the Royal Engineers, it was called a "holiday posting," because of the weather. Malta's sunny Mediterranean climate meant you could go swimming and play cricket and tennis all year round, Dad said. This sounded brilliant. What could be better, after the British weather we were used to? Some of

Margaret, confirmation day, Darlington 1938.

the officers, Dad had heard, owned yachts and were members of the Royal Malta Yacht Club. Local leave from Malta meant you could visit Africa, Sicily and even Rome. Friends at work had slapped Dad on the back and said he was "jammy," slang for lucky, to be going to Malta.

All military personnel posted to Malta were given a little handbook which Dad brought home for us to read. This is part of the introduction:

> Malta is like a jewel set in a sea of sapphire. With its equable climate, as a health resort it has no peer in the Mediterranean. Nothing can be more delightful than a sojourn there during the winter months. While northern countries are enveloped in fog, drenched in rain, or covered with snow, the Maltese islands are bright with sunshine, blue sea and charming flowers.[11]

I've always been a bookworm, and as soon as Dad's posting was confirmed, I went to the public library and borrowed every book I could find about Malta. Ed loved me to read to him and while he was happy to listen to pretty much anything—apart from books by Enid Blyton which he said were cissy—he particularly enjoyed history books and so did I. We loved reading about Malta and couldn't wait to go.

School broke up a week before Christmas. We helped Mum and Dad to pack everything up, then a removalist company called Binns came and collected all our furniture and a few cartons which were to go into storage while we were in Malta. The electrical items Dad had ordered at the Ideal Home Exhibition were delivered while we were packing, so we left them in their boxes, to go straight to Malta. Dad ordered lots of non-fiction books to take with us. He loved his books.

Dad sold his car which was too small for the seven of us to travel any distance and borrowed a Ford station wagon from one of his friends for a couple of weeks. We all piled in and headed north to spend Christmas and New Year in Brigg, with Granny Kenny. As Dad had 10 half brothers and sisters living in and around Brigg there were lots of cousins to play with. He showed us where he had gone to school and all his old haunts. Granny told us stories about Dad when he was a naughty little boy, which we loved.

My brothers and I pooled all the money we had in our piggy banks and had just enough to buy Dad a bottle of Old Spice aftershave and Mum some 4711 perfume for Christmas.

We were all very excited about the move.

A BRIEF HISTORY OF MALTA

With a mix of Maltese, Italian, British, Arab and North African influence, the ethnic makeup of Malta is diverse. The culture is a fascinating mix of traditional Mediterranean customs and more modern European influences.

The history of Malta is shaped by its location, colonisation and conquest. The earliest inhabitants are believed to have arrived around 5,000 BC from Sicily and North Africa and were likely a mix of Berbers, Phoenicians and other groups.

In 218 BC, Malta came under the control of the Roman Empire and was part of the Roman, Byzantine and Arab empires for the next 700 years. During this time, Malta was inhabited by a mix of Berbers, Arabs and other groups, so the island's language and culture were heavily influenced by these different civilizations.

The Arab conquest of Malta occurred in the 9th century, during the expansion of the Islamic Empire. At the time, Malta was part of the Byzantine Empire, which had controlled the islands since the 6th century. However, their presence on Malta was weakened by a series of attacks by North African raiders and, in 870 AD, the island was conquered by an Arab fleet who were able to overcome the Byzantine garrison.

After taking control of Malta, the Arab conquerors established a garrison and a naval base on the island. They also began to develop the agriculture and economy of the island, which had been neglected by the Byzantine authorities. The Arab rulers encouraged the cultivation of citrus fruits, cotton and other crops. They also developed a thriving trade in textiles and other goods.

The Arab period of Malta's history lasted for about two hundred years. During this time, the island was part of a larger Muslim world that stretched from Spain to India. The Arab conquerors left a lasting impact on Maltese culture, introducing new customs, language and architecture. Many Maltese words and phrases have Arabic roots and some of the island's most iconic landmarks, such as the fortified city of Mdina, were built during the Arab period.

In the 11th century, the Arab presence in Malta was weakened by a series of internal conflicts and invasions by Norman forces from Sicily, who conquered the island in 1090. Malta became part of the Kingdom of Sicily. The Normans introduced Catholicism to Malta and their language, which would later become Maltese.

Throughout the Middle Ages, Malta was ruled by a series of foreign powers, including the Sicilian and Aragonese kingdoms. In 1530, the island was granted to the Knights of St John. During their rule, Malta experienced a period of economic and cultural growth. The island's architecture, art and literature flourished.

In 1798, Napoleon Bonaparte invaded, and Malta was briefly ruled by the French. The British took control of Malta in 1800 and ruled for the next 164 years. During British rule, Malta developed into a major naval base and played a vital role in the First and Second World Wars.

The British left a lasting legacy on the island's culture, including the English language and the sport of cricket. But it was the island's strategic military position that made it into a rope in the tug-of-war of military powers. This would especially be the case during the Second World War which, though we didn't know it when we moved to Malta, was imminent.

LANGUAGE

The Maltese language is the only Semitic language spoken in the European Union. The Semitic languages are a branch of the Afroasiatic language family.

Maltese has a fascinating history that spans thousands of years. The language has Phoenician roots. This ancient civilization of seafarers and traders once lived in what is now Lebanon, Syria and Palestine. They established colonies throughout the Mediterranean, including on the island of Malta. It was the Phoenicians who first introduced their language to Malta, which was then known as Melita and can be traced back at least 2500 years.

Melita was influenced by various other languages over the centuries, including Arabic, Italian and Sicilian. It has its own unique grammar and vocabulary. It was traditionally written using the Arabic script, but since the 20th century, has been written using the Latin alphabet, with some modifications.

When the Knights of St John established their capital in Malta, they brought with them several languages, including Italian, Spanish and French. This had a significant impact on the development of the Maltese language and many words and phrases from these languages can still be found in modern Maltese.

In 1869, a Maltese linguist named Mikiel Anton Vassalli published a book with the first comprehensive grammar of the language. It helped to establish the Maltese language as distinct from Arabic. In 1934, Maltese was recognised as an official language of Malta, along with English. This was an important milestone, giving it a greater degree of recognition and legitimacy. In 2004, Maltese was officially recognised as a European Union language. Today, it is spoken by around half a million people who live in Malta and some parts of Sicily and North Africa.

The Maltese language is like a tapestry of Mediterranean history. New words and phrases introduced from other cultures sit like demarcations in the country's timeline.

Before we left England for Malta, I found a little tourist book at the library which included a few pages of Maltese vocabulary. I didn't know if my pronunciation was correct, but I soon learnt some basic words and sentences. I was looking forward to trying them out when we got to Malta.

THE KNIGHTS OF MALTA

The Order of Knights of Malta, also known as the Sovereign Military Order of Malta, is one of the oldest religious orders in the world. Its origins can be traced back to the 11th century, when a group of monks established a hospital in Jerusalem to care for pilgrims.

The hospital was initially run by a religious order known as the Hospital Brothers of St John of Jerusalem. They were primarily responsible for tending to the sick and wounded, but they soon extended their role to provide protection for the pilgrims who were frequently attacked by bandits during their journey to Jerusalem.

In 1113, the Hospital Brothers were recognised as a religious order by Pope Paschal II and became known as the Knights Hospitaller. The Knights were given the status of a military order in 1136, which meant that they were authorised to engage in combat against the enemies of Christendom.

In the years that followed, the Knights Hospitaller became a powerful force in the Holy Land and played a key role in the defence of Jerusalem during the Crusades. They were also responsible for the construction of many significant buildings in Jerusalem.

When Saladin, the first Sultan of Egypt, captured Jerusalem in 1187, the Knights were forced to move north to Acre. In 1291, they relocated to the island of Cyprus, where they continued their work for the next 18 years. Their departure from Cyprus, because of their involvement in temporal politics, coincided with a movement in Europe against a parallel brotherhood of priest-knights called the Knights Templar.

In 1307, on Friday the 13th of October, French King Philip IV the Fair launched a secret operation: the mass arrest of all the Knights Templar in the Kingdom of France. This is the origin of the modern superstition that bad things happen on Friday the 13th.

The abrupt fall of the once hugely influential Knights Templar prompted the Knights Hospitaller of St John to move and consolidate. They were a strong military force and decided that, if they hunkered down on a fortified island, they could withstand any foe. After four years of campaigning, the Knights of St John captured the island of Rhodes in 1309. There they established a naval fleet, which they used to protect Christian shipping in the Mediterranean. They also occupied territories on the mainland during this time, such as Smyrna, in Anatolia, which today is Izmir in Turkey.

Rhodes was a strategically important island that served as a gateway between Europe and the Middle East. The Knights of St John recognised its value as a key location for their defence against Muslim expansion in the region. They built a formidable fortress, the Palace of the Grand Master, which became the centre of their operations on the island.

In 1522, the Ottoman Empire, under the leadership of Sultan Suleiman the Magnificent, launched a massive siege of Rhodes with an army of over 100,000 soldiers and a fleet of warships. The Knights of St John were vastly outnumbered, with only 6,000 soldiers and a handful of ships. Despite the odds, the Knights held out against the Ottoman forces for six months, using their superior knowledge of the terrain and expert military tactics to inflict heavy losses on the enemy. The Ottoman army was further inhibited by bouts of disease and food and water shortages.

The Knights were eventually overwhelmed by the sheer size of the Ottoman army and, in December 1522, they surrendered. The terms of the surrender allowed the Knights to leave Rhodes unharmed, taking their holy relics and other valuables with them.

In 1530, the Knights Hospitaller were given the islands of Malta and Gozo by the Holy Roman Emperor Charles V of Spain, in recognition of their services to the Catholic Church. The Knights moved there to continue their mission of defending Christianity against Muslim expansion in the Mediterranean and became known as the Knights of Malta. They established their headquarters in Vittoriosa (present-day Birgu), carried out improvements to Fort St Angelo and began to transform the island into a powerful military fortress–the original "Fortress Malta."

Over the next few decades, the Knights of Malta became one of the most powerful military forces in the Mediterranean. They successfully repelled several attacks by the Ottomans, including the First Siege of Malta in 1565, which lasted for several months and ended in victory for the Knights.

The Knights built a series of bell-shaped pits, covered with circular stone slabs, for storing grain. They are located throughout Valletta and Floriana and were used right up to and during the Second World War. They were a perfect way to store provisions in case of siege.

The Knights became known for their acts of charity and philanthropy, establishing hospitals and orphanages throughout Europe. They also provided relief to the victims of natural disasters and other crises.

The 18th century was a difficult period for the Knights. They were caught up in the geopolitical struggles of the time and suffered a series of military defeats at the hands of their enemies. In 1798, the island of Malta was occupied by French forces under the command of Napoleon Bonaparte and the Knights were forced to flee.

They continued to exist in exile and gradually regained some of their former power and prestige. In 1834, the Order established its headquarters in Rome and was recognised as a sovereign entity by several European powers.

Whether it is referred to as the Order of St John, The Knights Hospitaller or The Knights of Malta, this body is known for its charitable work in disaster relief, providing aid to victims of earthquakes, hurricanes and other natural disasters around the globe. The best-known activities are those of the St John Ambulance Brigade, but the Order also operates hospitals, clinics and other healthcare facilities, providing assistance to those in need, regardless of race, religion, or social status.

THE FIRST SIEGE OF MALTA

The First Siege of Malta, between 1565 and 1566, was a major battle between the Ottoman Empire and the Knights of Malta.

The Ottoman Empire, under the leadership of Suleiman the Magnificent, had been expanding its territory throughout the Mediterranean for several years. In 1565, Suleiman set his sights on Malta, which was an ideal seat for control of the Mediterranean. For veteran Knights, this must have been a horrific feeling of déjà vu—they had come to Malta after being driven out of Rhodes by the Ottomans in 1522, some 40 years earlier.

The siege began on 18 May 1565, when an Ottoman fleet of around 200 ships, carrying an estimated 40,000 soldiers, arrived off the coast. The Knights, led by Grand Master Jean Parisot de Valette, had a much smaller force, with around 500 knights and approximately 8,000 soldiers and civilians.

Despite the overwhelming odds, the Knights were determined to defend their stronghold. They had spent years preparing for an attack, building walls, fortifications and gun emplacements. They had learned Ottoman tactics through their failure to defend Rhodes.

The Ottomans launched a series of attacks on the city but were repeatedly repelled. The Knights were helped by the local population, who provided food and supplies, as well as by a small force of Spanish soldiers who arrived to reinforce the defenders. Pushed to their limits, with supplies dwindling, the Knights refused to give up. In September, the Ottomans launched a massive assault on the city, but the Knights were able to keep them out.

In October, a relief force arrived from Sicily. The Ottomans, realising that their position was untenable, decided to withdraw. The siege had lasted for 115 days and had cost the lives of thousands of soldiers and civilians on both sides.

The siege marked a pivotal moment in the struggle between the Ottoman Empire and the Christian powers of Europe and solidified the reputation of the Knights of Malta as a formidable military force. It also had a profound impact on the people of Malta, who saw it as a heroic moment in their history. A symbol of their resilience and determination in the face of adversity. Nor would it be the last.

While the Knights had successfully defended the island against the Ottoman attack, the conflict highlighted the need for a more fortified and strategically located capital city than Mdina, the capital of Malta at that time. Grand Master Jean Parisot de Valette, the leader of the Knights of St John, commissioned the construction of a new city on the Sciberras Peninsula, a narrow strip of land overlooking the Grand Harbour. The city of Valletta was named after him and was designed by Italian military engineer, Francesco Laparelli.

Given the objective of improving the fortifications of the island, Valletta was built in a grid pattern, with straight streets and wide squares, fortified by massive walls, bastions and gates, making it virtually impregnable. Narrow streets, rising steeply as they got closer to the centre of the city, would make it difficult for enemy troops to move in significant numbers. The streets had steps that were built in such a way that Knights in heavy armour would be able to climb them.

Valletta was completed in 1571 and quickly became an important centre of trade and culture in the Mediterranean. The Knights established their headquarters there and the city became the administrative centre of the Order's possessions throughout the region.

To further strengthen their landward defences, in 1635 fortification lines were designed by another Italian military engineer, Pietro Paolo Floriani. The area between these lines and Valletta was named Floriana, in his honour.

During the 16th and 17th centuries, Valletta was a hub of artistic and intellectual activity, home to numerous artists, writers and musicians who played an important role in the development of Baroque art and architecture in Europe.

It was during this period that the famous St John's Co-Cathedral, dedicated to St John the Baptist, and St Paul's Co-Cathedral, with its 60-metre-tall dome, were commissioned by the Knights. A co-cathedral is the co-seat of a bishop, sharing the diocese under a bishop's control.

During the 18th and 19th centuries, Valletta continued to develop as an important centre of trade and commerce. The city's strategic location made it a vital port for ships travelling between Europe, Africa and Asia.

THE SECOND SIEGE OF MALTA

Napoleon Bonaparte arrived in Malta in June 1798 with a fleet of more than 400 ships and an army of 30,000 soldiers. He had managed to keep his plans to invade Malta a secret and the Knights were caught completely off-guard.

Valletta was crucial to the success of his plan to control the Mediterranean, expand the French Empire and thwart his main rival, the British, by disrupting their trade routes. Despite fierce resistance, Napoleon's forces were able to take control of the island in a couple of days. While the Knights had the means to withstand a siege, a series of circumstances, including discontent among their own French members, as well as the native Maltese population, led to a truce which ended with the capitulation of the Knights.

They were allowed to leave the island with their ships, holy relics, weapons and valuables. Estranged from their island, the Knights dispersed. Some travelled to St Petersburg to seek help from their protector Emperor Paul I, who gave them a splendid palace there.[12]

Once Napoleon secured Malta, he established a new government, appointed a new governor and set about consolidating his position in the Mediterranean. A few months after the invasion, unpopular governmental reforms led to an uprising which resulted in a blockade of the French garrison by Maltese insurgents, aided by the British,

Neapolitans and Portuguese. The Second Siege of Malta lasted for two years and ended with the French surrendering to the British in 1800, making Malta a protectorate and initiating 164 years of British rule.

The Maltese people had sought assistance from Britain to drive the French out of their country. As a token of appreciation for the British intervention and success, Malta voluntarily became a British colony and remained under the direct rule of Britain as a protectorate till 1964 when it became independent.

It was as a British Protectorate that the Third Siege of Malta occurred, during the Second World War.

ON OUR WAY TO MALTA

We sailed from Southampton on 16 January 1939 on HMS Somersetshire. In September that year, the ship was requisitioned and converted into a hospital ship, but it would be many months before Britain needed floating hospitals.

The ship was gleaming white with dozens of windows which shot back limited sun through the grey clouds. A rope lined with flags, like charms on a bracelet, was hung from the mast, where it danced in the wind. I ran down the deck, running my hand along the polished wooden balustrade that wrapped around its length.

So many Army families were leaving on that ship that the BBC were there to record the event. Masses of people waved goodbye from the wharf. There was a sense of adventure and a good deal of luxury for families like us, of the higher ranked officers.

It was a cold grey day, as we sailed away towards the promise of sunshine. My older brother Pat, 11 at the time, had a lovely voice and lots of self-confidence. As we slowly pulled away from the shores of England, he jumped up onto a chair in the saloon and sang "Wish Me Luck as I Go On My Way," earning a huge round of applause.

I went on deck to watch as we passed the Needles, a row of three stacks of chalk that rise about 30 yards out of the sea off the western extremity of the Isle of Wight in the English Channel. Then we headed south into the gloom of the night. Everyone was seasick crossing the

Bay of Biscay, on our way to Gibraltar which was our first stop. We spent two days there and, after the wintry weather of England, enjoyed seeing the sun.

There were several parties and other activities for the children on board and we had a wonderful time. Apart from swimming, there were all kinds of games—sack races, egg and spoon races, deck tennis and even horse races using mechanical horses. The games weren't just for the children—they were also very popular with the adults.

We travelled First Class, while the families of the lower ranks travelled Second. Through the bars of the gate which separated us, I made friends with a girl my age called Joyce Palmer. She wasn't allowed to come into the First-Class area, but we spent hours chatting through the gate and became firm friends for life.

My father spent a lot of time in the saloon with the other military men, talking about the threat of war. It seemed so remote, and never even occurred to us children as a possibility. We overheard things, but with so much excitement, nothing ominous registered. Some of the parents were convinced it would happen. Others were convinced it would not.

The officers chatted through a thick fog of cigarette smoke that hung in the saloon. We would sit under one of the tables, below the smoke screen, and listen to the conversations about war. When we discussed it afterwards, my brothers said it sounded very exciting. War in the hypothetical is exciting. We had no concept of the folly of this romantic view.

The journey to Malta took 10 days. We were having such fun; I'd have liked the voyage to have lasted longer. Little did I know that I was about to embark on the six most memorable and often terrifying years of my life.

PART 2

MALTA

ARRIVAL IN MALTA

The sea was rough as we entered the Straits of Messina, which separates Sicily from Malta, early on the morning of 24 January 1939. There were huge, rolling waves. But once we passed Valletta's breakwater, we were into the calm depths of the Grand Harbour. I watched through a porthole as we sailed into the port. With Fort St Elmo on one side of the harbour and Fort Ricasoli on the other, it felt as if we were sailing into a history book.

It was a beautiful clear day with a deep-blue sky and an even deeper blue sea: two different but equally dazzling shades of the same colour. It made me think of two precious stones, lapis lazuli and blue sapphire, lying side by side.

Valletta, the capital of Malta, looked like a giant castle which someone had carved out of pale gold honeycomb. The city was on a rocky limestone promontory, with castle walls that went all the way down to the sea. The buildings sparkled in the bright sunshine. It took my breath away.

Before we arrived, Dad had explained that a Maltese civilian named Tony Cefai had been assigned to work as his personal assistant, known in the Army as a "batman." This part-time job entailed looking after my father's uniform, collecting the mail and running errands. Tony was on the landing stage in front of Custom House when we arrived. An Army officer called Major Fowler was also there to meet us and he introduced Dad to his new batman. Dad then introduced us all to the Major and the batman. We were to call him Mr Cefai, while my father called him Cefai, which was pronounced "Shefai."

Dad's new assistant was in his late 20s, an inch or so shorter than my father, with a solid build, very dark brown, almost black wavy hair and brown, friendly eyes. He wasn't wearing a uniform, but was smartly dressed in a cream jacket, white shirt and tie. On the bottom half, he wore knee-length khaki shorts, long socks which came to just below the knee and were turned over at the top and very stylish brown and white Oxford brogues, which he told me later were a gift from Dad's predecessor.

Our luggage appeared from the hold and while my father checked to make sure it was all there, we chatted to Mr Cefai. He pointed out that, on a clear day, you could see a volcano called Mount Etna on the island of Sicily, some 60 miles away. We all stood on tiptoes to check. What I had thought were cliffs around the edge of the harbour, like those I had seen in the south of England, were defensive walls, called bastions. They'd been built by the Knights of St John several hundred years ago, to keep the enemies out. The Grand Harbour was surrounded by the bastions of five forts: Fort Saint Elmo, Lascaris, Ricasoli, Saint Angelo and Saint Michael. That's why Malta was often called the Fortress Island, Mr Cefai explained. He said the harbour was very deep, making it perfect for big ships like the one we had arrived in. He was a mine of information and we liked him immediately.

While the officials were checking our papers, I noticed lots of cats waiting patiently for the laden fishing boats to arrive. If there were so many stray cats in Malta, I thought, perhaps I could get one of my own? In the blue expanse above, gulls wheeled, complaining noisily as they watched the haul of fish with their beady eyes, to make sure they didn't miss out.

A number of barefoot children were begging or offering to carry people's luggage. A group of women chatted animatedly while they waited to be allowed on board our ship to sell their lace tablecloths. Crates of food and water were being loaded on board, for the onward journey. The next port of call was Port Said, and the final destination was Sydney, Australia. A few people boarded in Malta for those destinations.

Mr Cefai said that P&O ships on their way back to England from the Far East called in every other Friday. People living in Malta used this service to go to England for business or a holiday. There were no commercial flights back then. A Second-Class ticket cost £14 and First Class was £20.[13]

We piled into three vehicles with all our belongings and set off towards our new home, which was in a suburb called Dragonara. All the houses we passed were square with two or three stories and flat roofs dotted with colourful pumpkins and melons, which were set there to ripen in the sun. Most houses had enclosed balconies and painted wooden shutters. Dark green and red were popular colours and the large timber doors, many with stout brass door knockers, were painted to match. Everywhere I looked, Malta's honey-coloured limestone dominated the landscape.

England had lush green grass everywhere, but there was virtually none to be seen in Malta. Just a few dried-up shrubs and trees. Water, I discovered later, was the key to making things grow. And to survive.

All the houses in Malta had a name and ours was called Carmen. It was on a promontory, right next to the sea and close to Dragonara Palace, a summer residence owned by the Marquis Scicluna. The house had three small bedrooms upstairs: one for my parents, one for the twins and me and one for my brothers. Downstairs there was a living room, a dining room and a kitchen. The primitive bathroom, which had obviously been added on after the house was built, was a lean-to affair in the back garden. Carmen was a terraced house, joined to our neighbours on each side. It was very dark inside; the furniture was old and shabby, and I didn't like it very much. Fortunately, as it turned out, we didn't spend too long living there.

Major Fowler had kindly brought a picnic lunch prepared by his wife. We ate it in the small garden at the back of the house, seated around an old metal table under the vines. There were two loaves of crusty bread, a large chunk of local cheese, a big salami sausage, tomatoes and fat green olives. I had never tried olives before and thought they were delicious. Ed, who was always very fussy with food, said he didn't like them. I told him that one small nibble was not enough to pass judgement.

Dad and Major Fowler drank beer, while Mr Cefai, Mum and we kids drank lemonade. Before he left, Major Fowler took a photograph of us all on the steps of our new home with Dad's camera. In the photo (on the front cover of the book), the boys and I are all wearing our brand-new roller skates. We got them for Christmas but had not been allowed to use them on board the ship. Camera film was black and white back then and photos were only taken to mark special occasions and holidays. It was a long way from today's world of constant clicking with our iPhones. This was partly due to cost, as every photo had to be developed and paid for.

We were desperate to explore our new surroundings, but Mum said we had to wait an hour for our lunch to go down. Pat, Ed and I then headed off, at breakneck speed, clutching a big chunk of Mrs Fowler's chocolate cake. We couldn't wait to swim in the crystal-clear water. Surprisingly, the sea wasn't too cold, even in the middle of January. Pat showed off by jumping into the sea from a very high rock, as he always did. Ed and I both declined to follow suit. Then we walked to the end of the promontory to have a better look at the Palace. It had white pillars all the way round the outside, like the Parthenon in Greece I had learnt about in school.

Two days later, we all started at the Army School at Saint George Barracks, a short walk from our house. My father began work as Clerk of Works in Floriana and my mother started to get the house organised.

A PARTY AT THE PALACE

Every few months the Governor of Malta, Sir Charles Bonham-Carter, and his wife Gabrielle, hosted a party for all the new arrivals to Malta at Grandmaster's Palace in Valletta. They lived in another palace called San Anton's but used Grandmaster's for official functions. There was a cocktail party for the adults and a separate party for the children, held at the same time. We wore our Sunday best and were on our best behaviour.

Dominating St George's Square, the Grandmaster's Palace took up a whole block in the centre of Valletta. It was the first building constructed by the Knights of St John when they built their new capital city.

At the appointed time, about 30 adults and as many children assembled outside the palace. We all trooped in through huge carved doors. There were two stories, with a beautiful marble staircase leading upstairs from the entrance hall. The floors were covered with marble or blue and yellow majolica tiles. Along the walls stood suits of armour, flags, shields, Maltese crosses and antique weapons—a reminder that this beautiful place had often been engulfed by war. Portraits of kings and grandmasters and exquisite tapestries and fabrics, such as gold damask and brocade, hung on the walls. The legs of the chairs had large gilt claws for feet. There was furniture made of mahogany and rosewood, inlaid with other woods, ivory, or tortoiseshell and huge porcelain vases. Everywhere I turned, I marvelled at gilt-edged mirrors, friezes and frescoes. Enormous glass chandeliers hung from the ceilings. I was mesmerised.

We all queued up to meet the governor and his wife. Sir Charles (great grandfather of the British actor Helena Bonham-Carter) was in his mid-60s, slightly above average height with thin lips and hair that was only barely there. You wouldn't have called him handsome, but he had kind eyes. His wife, Lady Bonham-Carter was quite tall for a woman, but equally unremarkable. You could tell by their clothes that they had been born in the Victorian era when fashion was conservative and dowdy. They looked like the sort of people who would have felt at home at embassy parties and evenings at the opera and ballet. They were friendly enough and smiled when we shook hands.

The food was memorable, although I must admit that we weren't hard to impress. My mother was never much of a cook. We always ate very simply at home.

At the party my parents met Miss Foss, headmistress of a private school for young ladies and Father Joseph, a Jesuit priest who was headmaster of a private school for boys. My parents were impressed, and our fate was sealed. Within a few weeks, we had all changed schools—me to Chiswick House with Joan and Daphne and my brothers to St Aloysius College. The twins were seven, I was nine, Ed was ten and Pat was eleven.

On 20 January 1940, at the age of 39, having been in the Royal Engineers for 20 years, my father was commissioned Lieutenant and three months later he was promoted to Captain. His role as Garrison Engineer made him Deputy Commander Royal Engineers (DCRE), with the acting rank of Major. In this position, he was responsible for overseeing the security of the south of the island. This covered the main harbours and aerodromes, including the submarine base in the middle of the harbour at Manoel Island.

The promotion meant that we were entitled to better accommodation, so we moved to a large limestone residence standing in its own grounds in a suburb called Floriana.

Sam Staples in uniform, Malta 1940.

MAISON NOTRE DAME

The fortified town of Floriana was built on the Sciberras Peninsula, just outside Valletta. It was named after Pietro Paolo Floriani, an Italian military engineer who designed the bastions called the Floriana Lines, which were built in the 17th century. The name Floriana comes from Latin and means flower or blossoming. I have always loved flowers and I decided that, when I grew up and bought my own house, I would call it Floriana.

The British developed Floriana into a garrison town in the 19th century, with the addition of barracks and the development of facilities along the wharfs on both sides of the peninsula, including schools and several hospitals. During the First World War, Malta became one big hospital, receiving wounded soldiers from the Dardanelles in Turkey and the campaign in Salonica. The island was a major recuperation centre for soldiers on several fronts.

Dad had bought a second-hand car from a colleague who was leaving. It was hardly big enough for seven, but we all squeezed in for the 20-minute drive to our new home: my parents in the front with Daphne on Mum's lap and the rest of us in the back, with Joan on Pat's lap.

The house was halfway up Sa Maison Hill in north Floriana. Compared with anywhere we had lived before, it was a mansion. A dozen white steps led from the road up to a large gate. Dad stopped the car and got out to open it, but before he could do so, two young Maltese men suddenly appeared and opened it for him.

Pat, Ed and I leapt out of the car and ran up the drive, through the beautifully landscaped garden. There were masses of flowers, including pink climbing geraniums, sweet-scented honeysuckle and others, the names of which I didn't know. A shocking pink bougainvillaea cascaded in mad profusion down one side of the house. There were orange, grapefruit and pomegranate trees, as well as grapevines, a vegetable patch and even a chicken run. No wonder we needed two gardeners to keep it all shipshape and to water everything.

The name of our new home, Maison Notre Dame, was displayed on a plaque to the left of the front door and the year it was built, 1910, was above. It was a large, square, two-storied house of pale golden limestone, with dark green wooden shutters. Downstairs there was a kitchen, a study, a laundry, a small sitting room and a dining room. All the rooms had very high ceilings and the floors were made of limestone flagstones. The main sitting room was upstairs and opened onto a large veranda about 40 feet above the road, with spectacular views over Pietà Creek and Sliema harbour. The rattan furniture on the veranda had bright blue and yellow cushions.

Maison Notre Dame.

Maison Notre Dame name plate.

In a time before air conditioning, Maltese houses were built to minimise the amount of sunlight that came in, thereby keeping them as cool as possible. Compared with the house where we had been living in England, the inside of Maison Notre Dame was quite dark, which kept it reasonably cool. Two tall pepper trees at the front of the house provided shade from the afternoon sun.

The three bedrooms were upstairs. Mum decided that the three girls would share the biggest one, at the front of the house, and the boys would share the one next to it, which was slightly smaller. My parents' bedroom was at the back of the house, next to the sitting room and beside a proper bathroom with a large bath. We ran around exploring with great excitement.

The dining room and Dad's study were lined with dark wood panelling and furnished with dark wood furniture, which made them rather sombre. The kitchen had wooden cupboards painted pale lime green, a free-standing gas cooker and a huge white sink. There was a larder for storing perishable food. It had air vents covered in wire mesh, to let the air in and keep the flies out. My father was disappointed to see that there was no refrigerator and said that, if he couldn't buy one locally, he would get one sent from England.

We had left our furniture in storage in England, so the beds, sofas, tables and chairs in our new home all belonged to the Army. We had brought a lot of other personal effects, such as linen, cushions, paintings, crockery, our wireless (which was the size of a small television) and books. And, of course, our brand-new washing machine, vacuum cleaner and toaster. Mum said the vacuum cleaner, which we always called the Hoover because of the brand, would be useful for cleaning the numerous rugs which covered the flagstone floors.

When our bedroom was set up with our familiar floral eiderdowns, it looked like home. Next door, the boys had fun sticking up all the posters they had brought from England. Their eiderdowns were made from a green, blue and red tartan fabric. My parents' bed was covered in a white, hand-embroidered cotton bedspread which Mum had bought when we lived in Hong Kong. Dad spent hours organising the books in his study, grouped by subject matter. Woe betide anyone who borrowed a book and didn't put it back in the right place.

I fell asleep that night with a smile on my face and a jasmine-scented breeze wafting through the half-open windows.

PARADISE

After the cold English winters, Malta was a child's paradise. Sunny skies and balmy weather meant we could swim every day. We thought we were on a permanent beach holiday. Figs, almonds, pomegranates and lemons grew everywhere. I had never seen pomegranates before, and they quickly became my favourite fruit.

Each morning a driver with a horse and buggy, called a *karozzin*, arrived to take me and my sisters down to the wharf in Valletta. From there we caught the ferry across to Sliema, a short walk from Chiswick House School, which was at number seven Windsor Terrace. My mother insisted we wore big floppy hats to stop us from getting burnt.

We drove past fragrant citrus groves, nestled between the craggy stone walls, vineyards and olive trees, all growing in the orangey-brown soil. As we approached the shoreline, the air tasted of salt and seaweed. Fishing boats in bright primary colours—reds, blues, yellows and greens—bobbed up and down in the sapphire-blue water. The fishermen and women, busy mending their nets, waved enthusiastically as we went past. Each boat had the all-seeing eye of Osiris painted on its bow. Even the water taxis, called *dghajsas*, had them painted on either side. The fishermen believed the eyes would protect them when they were at sea. This was a holdover from the history of Malta as a multicultural centre, with this exotic decoration a hand-me-down from Egypt, and still present despite Malta's many centuries as a Christian country.

The driver didn't speak much English, but he often let me take the reins, which was great fun. My sisters were jealous, but he said they were too small. Meanwhile, my father took the boys to St Aloysius College in Birkirkara, a 15-minute drive by car. Not nearly as exciting.

Once a week, my mother went into Valletta to get her hair done. She found a dressmaker called Georgina and had some summer dresses made. She never learnt to drive, so Mr Cefai would pick her up in my father's car. We hired a housekeeper whose name was Carrie, short for Caroline. She was 14 years old and had grown up helping on her parents' farm in the countryside. She had never been to school. Carrie earned £2 a month plus board and lodging. My mother was pleased to have help in the house.[14]

A week after we moved in, Carrie plunged into manic spring-cleaning mode, moving all the furniture, and hanging all the carpets and bedding outside in the sunshine. Then, according to Mum, she would "beat the bejeezus out of them" with a paddle-shaped carpet beater made of rattan which she had brought from home.

In mid-summer the air became heavy and humid. Sometimes it felt as if we were living in an oven. Before dinner, we would join our parents on the back veranda for a glass of freshly squeezed lemonade, the heady scent from the citrus trees wafting up from the garden. We looked forward to the cool breeze which arrived each evening at sunset, after the blazing sun disappeared below the hazy horizon.

As summer turned into autumn, the air freshened. All the rain fell in winter, a season confined on the island to December and January, and while it was a lot cooler than summer, after England we didn't find it cold. We used the back veranda for most of the year.

There were virtually no cattle on the island, which meant no fresh cow's milk or cheese. Every morning a man came to our front door with a small herd of goats. Mum would get him to fill a couple of big jugs, straight from the udder, with the slightly sweet milk. Sometimes he brought goat cheese. The goats wore cotton brassieres to stop their udders from dragging in the dust and contaminating the milk. A man selling vegetables also called in and the poultry man brought chickens and plump pigeons. Twice a week a young girl stopped by with a basket full of eggs. We only bought some if our hens were off-lay.

Few Maltese houses had ovens and the one we had was very small and temperamental. When my mother heard that the locals took their Sunday roast to be cooked by the baker in his huge oven, we did the same. We dropped off the roasting pan on our way to Mass and picked it up afterwards. You couldn't buy lamb, but a roast leg of goat tasted very similar. Mr Cefai showed my mother how to cover it with slices of fatty bacon, so the lean meat wouldn't dry out during cooking.

Mum was thrilled when we took delivery of a fridge. It meant she could buy fresh food once or twice a week instead of every day. Refrigeration in the home was still very new in Malta and few people had a fridge.

I loved to go with my mother to the covered market in Valletta, called the Is-Suq tal-Belt. Entrance to the market was through big arched doorways. The inside was divided into five avenues of stalls selling pretty much everything from meat, poultry, fish, fruit, vegetables and cheese, to coffee, tea, sweets, fresh flowers and kitchen utensils.

Plastic bags and bottles and aluminium cans weren't in common use until about 25 years later. Vendors tipped the fruit and vegetables straight into our shopping bags. Meat, fish and cheese was wrapped in greaseproof paper and items like honey and dried legumes were tipped into our own containers that we took with us. Beverages and other liquids came in glass bottles, which were recycled.

Most Irish people have "the gift of the gab" and talk to everybody. It's a trait we all inherited from my mother. Mum soon got to know some of the stallholders at the market and they would keep things for her, under the counter. I always felt sorry for the poor rabbits hanging up, completely skinned, but with their little pom-pom tails still intact. One of the stallholders explained that they left them on so people knew they were buying a rabbit and not a cat. If it didn't have its tail, he said, you couldn't be sure. I helped Mum to carry the shopping baskets and she always bought me an ice cream or some sweets.

Nothing was wasted in our house. Any food we didn't eat was given to the chickens or put in the compost bin. Our weekly rubbish was minimal, and Mr Cefai burnt it in an incinerator at the bottom of the garden.

British Army families had access to the Navy, Army and Air Force Institutes (NAAFI)—a not-for-profit organisation which ran canteens and shops everywhere British troops were stationed. At the outbreak of the Second World War, the NAAFI grew exponentially to support the troops on active service around the world. The number of employees rose from 8,000 to a peak of 110,000 and the number of trading outlets grew from 1,350 to almost 10,000. The NAAFI shops sold groceries, cigarettes and alcohol, mostly brought in from Britain, to servicemen and their families. The Maltese didn't have access to these facilities, which were dotted over the island. There were fewer than 20 in Malta when the war started but the number would more than quadruple by 1942. Tragically, 550 NAAFI employees lost their lives supporting the war effort overseas.[15]

Mum had a weekly order at the NAAFI, which sold mostly non-perishable food, and Tony would pick it up every Friday. Apart from alcohol and cigarettes, we bought jars of Heinz salad cream and jam, Nescafé instant coffee, Nestlé tinned cream, evaporated milk and powdered milk called KLIM, Twining's tea, cans of ham and corned beef, peaches, pineapple and mixed fruit salad. Living in a country which had such an abundance of fresh fruit, I don't know why we bought fruit in tins, but everyone did and we loved it. The NAAFI also sold English chocolates such as Rolos, Mars Bars and Maltesers,

Kellogg's corn flakes, biscuits such as Digestives, Custard Creams and Ginger Nuts and fizzy drinks. We consumed far too much sugar as children, but we expended so much energy in walking, swimming and exploring that we soon burnt up the calories.

The Maltese people were friendly, smiley and helpful. I quickly added to the few words of Maltese I had learnt before we arrived, so I could communicate with them. They loved it when I said something in Maltese. Country people, like our gardeners, went about barefoot, spoke no English and were illiterate. School was not compulsory at the time. I noticed that the buses running to and from Valletta were each a different colour: green for Sliema, red for Birkirkara. Mr Cefai explained that it was so that people who couldn't read knew which bus to catch.

Our two gardeners were delighted when my father took an interest in the garden, acquiring seeds so they could plant tomatoes, onions and potatoes in the vegetable patch. Pretty much anything will grow in Malta, we discovered. You just need water. There were several vegetables which we had never seen before, neither in Hong Kong nor in England. Pumpkins, for example, which Carrie made into a delicious soup, as well as aubergines and courgettes. Jerusalem artichokes had been planted by our predecessors. In summer, they grew into very tall plants with a large yellow sunflower on top. In winter they died down, leaving nothing above ground. One of the gardeners showed Dad where to find these weird looking tubers. Carrie was familiar with them and said you could cook them any way you cooked potatoes—roasted, mashed, or puréed into soup. We always called them "fartichokes," because they gave you terrible wind. They tasted a bit like parsnips which we had eaten in England but which we never saw in Malta.

SA MAISON GARDENS

Mr Cefai always brought a packed lunch from home, neatly wrapped in a red and white chequered napkin. It consisted of a big chunk of bread with a hole scooped out and slices of tomato and cheese, olive oil and garlic stuffed into the hole. He used a very sharp penknife to remove slices. When he had finished, he would carefully wipe his mouth with the napkin, fold it neatly and put it into his pocket with the penknife.

One day after school, I was chatting to him as he sat on the front steps eating a late lunch. I asked him if we could visit Sa Maison, a stately home not far from our house. I had been dying to have a look around the gardens ever since we arrived. Mr Cefai said he had a couple of hours free, so we called the boys and set off.

Sa Maison was built into the Floriana fortifications, overlooking Marsamxett Harbour. Mr Cefai said that a man called Chevalier Caille Maison had built the house in the middle of the 18th century as a shooting lodge. In the late 19th century, the grounds were used by the British Army as an observation and defence post for the Port of Marsamxett and we found two canons on the bastions which dated from that time. A British lady called Lady Julia Lockwood had rented the house from 1842 to 1856, which is why all the locals called it Her Ladyship's Garden.

The government had taken over maintenance of the property at the turn of the century and they weren't doing a very good job. The house was all boarded up, the gardens run-down and in need of attention. They were on five levels, with ramps and steps to get from one to another. While there were still lots of beautiful trees and palms, the garden beds were overgrown and desperately in need of water. We found a greenhouse, but most of the panes of glass were broken and the potted plants inside were dead.

There was one plant in particular that was thriving. Mr Cefai said it was called Angel's Trumpet and warned us not to touch it because it was very poisonous. The plant was the size of a small tree, covered in huge, trumpet-shaped white flowers which radiated an intoxicating perfume. When I got home, I looked it up in our Encyclopaedia Britannica, which ran to 32 volumes. We had brought it with us from England and it was our equivalent of the internet.

The proper name, I discovered, is Datura Innoxia, and it has long been used for hallucinogenic love potions and poisonous witches' brews. It comes in a myriad of different colours and belongs to the nightshade family. The flowers are highly toxic and can lead to death, even if consumed in minute quantities. A good topic for an Agatha Christie mystery murder, I thought.

I tried to imagine how the garden would have looked when Lady Julia lived there.

CARNIVAL TIME

Malta's annual Carnival dates to the 15th century and takes place in February, in the week leading up to Ash Wednesday, the first day of Lent. The name Carnival comes from *Carne Vale* which means "remove meat." For the 40 days of Lent, from Ash Wednesday until Easter, meat was not allowed, according to Roman Catholic tradition.

Mr Cefai invited us to attend the Carnival parade, followed by refreshments at his house. He wanted us to meet his mother and three sisters. The parade started at ten in the morning in Floriana and ended in the main square of Valletta. Hundreds of people lined the street, as we waited for the festivities to start. We found a good spot, not far from Mr Cefai's house at the Granaries in Floriana.

Suddenly there was loud music and decorated floats started slowly moving past. People walked and danced in between, wearing colourful costumes, some with huge heads. The Maltese had decorated their cars, their karozzins and even their horses to take part in the parade. There were musicians and dancers dressed in traditional Maltese costumes. The convivial atmosphere reminded me of the Chinese New Year celebrations we had seen in Hong Kong with the dragon dance and the lion dance. I wondered why we didn't have parades like that in England.

Afterwards we went to Mr Cefai's home, to meet his family. A magnificent purple Morning Glory vine spilled over the otherwise plain entrance to the house. Mrs Cefai, whose name was Carmela, greeted us at the door and gave everyone a kiss on both cheeks. A small lady with short steel grey, curly hair, she was dressed in black, as her husband George had died some years earlier. Once widowed, Maltese women invariably wore black. Tony's sisters, Josephine, Geatana and Lily, were in their early twenties and, like their older brother, spoke very good English.

They were clearly delighted to welcome us into their modest home. It was small but impeccable, with Maltese lace doilies adorning the dark wooden furniture. The floor was tiled with limestone flagstones, like most of the houses we had been to. In the corner of the living room, a small statue of the Virgin Mary stood in a little niche cut into the wall, with a candle burning and a vase of flowers.

While Tony found some extra chairs, Mrs Cefai served everyone a delicious drink of Orzata, an almond syrup, mixed with soda water. The twins sat on a big cushion on the floor. There were lots of homemade delicacies, including sweet spicy biscuits called *ottijiet*. My favourites were some little savoury pastries called *pastizzi*. Mrs Cefai gave us each a bar of nougat to take home and told us about a shop in Floriana where we could buy more. Packed full of roasted almonds, pistachios and hazelnuts, I couldn't wait to take a bite.

Lily told us that the Carnival events would continue for four days. She had been invited to a masked ball the following evening and was very excited. She showed us what she was going to wear and promised to take me the following year.

SUMMER ACTIVITIES

Almost every weekend, from May to September, one village or another had a "festa" dedicated to the patron saint of the parish church. Like the Carnival in February, these celebrations were colourful events with lots of music and dancing. A painted wooden statue of the saint was paraded through the streets alongside marching bands, floats and plenty of people selling food and drink. After the sun went down, there were often fireworks, and we went to watch with Mr Cefai or my parents. In August, we caught a ferry across to the island of Gozo for the Festa of St George. The boys loved the horse races which took place in the main street of Victoria, the capital of Gozo, with horses galloping past, right in front of us.

On Sundays during summer, a busload of military families would often go for a picnic to Ghajn Tuffieha Bay, Maltese for Apple's Eye, which had a lovely sheltered, sandy beach. Mum always made sandwiches for a picnic lunch containing hardboiled egg and Heinz salad cream, as well as a few tomato sandwiches with a bit of raw onion, which was Dad's favourite. Afterwards we ate fresh figs and pomegranates from the garden.

The sea in Malta was the cleanest and bluest I had ever seen, and I loved the feel of the warm sand between my toes. Sometimes I was allowed to bring one of my school friends. We made sandcastles and played beach volleyball. We swam for hours, diving down to collect pretty shells, then lay on our tummies on our towels, while the hot sun dried the water off our backs, leaving a salty residue.

A rowing regatta was an annual event held on 8 September, a public holiday to mark Victory Day and the end of the Great Siege of 1565. The racing route was in the Grand Harbour, and we all went down to watch. Different coloured flags were tied to the rowing boats so that the clubs taking part could be easily identified. We each chose a boat that we liked the look of and cheered until we were hoarse. The races went on for several hours and we bought lunch from the street vendors.

Once a month, a dinner-dance was held at Fort St Elmo, another magnificent building from the time of the Knights of St John, for the senior military men and their wives. You had to be invited to attend and invitations were highly sought after. The first time my parents went, Mum wore a beautiful floor-length evening gown in jade green satin, made by Georgina, her new dressmaker. In her hair, she wore a comb with pearls and feathers in it. She had quite a collection of hair adornments she had bought when we lived in Hong Kong. I loved helping her choose which one to wear. Dad wore what he called his "number one dress uniform." They looked stunning.

Mr Cefai came to pick them up and take them to Sliema Wharf. From there, they went by naval launch, across Grand Harbour to Fort St Elmo in the gathering dusk. Next morning, they told us all about it and we hung onto every word. Tables and a dance floor had been set up outside in the courtyard, under the clear, star-studded sky. Cocktails were served on arrival, then everyone sat down to a sumptuous dinner. Laughter and music floated around, with the soft candlelight providing a romantic atmosphere. While the temperature had dropped with the setting sun, the cool sea breeze was welcome. Mum said she didn't need her fox fur stole, with its little tails hanging down, until midnight, when it was time to leave. My parents had fun showing off their fancy dance moves and got lots of compliments. Mum was in her element when she was dancing, and Dad was her favourite partner.

My father was a happy, loving man, but he was quite strict, especially with my brothers. A typical military man, he was always trying to bring some discipline and order into our lives. Once we were settled in at Maison Notre Dame, he pinned a notice on the kitchen door with our daily orders, which began "7:30 am dining room breakfast." My mother pulled it off the door, screwed it into a ball and said, "Go away little boy. Don't annoy me. We're not in the barracks." And that was the end of that. She always called my father "little boy" when she was cross with him. He had learnt early in the marriage that arguing with Mum was futile. She nearly always got her own way.

TWO ADDITIONS TO THE FAMILY

Dad was driving through the village of Tal-Handaq in the countryside when he saw a stray dog with three puppies. He stopped the car and, on the spur of the moment, decided to bring one home. While the mother was looking the other way, he popped a male puppy into his car. Back at the barracks, he spread a newspaper on a table and smothered him in Keating's Powder. The number of insects which came tumbling out was unbelievable, but that was the last time he was flea-ridden. He was black and tan with large droopy ears and we called him Handak, after the village where he was born.

I found some kittens in an abandoned building, not far from our house in Floriana. I took one home and named him Timmy. He was a tabby cat with a distinctive M-shaped marking on his forehead. I was sure it was M for Margaret. I've always loved cats and when he was little, I carried him around in my pocket. He got on well with Handak and they went around the garden together, hunting for lizards which they ate, half each.

We were a happy family of seven living in a comfortable home in paradise. We had Carrie to help my mother, a dog and a cat. Life couldn't get much better. It could, however, get worse.

MY MOTHER

My mother was an attractive woman of 45 when we arrived in Malta. You would never have guessed that she was six years older than my father. Apart from lipstick and a little powder on special occasions, she didn't wear makeup. She had beautiful fair skin, so she didn't need it.

My mother was invariably called by her full name, Hilda Mary. Too busy looking after five children, she didn't have time for any hobbies or pastimes. She never learnt to drive or swim, which limited her activities to a certain extent. We tried to persuade her to come into the sea with us, but she said she preferred to sit on the beach under a parasol and watch.

Mum rarely drank alcohol but could sometimes be persuaded to have a couple of nips of Irish whiskey, which she called "a drop of the craythur." Mum said that "craythur" meant creature in Irish and the expression was something to do with whiskey being a creature comfort. Whatever the explanation, it was always Mum's "tipple." On the rare occasions when she indulged, we would ask her to entertain us with some traditional Irish dancing, which she would do with her arms held rigidly by her sides, like the famous River Dancers. She loved dancing and singing and knew the words to hundreds of songs. She taught us to sing an Irish jig which could be used as dance music. She called this music with nonsensical words "gob music." In time we all became experts.

Mum was very sensitive about being six years older than my father. I don't think she ever told him the year she was born. Once I asked her how old she was.

"I can't remember. Go and ask your father," she replied.

When I asked my father he said,

"I don't know, ask her yourself."

THE TWINS

My twin sisters were not identical and had very different personalities, but they were inseparable. Sometimes I thought that Daphne leaned on Joan, but at other times I thought the opposite. They just needed each other.

Daphne had a petite, svelte figure, perfect for achieving her dream of becoming a ballerina. She was always the prettier twin, softly spoken and what you might call a delicate little flower.

Someone told her about a Russian Princess who ran ballet classes in a studio in Tigne Street in Sliema. Princess Nathalie Poutiatine (Romanised from the Russian Putjatin) was born in 1904 in St Petersburg. She took classes with the prima ballerinas Tamara Karsavina and Felia Dubrovska. Her family was forced to flee Russia in 1919, following the uprising of the Bolsheviks and the assassination of Tsar Nicholas II. The historical abdication document, which brought an end to 300 years of Romanov rule, was allegedly signed at the Poutiatine home, on a page torn from one of Nathalie's exercise books. It was signed by Grand Duke Michael, successor to Tsar Nicholas II, who had taken refuge there.

The family arrived in Malta on the SS Bermudian in 1919 and remained for two years. About 800 people fled from Russia to Malta at that time, mostly professionals, such as doctors, lawyers and artists. In 1921, when Princess Nathalie was 17, her family moved to Paris where she was able to continue with her ballet training under the well-known Russian prima ballerina, Lyubov Egorova, who had turned 40 and retired from performing. Princess Nathalie met her future husband, a Maltese businessman called Edgar Tabone, in Paris.

In 1927 they decided to move back to Malta and make it their home. Princess Nathalie opened the first ballet school in Malta and performed regularly at the Royal Opera House in Valletta. In a celebratory concert for the birthday of King George V, on 2 June 1929, she danced *La Danse de la Tsarevna*.

It was thanks to this Russian Princess that many Maltese had their first exposure to classical ballet. She and Edgar had no children, but by the time Princess Nathalie retired from teaching ballet in the early 1980s, other ballet schools had been set up in Malta by her ex-pupils. Her legacy continues to flourish.

Wearing a black leotard, pale pink tights and ballet pumps, her hair held back with a white headband, Daphne started weekly classes with Princess Nathalie. She loved it. Having never met a real princess, I was desperate to meet this royal ballet teacher. One day Mum asked me to go and pick Daphne up after her lesson and I got my wish. Princess Nathalie, as the students called her, was in her late 30s and very beautiful. She had thick dark brown, wavy hair, full red lips and a graceful, slim figure. Apart from that, she looked just like a normal person, and she wasn't even wearing a tiara. I was a bit disappointed but nonetheless in awe of her royal status.

The Royal Opera House in Valletta was designed by the English architect Edward Middleton Barry who had designed Covent Garden in London. It was completed in 1866, extensively damaged by fire in 1873, but restored by 1877. With a seating capacity of over a thousand, it was one of the most beautiful buildings in Valletta.

On Friday 2 June 1939, Princess Nathalie organised a concert at the Royal Opera House so that her pupils could perform for their families and friends. We all went to watch the show and the Opera House was almost two-thirds full. The tickets were inexpensive, and this annual event was a highlight in the Maltese calendar.

We sat in the second row and had a fantastic view. The show featured three short-story ballets, including an adaptation of *Swan Lake*, and a series of six shorter dances, including *Le Ballet au Temps de Degas*, about a ballet school in Paris during the nineteenth century. The Princess danced a couple of solos and most of her pupils took part in the show. There were only a couple of boys and one of them was the Princess's nephew.[16]

Daphne wasn't chosen to take part in the show because she had only been dancing for a few weeks and Princess Nathalie had very high standards. My sister put on a brave face and said she didn't care. She was confident that next year she would be up on the stage with the other girls, dancing in a white, diaphanous dress.

Unfortunately, the war put an end to such aspirations and the Opera House would be flattened by a direct hit in April 1942.

Joan wasn't interested in ballet, but she had a good singing voice. She was stockier than Daphne, with more angular facial features and straight brown hair, compared to her sister's heart-shaped face and auburn waves. Joan was a very caring child and, unlike Daphne, she didn't faint when she saw blood. She wanted to be a nurse when she grew up. When we started putting on family shows to entertain ourselves and our friends Joan always took part, but she was a shy, sensitive child, especially with people she didn't know.

MY BROTHERS

They were also very different from one another. Patrick, the eldest, was a born leader. Outgoing, boisterous and self-confident, Pat was a good singer with a beautiful voice. Once he learnt to play the piano, the sound of him thumping away and singing at the top of his voice became common in our house. He favoured happy tunes such as those by the likes of Fats Waller, whom he impersonated singing "Ain't Misbehavin.'" He was happy to perform whenever the occasion presented itself. Pat was always getting into trouble, but he was fun to be around. He made me laugh and I loved him. He was also very protective of his younger siblings.

Ed was the complete opposite. Quiet, sensitive and a follower rather than a leader, he lived in Pat's shadow. Although he was a year younger, Ed was taller and leaner. Both boys had ears which stuck out more than they liked. Mum said it must have come from Dad's family as none of the Hastings had them. I was glad I didn't have them. Both my brothers wanted to be in the Army when they grew up, which is just as well, since conscription didn't end until 1960.

Ed was only a year older than me, and we were very close. We used to share our deepest thoughts and feelings and he never teased me the way Pat did. Ed often said that he felt as if he was missing something, as if he had lost an arm or a leg. It was a long time before I found out why he felt that way.

My brothers turned 11 and 12 the year we arrived in Malta, and we were there for six years. I can't remember exactly when it happened, but when they started to take an interest in girls—especially Pat—they didn't want me tagging along.

One evening they went off to check out the red-light district in Valletta. It was located in a cobblestone alleyway called Strait Street and known as The Gut. They had heard about a bar called Captain Caruana and another called Maxim's where all the pretty girls went. Boyfriends on the island were two a penny. Girlfriends were hard to find.

They wouldn't take me with them, and I was sworn to secrecy regarding their destination. They told my parents they were going to the cinema. I insisted on getting a full report when they returned, in exchange for maintaining my silence. Apart from sailors and airmen who had been drinking far too much local wine, known as "Stuka juice," they said they had seen lots of prostitutes. I had to look the word up in the dictionary. Pat and Ed were also smoking the odd cigarette and I was sworn to secrecy on that, too.

Pat had started shaving and surreptitiously using Dad's aftershave, when he wanted to impress the girls. Dad didn't have a very good sense of smell and he never discovered the reason why his Old Spice aftershave was disappearing so quickly.

Ed was very handsome, and several of my schoolfriends told me they liked him. When I told Ed, he just blushed and gave me his little half-smile. He acted young for his age and was very shy with girls he didn't know. Pat, on the other hand, had several girlfriends while we were in Malta, but I never got to meet them.

THE STAPLES FIVE

With dark wavy hair like my mother, bleached auburn by the Maltese sun, I was taller than the twins. I don't know where my hazel eyes came from, as both my parents had blue eyes. I loved swimming, although I was never as confident as my brothers. Pat was the fastest swimmer in his age group in freestyle, but Ed could beat him in breaststroke. I could swim but I couldn't beat either of them. Apart from swimming

I was never very sporty. I wanted to be a singer or an actress when I grew up.

As a child, I had to choose between playing with my two sisters or my two brothers and neither choice was ideal. Joan and Daphne were two years younger and happy to amuse themselves. When I joined in with one of their games, I would try to take charge and they would tell me to go away because I was too bossy. My mother would say:

"Leave them alone. They were perfectly happy until you came along."

With two older brothers who always did everything together and two younger sisters who did the same, I sometimes felt like the odd one out. I spent quite a lot of time on my own, reading or painting.

Like any family, we had arguments from time to time, but the Staples Five were a united team, especially when it came to performing. Within a year of arriving in Malta, we had developed a fairly slick Staples Family Show, to entertain ourselves and our friends.

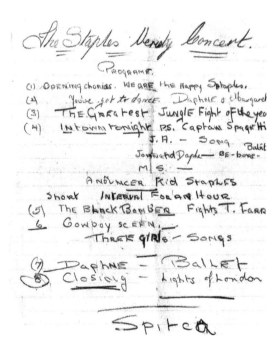

Staples Five Variety Show programme.
Note: Short interval for an hour!

92

We acquired a second-hand piano from a family that was leaving the island and we all started piano lessons. The teacher's name was Mr Marmo and I didn't like him. He was a bit too "touchy feely" and he had bad breath. Joan was scared of him. I told my mother, and she found another teacher. At that point, I decided to stop piano lessons and Mum organised singing lessons for me instead.

Pat was the most gifted pianist of the five of us and always accompanied the singers in our shows. Mr Cefai loved to watch us rehearsing and taught us a couple of Maltese songs. When Dad wasn't around, he let us call him Tony. He was like an older brother, and we all loved him. His favourite song was "My Old Man Said Follow the Van" and it wasn't long before he knew all the words and was able to sing along with us.

We were often asked to perform when we had visitors and my father was very proud of us. He wrote:

It is a grand thing to get children to dance and sing. It gives them confidence and audiences never tire of seeing talented children perform.

WAR STARTS

On 3 September 1939, Germany invaded Poland and Britain declared war on Germany. We sat around the dining room table and listened to the announcement on the wireless. I had no idea what it meant and couldn't understand why my parents looked so worried.

"Malta is a long way from the war," my father said. "There's no need for you to worry."

He was just trying to reassure us. My brothers thought war sounded rather exciting. They couldn't wait to see some action and ran around the house shooting Germans with their imaginary guns.

My friend Joyce Palmer didn't go to Chiswick House because her parents couldn't afford it. She went to the Army school at St George's Barracks, where we had also gone before we changed schools. Joyce lived at St Andrews Barracks and some of the girls at Chiswick House also lived there. If I could organise a lift with one of them, I'd go to Joyce's house after school instead of going home. My father would pick me up before it got dark.

Joyce was fun-loving and easy-going. We laughed a lot and shared our dreams and secrets. I was jealous of her long plaits. My mother wouldn't let me grow my hair long because she said it was much tidier if it was kept short. Joyce was good at maths and helped me with my homework when I got stuck.

The day after war broke out, I went to Joyce's house. We found an atlas amongst her parents' books and located Germany, then we sat on her bed to discuss how the war might affect us. It seemed to be quite a long way from Malta, so we decided we would be okay. Later that month I turned 10.

To begin with, the war didn't affect us. But we were in a fool's paradise.

THE THIRD SIEGE OF MALTA BEGINS

"Air raid warning, Air raid warning. Shut your doors and windows."

The Rediffusion blared out in English and then in Maltese, at 6:55 am on the morning of 11 June 1940.

It was the day after Mussolini allied himself with Hitler and declared war on the Western Powers. The day the third siege of Malta began. The day our little island entered the conflict. Just ten minutes' flying time from the Italian island of Sicily, suddenly we were very close to the enemy.

Italy wasted no time in sending bombers to attack Valletta.

The Rediffusion Relay Service was the first radio broadcaster in Malta. It started in 1935, authorised by the Government of Malta to operate sponsored radio programmes, as well as commercial radio programmes. It was launched with the aim of countering Fascist propaganda from Italy and rebroadcast all the BBC news. Not everyone had access to the Rediffusion service at home, so loudspeakers were placed in public squares. It warned everyone when an air raid was coming and when it had ended.

This was the first of many times we would hear that warning. The day our lives changed.

My father was in the middle of getting dressed and still in his underwear. He shouted for us all to go downstairs to the kitchen. We sat on the floor, under the window, listening to the tremendous noise. It went on for over an hour and was our first experience of an air raid. It sounded like a big thunderstorm and we were all terrified.

When we went outside, we were shocked by what we saw. Huge piles of broken masonry and glass lay all over the street where we lived. Several people had been killed, one near the Porte des Bombes, just 300 yards away. I saw my first dead body, an elderly man who was missing an arm.

We spent that night in a donkey stable under a road ramp near Maison Notre Dame, with several other families. People brought mattresses and blankets, but there wasn't much sleep.

The next day, my mother sent me to buy a few groceries from a small shop in Floriana. It was all boarded up and I came back empty-handed. Mr Cefai said the man who owned the shop had been deported. I asked him what that meant. Mr Cefai said he was an "Eyetie-lover" and went on to explain that some Maltese people supported the Italians and were a threat to everyone else. He said that, in wartime, they couldn't be trusted, so they had to go.

When Italy joined the war effort, the Maltese authorities interned or deported many Italian sympathisers. It wasn't difficult to understand why some people felt closer to the Italians than they did to the British. The Maltese language has a lot of Italian words, the food is strongly influenced by Italian food and many street names in Malta are Italian. More importantly, it was only 20 years since 7 June 1919, when a series of riots by the Maltese population culminated in British troops firing into the crowd and killing four people. This led to increased resistance to the colonial government and support for those who challenged the British presence on the island. The Maltese national holiday Sette Giugno (Italian for the 7th of June) commemorates this event.

Within days of the first Italian attacks, many young Maltese men over 18 volunteered for the newly established Malta Defence Force, to defend the islands from parachutists. The Governor, General Dobbie, a Scottish man who had replaced Sir Charles Bonham-Carter in 1940, and the General Officer commanding troops, Major General Scobell, toured the villages and inspected the newly formed groups. The men were issued with steel helmets and an armband and were trained by British and Maltese instructors.[17]

In 1941, conscription was enforced in Malta for all males aged between 16 and 56, although many had already joined up by then. Domestic work at home still needed to be done, but women of all ages, some as young as 14, took on additional jobs to fill the gaps and keep the country running. Some worked as drivers and office workers for the Army, Navy or RAF, others ran laundries, schools, hospitals, entertainment venues and so on.

The most influential newspaper, *The Times of Malta*, was run entirely by women during the war. A doctor called Irene Condachi single-handedly inoculated at least 20,000 children in war conditions by visiting all the government schools.[18] Dr Condachi was joined by a female ophthalmic doctor and a dentist and together they started The School Medical Service.

There were many unsung heroines, like these women during the war, but women didn't get the vote in Malta until 1947, after the war had ended.

WHY HITLER NEEDED MALTA

Look at a map of the Mediterranean and you will see the familiar boot of Italy, with the Italian island of Sicily sitting to the west of the toe. Look more closely and you can see a tiny dot, just south of Sicily. That's Malta. Right in the middle of the Mediterranean.

Malta has three inhabited islands—Malta, Gozo and Comino—and several uninhabited islets. Sicily is 58 miles to the north and Tunisia is 194 miles to the west. The main island, Malta, is 120 square miles, making it slightly smaller than the Isle of Wight, off Britain, and twice the size of Washington DC.

Gozo and Malta are composed mainly of limestone. The southwest side of Malta is covered in hills, which climb abruptly from the sea to a height of about 800 feet. The highest point, in Gozo, is over 1000 feet. Two magnificent natural harbours are both on Malta, the Grand Harbour and Marsamxett harbour, providing safe anchorage for large ships.

When the Second World War began, Malta was part of the British Empire which, having recently acquired Germany's East and West African colonies and Samoa in the Treaty of Versailles, at the end of the First World War, was at its largest.

At that time, Britain could send a ship from England to Australia, stopping at British ports all the way. After sailing south past France and Portugal, the first stop was Gibraltar—at the southern tip of Spain—the gateway to the Mediterranean. From there, ships headed into the Mediterranean, stopping in Malta on their way to Port Said in Egypt.

From Port Said, they would sail through the Suez Canal and cross the Arabian Sea to Bombay in India—now called Mumbai—then on to Colombo in Ceylon—now called Sri Lanka. Next stop was Penang in Malaya—now called Malaysia, then Singapore. From there, ships sailed to Hong Kong or Australia.

Egypt had gained independence from Britain in 1936, when the Anglo-Egyptian Treaty was signed. However, the treaty allowed Britain to maintain a large garrison of troops in the area, to defend the Suez Canal and protect Britain's oil supplies from the Persian Gulf.

While Egypt remained formally neutral during the Second World War, the country hosted thousands of British and Commonwealth troops and the Suez Canal was still under British control. In addition, thousands of Egyptian civilians were employed to work in the British military bases and camps.

The British Empire had a large part of the world all sewn up.

As a result of the loss of Germany's overseas possessions following the First World War, Hitler had no such network. But he did have a foothold in North Africa from November 1942 until May 1943, when Vichy-controlled Tunisia and Algeria were occupied by Germany.

British control of Malta was essential to the Allied war effort, allowing them to disrupt German supply lines to their armies in North

Africa. Hitler soon realised its strategic importance. Eliminating Malta as a British air and naval base would have secured an uninterrupted flow of supplies from factories in Europe to the German troops in North Africa, by way of the Mediterranean Sea.

Malta had its British military and naval base, including deep natural harbours with good protection for submarines, and several military hospitals where injured servicemen could recuperate. Indeed, so many men were hospitalised in Malta during the First World War, that the island was nicknamed The Nurse of the Mediterranean.

But when the war started Malta could hardly be called a British stronghold.

With just three Gladiator biplanes, nicknamed Faith, Hope and Charity, Malta was totally unprepared for war when the island first came under aerial attack. Aviation was in its infancy. The RAF had only been in existence for a couple of decades, since 1918, and its airbase in Malta, RAF Hal Far, was only about a decade old.

When Hitler ordered that Malta be captured, he may have thought it would be a pushover, given its size. As other invaders had discovered before him, he was wrong. Even when Italy joined the Axis and aircraft could launch attacks from Sicily, just 10 minutes' flying time from Malta, rather than having to fly all the way from Germany, Malta still held out.

In May 1941, nearly two years after the war had begun, General Rommel, the legendary German commander of North Africa, said "Without Malta the Axis will end by losing control of North Africa."[19]

If they were going to avoid capitulation, Britain's neglect of Malta's defences had to be remedied. As the war progressed and aerial attacks on Malta worsened, Britain started to try and address this imbalance. They sent Spitfire aircraft by convoy to Malta, to boost the air defences on the island. Unfortunately, many of these aircraft were destroyed by the enemy, either when they were en route or before they could become operational.

It took until May 1942 for Malta to reach a degree of parity with the enemy in terms of air power. Even when they did, the rough ride continued.

I liked Carrie, our housekeeper. With her curvaceous body and thick black, wavy hair, which she always wore tied back in a ponytail, she was like an older sister. We spent hours chatting and she would tell me all about the boys who were sweet on her. Sometimes Mum got cross and said I needed to let her get on with her work. Mum didn't mind if we were doing a job together, such as hanging out washing, which the Maltese sun dried almost as soon as we pegged it out, bringing it in and folding it, changing sheets, or peeling vegetables.

Carrie had nine brothers and sisters and I had trouble remembering all their names. Two of her older brothers were in the Royal Malta Artillery, manning the guns around the harbour. They had joined up when they turned 16. One of Carrie's older sisters was married, and she had two nieces and a nephew.

Carrie knew how to run a house. She was a good cook and took pride in her work. Having grown up on a farm, she knew how to kill and pluck a chicken and milk a goat. We thought of getting a couple of goats at one point, when Carrie's Dad had some to sell. But my father found out that goats are escape artists. He was also told that while they will eat pretty much anything, given a choice they prefer to eat all the things you don't want them to eat. Dad had visions of a couple of Houdinis decimating his vegetable patch and then disappearing. The plan was shelved. Harry Houdini was a famous American escape artist and illusionist who had died in 1926.

Carrie taught me how to knit. Once I had learnt, I was desperate to make something, but you couldn't buy knitting wool locally. We found a couple of old jumpers my brothers had outgrown, and Carrie helped me to unwind the wool. We then washed it, dried it and rolled it into balls. From two old jumpers, I made one "new" one for Ed, which I gave him on his birthday. I didn't have enough wool to make it all in one colour, so the wristbands and waistband were in a contrasting colour, using a ball of wool Carrie had left over from something she was making for her two-year-old nephew. I was very proud of that jumper and Ed was thrilled.

One Saturday morning, soon after Italy joined the war, I was sitting in the kitchen with Carrie, in companionable silence. She was drying the breakfast dishes and I was reading a book. The boys had gone to a Scout meeting, my father was at work and my mother had gone to Valletta with the twins.

The doorbell rang and Carrie went to see who it was. When I heard hysterical screaming, I rushed out to see what on earth was going on. A Maltese official was standing on the doorstep looking somewhat embarrassed. He told me he had come to tell Carrie that her aunt had been killed in an air raid the previous night. He needed her to come to the mortuary to identify the body.

A makeshift mortuary had been set up in a disused building in Floriana, a bit further up Sa Maison Hill from where we lived, because all the hospital mortuaries were full to overflowing. It was supposed to be temporary but ended up being used right through the war.

Carrie was in a terrible state and begged me to go with her. We followed the Maltese official up the hill. When we arrived at the mortuary, he gave the man at the front desk a name and we were shown into a long room. I had no idea what to expect.

As I walked in, I looked to my right. A little girl who was about seven years of age was in a kneeling position, her eyes wide open, looking upwards, her face full of terror. She looked like a statue, covered in a light film of dust, a string of rosary beads twisted around her little fingers. As far as I could see there wasn't a mark on her. Dad had told me that when someone was killed by the blast from a bomb, the injuries took the form of internal haemorrhage and ruptured organs.

The room was full of bodies and there were bluebottle flies everywhere. A man in a khaki uniform had the top of his head missing. The sweet, sickly smell of death, which I would smell many times over the next three years, was overpowering. A feeling of nausea rose in my throat and I ran outside.

Carrie quickly identified her aunt and joined me. She wept inconsolably all the way home, using the tea towel she was still carrying to dry her tears.

My mother was furious with Carrie for taking a child to a mortuary.

But she was just a child herself, only about four years older than me. I had nightmares for many months afterwards. So did Carrie.

Everyone who visited the mortuary had to walk past our house. One day, a young woman was walking back down the hill, past our front gate, sobbing hysterically. She was surrounded by relatives who were holding her up by her elbows. We went out to see what was going on and someone explained what had happened. The poor woman had gone out to get food, leaving her five children in the care of the eldest. She came home to find a direct hit had destroyed her house and killed all her children.

My mother was also a mother of five. She wept, too.

MOVE TO ST ANDREWS

After a couple of weeks of heavy bombing, my father said that it was too dangerous to stay in Floriana. There were too many Axis targets near our house.

Dad arranged for us to move to the Officers' Mess at Saint Andrew's Barracks, some four miles north. Mr Cefai helped with the move and said he would feed the chickens until we got back. Handak and Timmy came with us.

We were one of the last families to arrive at St Andrews and nearly all the rooms had been taken. We ended up at the top of the building, sharing what had previously been servants' quarters, with Major Effenberg's wife and their son Frank.

We all slept in one room. There was no privacy, and my mother wasn't happy. My father said he would try and find something better.

While we were at St Andrews, my father lived at the Pavilion Barracks in Floriana and joined us from Saturday after lunch until Monday morning. Before he left, he took me aside and said: "I'm relying on you Liz. If there's an air raid, you're in charge."

My mother wasn't very good in emergencies. My two brothers were one and two years older than me, but my father had picked the one he thought was the most responsible. Teenage boys are often immature, and my brothers were no exception, as my father wrote in his diary:

The boys were naughty and had become a little too daring when it came to air raids. They had been doing some work after school at the telephone exchange at the dockyard. One day they were a little slow in getting down into the air raid shelter at the dockyard and were knocked down the steps by the blast. Afterwards, when they came out of the shelter, they found a man to whom they had been speaking a very short time before the raid. He hadn't made it to the shelter and was terribly maimed and dead as a doornail. After this they became much more careful.

The air raid shelters at St Andrews were in tunnels which had been dug out in Napoleonic times. To get there, we had to go down a narrow staircase from the fourth floor to the ground floor, then across Lieutenant Corkery's garden, down the steps and into the shelter. Lieutenant Corkery lived in a detached house next to the building where we lived. His wife liked gardening and there were lots of flowers.

We were shown where the tunnels were located the day we arrived. Officers' families, we were told, sat on the right-hand side of the tunnel, while the other ranks sat on the left. We were also told that the shelters were not deep enough to survive a direct hit. I wondered why they bothered to tell us that.

In the middle of that first night, the sirens wailed. My father, who usually took charge, wasn't there and my mother started to panic. "Follow me! Follow me!" I shouted as I ran down the stairs and through the Corkerys' garden to the shelter, my eiderdown wrapped around my shoulders, my mother, brothers and sisters all galloping behind me.

Once inside the shelter, I slept in a deckchair until the raid was over, then we all trooped back to bed. Most nights we were at St Andrews there was an air raid. Every time, I did the same thing, running through the garden, my eiderdown flapping around my shoulders, shouting out instructions to my family. My mother nicknamed me the Flying Swan. I could never remember any of it in the morning; it was always like a dream.

Animals weren't allowed in the shelters, but everyone liked Handak, and he was very well-behaved, so he always joined us. I took my cat Timmy in my schoolbag, and he was happy to stay there quietly. If anyone noticed, they never said anything.

LIFE AT ST ANDREWS

A couple of weeks after we moved to St Andrews, Mrs Alan, the senior officer's wife, came to our rescue and offered us the billiards room on the first floor. It was quite spacious, with lots of beds, some screens and a few additional pieces of furniture. Not perfect, but a great improvement on where we had been on the fourth floor. We had become good friends with Mrs Effenberg and Frank, so they joined us, and we were soon feeling quite settled. My father, two brothers and Frank made regular use of the billiards table which had been pushed to one side of the room.

New blackout measures were announced in a leaflet from the authorities:

All lights in Malta and Gozo shall be extinguished or so masked as to be invisible from the sea or from the air and to prevent any reflection being visible from the sea or from the air between the hours of sunrise and sunset.[20]

All the streetlights in Malta were turned off at night and you weren't allowed to light a cigarette in the street. Some of the officers' wives who were handy with a sewing machine made blinds from black fabric, which we used to cover the windows as soon as it got dark. We were all given gas masks, with special ones for mothers with babies. We carried them in cardboard boxes attached to a string which went around our necks. We had gas mask drills in the Corkery's garden, to practise putting them on.

One Saturday evening, we put on a Staples Family Show for all the families at St Andrews. Afterwards, Pat was given the nickname The Nightingale of St Andrews. Everyone loved the show and we were asked if we could put on another one soon.

THE GOVERNOR'S GARDEN PARTY

The Governor, General Dobbie, hosted a garden party at San Anton Palace in Attard, where he and his wife Sybil lived. It was a warm late October weekend, before the first rains arrived. It may seem strange to be hosting a garden party when all that bombing was going on, but everyone was trying their best to make life as pleasant as possible.

San Anton Palace had two storeys and a high square tower with a beautiful panoramic view of the surrounding area. It served as the official residence of the British Governor and is now that of the Maltese president. Malta has always been a popular place for making films because of the reliable, sunny weather, Roman ruins and beautiful old buildings. Decades later, scenes from the TV series *Game of Thrones*, as well as many movies such as *Troy* and *Gladiator* were filmed at San Anton Palace.

As we walked through the main gate and into the grounds, we passed the Eagle Fountain, which dates from the early 17th century, when the palace was built. The party was entirely in the garden, so we didn't go inside. I didn't care, as I have always loved gardens.

Mum and Dad went off to chat to the other guests while we kids wandered around the garden, admiring the wide variety of exotic trees from around the world: palms, cypresses, jacarandas, pine trees and avocado trees. There was an extensive orange grove, about ten times the size of the one we had at Maison Notre Dame, which produced a powerful heady perfume. Evergreen trees provided a canopy of welcome shade on one side of the garden. There were ornamental ponds, fountains, walled gardens and sculptures.

Bougainvillaea cascaded everywhere and there were dozens, if not hundreds, of rose bushes. The autumn flowers of the rose bush tend to have a more intense perfume and colour than the spring roses, because of the cooler weather. I closed my eyes and breathed in the heady, soporific perfume. Rhododendrons and azaleas provided a splash of colour in the shadier parts of the garden.

We found a hedge maze, where we had fun losing ourselves. There were families of ducks and swans on the ponds, and we found a small aviary which was home to lots of exotic, colourful birds. With perfectly clipped lawns and little bridges over the ponds, the grounds of the palace had been landscaped into an Arcadian vision.

After a delicious afternoon tea, we went back to St Andrews, the seven of us squashed into Dad's car. The sun was setting and it was going to be a warm, clear, starry evening. A few hours later, as the sirens wailed and we ran to the shelter, I couldn't help thinking how weird it was, after the tranquillity and beauty of the afternoon.

I dreamt about the beautiful garden I would make when I grew up.

MASS EXODUS

As the war situation worsened, there was a mass exodus of wives and children. Several families left just before Christmas 1940, for destinations such as Egypt or South Africa, where they stayed for the duration of the war.

After Christmas my father tried to persuade my mother to leave, but she refused, saying: "We will stay together, whatever happens. If the Maltese can take it, so can we."[21]

Dad wasn't happy about my mother's decision, but she was adamant.

Two of the families who had been living with us at St Andrews decided to leave. When the ship they were on was sunk by the enemy soon after it left the island, we knew my mother had made the right decision. We should have been on that ship. Was it the Staples Luck protecting us again? In any case, as things got worse, it was too late to change our minds.

Space became available and we eventually moved into three comfortable rooms on the first floor. We spent that Christmas at St Andrews and decided to put on a special show to entertain the few families who were still living there. Pat and I held auditions for the other children who wanted to take part, to make sure they were up to our high standards. Organising the show kept us very busy.

A week before Christmas, the remaining children at St Andrews were invited to a party hosted by the Marquis Scicluna at Dragonara

Palace. It was one of about 45 parties held across Malta and Gozo to provide Christmas cheer to the children most affected by the war. A national appeal had been set up to collect money, toys, groceries and sweets for these parties.

I had always wanted to see the inside of Dragonara Palace, but it wasn't as impressive as the Grandmaster's Palace in Valletta or San Anton's Palace in Attard. As we walked in, we were greeted by a huge Christmas tree covered in decorations. We played lots of games, then sat down cross-legged on the floor to watch a magician. He did some amazing tricks with a pack of cards—which Pat and Ed worked on solving when we got home—and there was a white rabbit which kept appearing and disappearing. There was afternoon tea with sandwiches, jelly, ice cream and cake. Someone dressed up as Father Christmas and gave each of us a small gift. We headed home with full tummies and a smile on our faces, uplifted with Christmas joy.

Everyone who lived at St Andrews had to eat at the NAAFI canteen because we had no means of cooking our own meals. It was an expensive way to feed a big family, as Dad wrote:

> My savings were running away, but my family had to be as safe
> as I could make them and St Andrews was the best option.

As the war progressed and food became scarce, my mother suggested, at one of the regular wives' meetings, that a Maltese caterer may have more contacts with local farmers than the NAAFI cook. She was slowly gaining confidence and was pleased when her suggestion was taken up. The Pisani family from the Sliema Hotel took over the NAAFI canteen and the food improved.

We felt safe at St Andrews, away from the harbours, although we were only four miles away. Fortunately, while we were there, the shelters never sustained a direct hit. We regularly sat on the roof, watching dog fights and counting the planes, like children today watching television.

Boats from the island of Gozo passed in front of Saint Andrews, carrying a cargo of vegetables. They were on their way to the main island, trying to reinforce our supplies of food. The enemy would dive bomb them and it always saddened me to watch.

Young RAF pilots, swinging from their parachutes after bailing out of their burning planes, also made attractive targets. Watching the German Messerschmidts swoop down and machine gun them made me realise the stark realities of war. If they made it to the sea, a launch would go out to pick them up. Sometimes the enemy would shoot at the launch. By this time none of us, not even my brothers, thought that war was exciting.

Pat and Ed did, however, collect war trophies, such as bits of shell, shrapnel and machine gun bullets, which they swapped with friends at school. They had to be careful what they picked up. Anti-personnel mines were designed to look like pens and other attractive items. They were dropped everywhere by the enemy. Despite radio warnings not to touch anything strange, children were attracted to such objects and were regularly maimed.

My father worked five and a half days a week, with Saturday afternoons and Sundays off. It wasn't practical for him to stay with us during the week as he needed to be close to the Pavilion Barracks to deal with any crises. He would spend two nights at St Andrews, then head back to work on Monday, after an early breakfast.

Early one Sunday morning, when he was at St Andrews with us, he got some terrible news. The soldiers on night duty at the Pavilion Barracks had seen a parachute descending. They went to retrieve it because parachute silk was highly prized for making ladies' underwear.

Unfortunately, the parachute turned out to be delivering a sea mine. Five men were blown to pieces, and one was seriously injured. The following day, my father attended a short ceremony at the Pietà Military Cemetery, where they buried five little parcels. His room at the Pavilion was only 10 yards from the explosion and was a complete shambles. A huge stone lay across his pillow, and the fireplace had been blown across the room, smashing the wardrobe to pieces. Tony Cefai, whose room was right next to my father's, was there to help salvage what they could.

Dad said that thanks to the Staples Luck they had been away that weekend.

Tony Cefai, unidentified Army Chaplain and Major Sam Staples.

BACK TO MAISON NOTRE DAME

My mother was keen to be back in her own home, so when there was a lull in the bombing in June 1941, we moved back to Maison Notre Dame. Everyone was sad to see us leave. They loved our shows and said it was more fun at St Andrews with the Staples family.

Some soldiers had been living in the house while we were away. They had started to dig a shelter in the garden which my father had designed. It was by no means finished, so we couldn't use it.

That first night back, we were all in bed asleep when there was an almighty explosion. The bedroom was as bright as day. As I sat up, I saw that our windows had shattered, and I was covered in glass. When I climbed out of bed, I started to bleed in several places. Joan sat up and started to scream. Daphne climbed out of bed and fainted. My father burst into our bedroom:

> I rushed in with my heart in my mouth, expecting to find the worst. I was so relieved to find everyone safe and sound.

A bomb had dropped just across the road and the front of our house had taken the full impact of the blast. My parents' bedroom was at the back of the house, so their windows hadn't broken. My hair and my sisters' hair was full of tiny shards of glass. The boys had very short hair and quickly removed the bits with a comb. It took me more than an hour to remove all the glass from Daphne's hair, while my mother worked on Joan. Then she did my hair. For once, I was glad I had short hair. Only a week before, one of my friends at school, who had long curly hair down to her waist, had to have it cut very short because her mother couldn't remove all the splinters of glass after a bomb landed near her house.

Dad put his arms around me and said everything would be all right. I breathed in the familiar smell of cigarettes mixed with Old Spice aftershave.

We couldn't go back to bed because there was glass everywhere and we were very badly shaken. Dad said we could have the following day off school. Mum made hot cocoa and we sat in the kitchen for the rest of the night. Dad read us a few chapters from our favourite book, *Swallows and Amazons*. As we listened to the adventures of the Walker family and sipped our hot drinks, we gradually calmed down, with the bells from numerous ambulances ringing in the background.

OUR OWN SHELTER

After that narrow escape, my father arranged for the shelter in our garden to be finished. He got some men to do the digging and designed the interior himself. The plan was meticulously drawn up and filed in his diary. To get to the shelter, we went down steps in the far corner of the garden, next to the Jerusalem artichoke patch. There were two sets of two bunks on each side, 8 bunks in all. Mum, my sisters and I slept on the ground level while Dad, the boys and Carrie slept on the top bunks. Dad's original plan had me sleeping up top but, having fallen out of a top bunk when we were sailing to Hong Kong, I preferred the lower level.

Dad made the beds himself, helped by Pat and Ed, and installed an electric light. It was far from bomb-proof—the ceiling of the shelter was only about 12 feet below ground level—but it was reasonably safe, unless we had a direct hit. Children love cubby houses and camping, so it wasn't too bad really. Anyway, there was no choice and we got used to it.

If you went out of our front gate, down the hill a few yards and turned right, you found yourself more than 20 feet below the level of our house, with a thick bastion wall on your right. Above it was our garden. Dad had a second entrance to the shelter made in that wall, with a black iron gate. We never used it, but Dad said it was good to have two ways in and out.

We slept in the shelter every night for nearly two years. Bombs often fell quite close to our house. That we survived is a miracle. Two Army buildings in Floriana—the Ordnance Depot, where ammunition was stored and the Army Service Corps Depot, where all the other provisions were stored—were both flattened.

When we weren't sleeping, we played cards, and I often did my homework with the light from that one bare bulb. Ed was good at maths and always helped me. I told him he could be a teacher when he grew up. Dad was good at maths too, but he quickly lost patience with me.

Timmy sometimes joined us, when he wasn't off somewhere, hunting for mice. Handak was our constant companion. When the bombing was really bad, he would climb onto my bunk, very quietly, so Dad wouldn't notice. His rule was no dogs on beds. The scent of Handak and the feel of his soft silky ears comforted me. I whispered to him softly and told him he was a doody, our family's word for a good dog. He closed his eyes and wagged his tail silently, imperceptibly, in response. I loved feeling his warmth under my fingers.

Carrie often wept during air raids, worrying about her family. Tears ran down her cheeks, but she made no sound. I would climb into bed with her, hug her tightly and try to calm her fears.

RAINING CATS AND CATS

Once we had our own shelter, we didn't wait for an air raid to use it. After dinner each night, we would all head down there and settle in. Dad was usually the last one to arrive because he would spend an hour or so reading in his study, which always smelled of stale cigarette smoke. He had an encyclopaedic knowledge on all kinds of subjects. If he was reading something interesting, he would tell us about it after dinner, then ask questions to make sure we had been listening. When Dad came down to the shelter at about 10 pm he would close the door and turn off the light.

It was the middle winter and I was in the middle of reading a book to Ed called *Rebecca* by Daphne du Maurier. We couldn't wait to find out what was going to happen next, so as soon as we finished dinner, we used the bathroom in the house to clean our teeth and get into our pyjamas, then went straight down to the shelter. Outside it was dark and raining heavily. We shared an umbrella and ran through the garden and down the steps to the shelter.

Ed and I were cosily ensconced under the covers in my bunk, and I was reading out loud. My parents, Pat and the twins were still up in the house, as was Carrie, so the door to the shelter was pushed to, rather than closed.

Suddenly we heard a scratching sound, as if someone or something was trying to get in. The door was metal and very heavy, to make it more bomb-proof, so it wasn't easy to push open. I jumped out of bed and opened it. There stood Timmy, soaked to the skin, with a tiny ginger kitten, equally wet, in her mouth. I say "her" mouth because that's when I realised that Timmy was female.

My mother kept an old wicker basket in the shelter, which she used to bring things to and from the house. It was in the corner, near the end of my bunk. I quickly put an old towel into the basket and Timmy dropped the kitten inside. Then, quick as a flash, she shot out the door again. The kitten was meowing pitiably. I opened the door and called for Timmy to come back and look after her baby.

Within a few minutes she was back, this time with a tabby kitten, also soaked to the skin, which she dropped into the basket. In due course, we counted five kittens: one ginger, two tabby and two black and white. So many different colours in one litter, but apparently that's normal with cats. When Pat and the twins joined us, we showed them the kittens. It was still raining heavily and Pat said that instead of raining cats and dogs, according to the well-known expression, on this occasion it had been raining cats and cats.

Timmy settled herself on top of her kittens and they stopped crying immediately. I pushed the basket under my bunk, hoping that Dad wouldn't notice, and went to sleep to the sound of suckling kittens and Timmy's contented purring.

MUM'S BEST FRIEND

My mother had a limited education, couldn't cook apart from the absolute basics and had very little experience with entertaining. In the company of the other officers' wives, she was out of her comfort zone.

Some of them could be very unfriendly. I started to notice the snide comments and the way Mum would switch to what she called her "Officers Mess English," in a desperate attempt to fit in. Her strong Irish brogue was impossible to shake off. Most of the commissioned officers had posh, public-school accents, as did their wives. They were the sort of people who had grown up with nannies and servants.

At home, Mum used a lot of Irish words and expressions which we grew up hearing and using. It wasn't until my friend Joyce made a comment that I realised nobody else understood them.

"You've got a couple of pillar beans this morning. Did you go to bed at all hours?" I asked Joyce one day.

"What on earth are pillar beans?" she responded. "And what time is all hours?"

I explained that, in my mother's lingo, pillar beans were small eyes, caused by lack of sleep, and all hours meant very late. When I shared some of my mother's other expressions with Joyce, she thought they were hilarious. She especially loved the expression "Your eyes are too close to your bladder" to describe anyone who cries easily. A messy house was said to be like Hanratty's, naughty children were "boollums" and anyone stupid was an "eejit" or a "proper eejit."

We made fun of Mum's pronunciation of films as "fillums" and rhubarb as "rhubub," to which she would say, "Go way ow that, or I'll show ye the back of my hand." But she was smiling as she said it.

She didn't use any of her weird Irish expressions with the officers' wives.

It was a world of rigid class barriers, where everybody knew their place. There was a hierarchy in society which meant that anyone in authority—the headmaster of a school, the matron of a hospital, the manager of a bank, anyone who had a title, such as doctor or a professor and anyone in uniform—was treated with respect. It was very different to today's world, where we're all on first name terms.

Malta was a very Catholic country and we felt an affinity with the people. When they saw us going to Mass and realised we were Catholics, it brought us closer. It was never them and us: we always felt as if we belonged in Malta.

Every Sunday, we went to Mass at the Sarria Catholic church in Floriana, a five-minute walk from home, with my mother. Dad walked a bit further to a Protestant church. Having a mother who was Catholic and a father who was Protestant was never an issue. We were all Christians and religion was never discussed. My father always said that his Protestant High Church was very close to Catholicism, and I often wondered why he didn't join us, but he never did.

My mother was popular with the locals. They loved to chat with her and practise their English. Unlike some of the Army wives, they never judged her. One Sunday, we were standing around chatting after Mass when someone introduced Mum to a Maltese lady called Dora Clarke.

Dora stood out from the crowd. Her thick black hair was cut short and neatly coiffed. She was wearing a well-cut suit, in black and emerald green, which came to just below the knee. Black patent leather shoes and a matching handbag completed the outfit. Bright red lipstick and matching nails made her look like one of the beautiful, sophisticated women I had seen in Hollywood films. I wanted to look just like her when I grew up.

Mrs Clarke was married to a British officer who, like Dad, wasn't a Catholic, so he didn't go to Mass. Dora, whose full name was Maria Dolores, was a couple of years older than my mother and obviously

Dora Clarke in London 1937.
She was always a sharp dresser.

came from a well-heeled background. She was born in Malta but had
married Major William Edward Clarke, who was also in the Royal
Engineers, like Dad. She spoke impeccable English with no accent.
Her two children, Edward and Dolores, were both grown up and no
longer living at home.

Mrs Clarke took my mother under her wing and became her
closest friend and confidante. After Mass every Sunday, she came back
to Maison Notre Dame for a cup of tea. We were constantly being
reminded that "children should be seen and not heard," so when adult
conversations were taking place, we kept quiet and listened. I heard
Mrs Clarke telling Mum that she knew how hard it was to fit in with the
officers' wives if you didn't come from the right background. Being
Maltese, she had been through it herself. Dora was 48 when the war
started and, having married at 20, she had been a part of Army life for
nearly 30 years. She had learnt a trick or two.

Dora had an aura of poise and self-confidence which my mother lacked. But mum's new friend was generous and kind and my mother was a quick learner. How to mix drinks and make canapés were skills Mum hadn't previously acquired. In Hong Kong, she had been too busy with five small children and Dad wasn't an officer then. A piece of fresh fig and a chunk of goat cheese on a toothpick was an easy and quick canapé to serve when friends came round for a drink. Dora was always showing Mum how to do things and I was learning, too.

Children never called adults by their first names when we were growing up, so Dora was always Mrs Clarke. She had a wardrobe of designer clothes, to show off her trim figure. Once a year, she went on a shopping spree in London. She said that after the war, when we could travel again, she would take my mother with her.

SPAGHETTI

We had never even heard of spaghetti, let alone tried it, until we came to Malta. Mrs Clarke taught Mum how to use it to make a small amount of meat go further, which she called "stretching." She also taught Mum to make a Bolognese sauce with a one pound can of Fray Bentos corned beef, which each Army family received in their fortnightly wartime rations.

We had onions and tomatoes in the garden and with that small can of corned beef, and Mrs Clarke's guidance, Mum learnt to make a delicious meal. She bought a bottle of sherry from the NAAFI shop because Mrs Clarke said that a good splosh made the sauce even better.

By helping to chop the onions and tomatoes and watching closely, I learnt how to make this recipe, which went on to become a family favourite. In normal times, it serves about four and you can use minced beef, browned with the onions, instead of canned corned beef.

To make it feed eight, including Carrie, my mother served it with lots of spaghetti. Unlike so many other things, spaghetti didn't have to come in by sea. It was made on the island and, until flour, the main ingredient, was severely rationed, you could buy it.

Having grown up in Ireland, Mum was used to frying food in lard and spreading butter or margarine on her bread. Margarine was invented in the 1870s and became a popular, cheaper alternative to butter in Britain during the First World War. In Malta during the Second World War, you could buy imported margarine and edible vegetable oil, but they were both rationed.

The Mediterranean climate in Malta is perfect for growing olives. Many locals pressed their own and used the oil for cooking and for dipping their bread. Mrs Clarke encouraged Mum to switch to this healthy option. Until then, we only had a very small bottle of olive oil which was kept in the medicine cabinet and used to treat earaches.

Carrie told my mother that her family in the countryside pressed their own olives and sold the oil. The next time my father took her home for a few days off, he bought several bottles of delicious extra virgin olive oil. It was like liquid gold and made a perfect base for Dora's recipe. Carrie's father had just finished harvesting his honey, which he did each year after the wild thyme had finished flowering and gave my father a big jar as a gift. We ate it drizzled on sliced fresh figs from the garden, for dessert. Until, quite quickly, it was all gone.

Carrie's father told Dad that his daughter loved working for us because she felt like one of the family. We felt the same about her.

We loved to arrive home from school to the sweet aroma of onions and tomatoes being sautéed in olive oil.

Mrs Clarke's Wartime Spag Bol

2 tablespoons olive oil
1 large onion, chopped
2 cloves garlic, peeled and crushed
1 can (1 pound or 450g) corned beef
1 pound (500g) fresh tomatoes, peeled and chopped
2 cups water
A good splosh of sherry
2 tablespoons tomato paste
Fresh or dried marjoram or oregano, to taste
1 beef stock cube, crumbled
1 teaspoon sugar

Salt and freshly ground black pepper to taste

To serve:
Spaghetti, cooked in boiling salted water and drained
Grated Parmesan or Cheddar cheese

Heat olive oil in a large, deep, frying pan and cook onion and garlic until soft but not brown. Add the corned beef and tomatoes and cook, stirring and breaking up the meat, for 10 minutes. Add water, herbs, stock cube, tomato paste, sherry, sugar, salt and pepper. Simmer the sauce gently for 20-30 minutes, adding more water if necessary. Serve the sauce with cooked spaghetti and top with grated Parmesan or Cheddar cheese.

Serves 4

RATIONING

The soil in Malta is shallow, but rich in phosphates, making it very fertile. Vegetables, such as tomatoes, onions, Jerusalem artichokes, potatoes, pumpkins and garlic were always grown in Malta, especially on the island of Gozo. Fruits such as melons, grapes, citrus, figs, olives and pomegranates also thrive in the Mediterranean climate. Other crops included wheat, barley, cumin, tobacco and a small amount of cotton, which was used for home spinning.

There was a small fishing industry, with 782 registered boats when war broke out, as well as some poultry, rabbits, a few cows and lots of goats. The Malta Export Brewery started making a lager called Cisk in 1929. It had a very distinctive gold colour and flavour, but when the war started that was the only locally brewed beer. There were but a few vineyards. Pretty much everything else was imported.

Producing only about 30% of its food requirements, Malta was alarmingly reliant on what came in by sea.[22]

During the war, vessels bringing food supplies from England to Malta were often sunk by the enemy before they could reach the island.

Often a ship would make it into the Grand Harbour only to be sunk before it was unloaded. This resulted in a great loss of life to Navy and Merchant seamen and depleted stores of basic commodities on the island. Space on the ships was also needed for fighter planes and armaments.

In April 1941, less than a year after Italy joined the war, the Government issued a Family Ration Book in the name of the head of each family, for basic supplies. The size of a family determined the amount of each item allotted per household and the amount of entitlement varied according to the availability of supplies.

To begin with, rationing affected coffee, tinned meat, sugar, tinned fish, soap and matches. Cheese, tinned milk, frozen meat, rice, tea, flour, bread, margarine and butter were not rationed. But gradually almost everything went on the list, as food supplies on the island depleted.

Fresh vegetables became scarce, unless you grew your own, and if you could find fresh meat, it was extremely expensive. Many of the goats, horses and chickens were gradually eaten, as the situation became more desperate.

Once rationing started, the NAAFI shelves quickly emptied, although they always seemed to have Dad's cigarettes—either Lucky Strike or Camel—Gordon's gin and Schweppes tonic water to make his favourite tipple, a G and T.

Many shops closed and were boarded up. A thriving black market emerged, where you could obtain most things if you were prepared to pay hugely inflated prices. Dad said that these racketeers were like vampires, using the war as a means of filling their wallets. It was illegal and discouraged, but it still went on. Posters appeared everywhere saying: "Do not buy from the black market. Report anyone to the police who is charging excessive prices."[23]

Fortnightly rations for my family included a one-pound tin of corned beef, a tin of sardines, a small bag of dried beans and sometimes tea and sugar. Occasionally, there were some dried eggs or powdered milk. When tinned milk stocks were running down, you could only get it for babies and the sick. Bread was rationed to one slice per person per day. Rations for servicemen were a bit bigger than for civilians, but not much.

Anything else that we needed my mother had to find on the black market. My father sometimes got angry when she paid exorbitant prices to put a meal on the table. But with eight mouths to feed, including Carrie, plus the dog, what else was she to do? One of the daily challenges of parenthood, the providing of meals, had suddenly become an almost impossible task.

My usually happy and fun-loving parents started to argue a lot, especially about food. When a can of corned beef went missing, it was like the Spanish Inquisition. Everyone denied knowledge and we never found the culprit. Dad bought a padlock and key for the larder.

You had to queue up for almost everything, including water, kerosene and bread. Sometimes my mother would send me to buy something, and I would wait for two or three hours, only to reach the front of the queue and be told they had run out.

When we first arrived in Malta and there was no rationing, Jerusalem artichokes were a tasty novelty. When we were forced to eat them because there was nothing else, I grew to hate them. If you ate too many, as I sometimes did when that's all there was, they gave you a terrible stomach-ache. One day I was so hungry I sat up in a fig tree for an hour eating ripe figs until I couldn't eat another one. The figs also gave me a stomach-ache, as well as sore lips, so I didn't do that again.

When we arrived in Malta, my father bought a dozen Maltese Black chickens which kept us in eggs. We fed them food scraps, but with rationing there were no leftovers in our house, so Mr Cefai brought them scraps from the Sergeants' Mess. In the early days, he would bring a bucket full. When we were on very short rations, my mother said one day, "Look at that, the poor lads." In the bottom of the bucket were half a dozen pieces of melon skin and nothing else.

Money became scarce and IOU (I owe you) cards appeared. They were used extensively and mostly honoured. Mum regularly paid the equivalent of a day's wages for one small fish on the black market.

When Timmy's five kittens were several months old, they had grown, but they were very thin and crying all the time. Timmy was also undernourished and no longer able to provide them with milk. One day I went to the kitchen, hoping to find something to give them. But there was nothing. Then I did a dreadful thing. I unlocked the larder and inside was just one tin of cream. I mixed it with water and gave it to my cats. My mother was furious and I cried bitterly when she shouted at me. She said it was time for the kittens to go. I managed to find homes for them with various school friends.

People started to make substitutes for tea and coffee, using all kinds of ingredients. Barley, chicory, or dandelion root were tossed in a hot frying pan until dark brown, then ground to a powder. It produced a not unpleasant, nutty, slightly bitter drink which was much improved by adding milk, if you could get any. Coffee drinkers said it was better than nothing. My mother wasn't a coffee drinker, but she really missed her tea. She wrote and asked her sister Kitty to send her some from Ireland, but it never arrived.

In July 1941, just three months after rationing began, all the bakers in Malta were told they had to replace 20% of the flour with potatoes, to make the flour last longer. It tasted awful and we complained.

Mum wasn't a good cook, but like all Irish girls, she could make soda bread, a simple but delicious bread which uses baking powder instead of yeast as a raising agent. It's best eaten the day it's made, slightly warm from the oven. We loved it when Mum started to make this traditional Irish bread, but it wasn't long before she had to stop because she couldn't buy the ingredients.

Irish Soda Bread

3 cups wholemeal or white plain flour
1 teaspoon each baking powder and baking soda
1 cup porridge oats
1 tsp salt
2 teaspoons sugar
2 tablespoon oil or butter
A pint (600ml) sour milk or buttermilk

Preheat the oven to 400°F (200°C). Mix all the ingredients in a bowl. The mixture should be soft and slightly sticky, like a scone mixture—not as dry as a normal bread dough. Don't over-mix or knead.

Tip dough onto a floured surface and use floured hands to shape it into a flattened round shape, about 3-4 inches (10cm) thick, place on a greased baking sheet and cut a cross into the top. Bake for 40-45 minutes, then remove from the oven and cool.

One day, Dad came home with a sack of grain, which the cook at the Sergeants' Mess had given to him. Recovered from the underwater wreck of a bombed cargo ship, it was soaked in sea water. We all helped to wash the grains and spread them out on the veranda to dry in the sun. The smell was disgusting, but it provided food for the hens for a while. They wouldn't eat it unless we washed it because it was too salty. When that ran out and we had nothing to give them, we let them peck around the garden. But that had to stop when they started to eat our vegetables. Eventually they gave up laying altogether, due to lack of food, and one by one they ended up in the stock pot.

We missed having our own eggs. Once Mum came home with half a dozen she had bought on the black market for a ridiculous price. She boiled them and gave us one each, and one to Carrie. She and my father went without. I cut my slice of bread into fingers, which we always called soldiers, and dipped them into the egg. I savoured every mouthful, fully aware that this was all I would get.

On another occasion, the same friendly cook gave Dad a big bag of sugar. Like the grain for the chickens, it had got damp and had solidified. We managed to break it up with a hammer and chisel. Carrie used it to make the most delicious grapefruit marmalade, with fruit from our garden. We gave a jar to Carrie to take home, a jar to Mrs Clarke and a jar to Mr Cefai. The remaining two jars didn't last long with a big family like ours.

Dad's friend at the Mess must have felt sorry for him, with so many children to feed. Another time, Dad came home with a big sack of porridge oats. Unfortunately, it was alive with weevils. Eventually we gave up trying to pick them out. But we were hungry, so we cooked and ate the porridge and played "loves me, loves me not," putting the cooked weevils around the edge of our plates, like stones from plums. When we had finished, we would count them. There was no prize for the winner but winning felt good all the same.

THE VICTORY KITCHENS

The Victory Kitchens were first introduced by the government at the beginning of 1942. They were like today's soup kitchens for the homeless. As the war progressed, Kitchens sprang up all over the island until there were over a hundred. A few were run by nuns and others by volunteers. The government confiscated a certain amount of the farmers' vegetable crops for the Victory Kitchens.

Whenever there was an air raid, the men who drove the Karozzins let their horses loose while they sought shelter. The horses were terrified and galloped around wildly. When one was accidentally killed in a raid, the meat went to the Victory Kitchens to turn into meals.

Most of the time during rationing there was only enough food for one meal a day and we ate ours in the evening. We began with a little vegetable soup from the Victory Kitchen, which I queued up for each day. You could either pay for the soup or forfeit a small portion of your rations. I took a saucepan with me, and they measured out our allocation, according to the size of our family.

They mostly made minestrone, which was our favourite. It was quite tasty and a generous portion for two, but not what you would normally serve to seven. We ate it with our daily bread ration and often that's all there was. One slice of bread and a little soup is not much for growing children, so we invariably left the table hungry. Occasionally there was another course, after the soup, such as a salad or vegetables from the garden.

Handak wasn't allowed in the dining room while we were eating. He sat outside, waiting. Dad often had to go back to work after dinner and, as soon as he had gone, Handak was in like a shot. Like us, he was hungry, and we all managed to save something for him, even if it was only a small piece of our already small slice of bread. He was part of the family and we loved him dearly.

When my father wasn't looking, my mother often cut her slice of bread in half and gave it to my two teenage brothers. Dad wrote in his diary:

> She denied herself of her share, behind my back, and got dreadfully thin.

At seven on the dot each morning, Handak would wake me, rubbing his cold nose and damp muzzle in my ear. Shifting his weight from left to right on his front paws, he would perform a little dance in anticipation of breakfast. You couldn't buy commercial dog food back then, so dogs ate table scraps. With rationing, these became increasingly scarce. It was my job to feed Handak, so when I got home from school each day I would walk down the hill to the Sergeants' Mess, to see if the cook had anything to spare for my four-legged friend. He was usually able to find a few bones.

When there was literally nothing to give to Handak, which happened more frequently as the war progressed, he would look at me with such sad eyes. I felt terrible.

TREASURE FLOATING IN THE SEA

Floating fish, stunned by bombs which had exploded in the sea, were picked up by anyone brave enough to go out and retrieve them.

Pat and Ed came home one day and said they had seen hundreds of tins of milk bobbing up and down in the sea. A ship had been sunk the previous day in the harbour and all the cargo had gone into the sea. The tins were glinting in the sunlight and the boys wanted my mother to give them a big bag, so they could go and get some. She would have let them go, but my father said it was too risky. Retrieving food from sunken vessels was a punishable offence.

One day Pat came home with a big wheel of cheddar cheese

wrapped in his beach towel. He was very good at free diving and had dived down to the wreck of a ship which had been sunk the day before, found the cheese and brought it to the surface, while nobody was looking. Terrified he would be caught, he ran all the way home.

My father turned a blind eye and said nothing. The cheese made several tasty meals and my mother invented this simple dish, served on our daily slice of bread. As the sauce cooked, the air thickened with the rich smell of the tomato sauce and our tummies rumbled in anticipation.

Staples Special

1 large onion, halved and sliced
2 tablespoons olive oil
1 pound ripe tomatoes, skinned and roughly chopped
1 teaspoon sugar
Salt and freshly ground black pepper to taste
12 ounces cheddar cheese, grated
6 slices of toast

Heat oil in a large frying pan and cook the onion gently, stirring from time to time, over moderate heat, until soft but not brown. Discard any accumulated liquid from the chopped tomatoes. Add them to the pan and continue to cook for a few minutes, stirring. Tomatoes should be semi-cooked and still chunky.

Add the sugar and salt and pepper to taste. Add cheese and when just melted serve on toast.

Serves 6

TWO SQUARES OF CHOCOLATE

One evening, the captain of a submarine in Marsamxett Harbour was invited to join us for dinner. He was very handsome, impeccably dressed and well-groomed. Mum served Mrs Clarke's Wartime Spag Bol, which had to feed nine on that occasion.

He gave my mother a bar of Cadbury's chocolate which she divided up, two squares each. It had been so long since we had eaten chocolate, I had forgotten what it tasted like, but I have never forgotten the exquisite taste of those two squares.

Ed annoyed me, as he took much longer than anyone else to eat his. How can anyone make two squares of chocolate last over an hour?

When the Captain had left, I overheard Mum asking Dad if the captain had a girlfriend. Dad said that he wasn't the marrying kind. At the time, I had no idea what she meant. In those days the word "gay" just meant happy.

MRS CLARKE'S SALT PANS

The salt pans in Malta were built by the Knights of St John in the 16th century. They extended quite a way out from the shoreline and consisted of containment walls, built to hold the sea water. When the tide went out the water caught in these pans was evaporated by the sun, leaving a thick layer of salt which could be harvested.

In a time before refrigeration, salt was a valuable commodity. Soldiers in the Roman army were sometimes paid with salt instead of money. Their monthly allowance was called *salarium—sal* being the Latin word for salt—which is where we get the word salary from.

In Malta, pork, fish, tomatoes, olives and other items were traditionally preserved with salt at the end of summer, to eat during the winter months.

Mrs Clarke rented the salt pans in Salina Bay near her house for £500 a year. In 1927 she took over the business from her family, who had been renting them before her. She soon recognised the potential in running it more efficiently in order to provide a good income for her family.

Sometimes a few fish got caught in the salt pans, unable to escape when the tide went out. Mrs Clarke would bring them to our house as a very welcome gift. If we had flour and margarine to make pastry,

Carrie would turn the fish, which was often a *lampuki* (a Common Dolphinfish in English), into a pie, with the addition of vegetables, olives, capers and raisins. The pie was covered with golden, crusty pastry and was absolutely delicious. We learnt to dry grapes from the garden on the back veranda, to make our own raisins.

Lampuki Fish Pie

1 lb puff or shortcrust pastry
1.5 lbs (750 g) fish fillets (lampuki or other firm white fish)
1 tablespoon plain flour
3 tablespoon olive oil
2 large onions, chopped
2 cloves of garlic, crushed
1 medium-sized cauliflower, broken into florets (or cubed courgettes)
3 large carrots, peeled and cut into chunks
2 potatoes, peeled and cut into chunks
12 black olives, stoned and cut into quarters
2 tablespoon capers
2 tablespoon tomato paste
2 tablespoon raisins, rehydrated in warm water then drained
2 cups fish stock
Salt and pepper to taste
1 egg, beaten or milk

To make the fish stock, break up the head and tail of the fish and put the pieces into a saucepan with just enough water to cover. Season to taste and simmer for about half an hour. Strain, keeping the liquid and discarding the solids. Cut the fish into bite-size pieces, discarding any skin or bones and mix them with the flour. Prepare the vegetables. If necessary, add water to make up the fish stock to 2 cups.

In a large frying pan, heat oil and fry onions and garlic. When soft but not brown add tomato paste, cauliflower florets, cubed potatoes and carrots, together with the fish stock and cook until the vegetables are tender. Add the olives, capers and drained raisins.

Line a pie dish with pastry. Place half the vegetable mixture into the pie dish, then cover evenly with the fish pieces and lastly the rest of the vegetable mixture. Roll out remaining pastry, cover the filling and crimp the edges. Brush the top of the pastry with beaten egg or milk and make a couple of holes for the steam to escape. If preferred, just put the pastry on the top of the pie and not on the bottom.

Bake at 350°F (180°C) for 30-40 minutes or until golden brown. Stand for 15 minutes before serving.

When we couldn't buy the ingredients to make pastry, Carrie made the fish into a delicious soup, with potatoes and carrots from the garden. Occasionally, Mrs Clarke gave us a few squid she had found stranded in the salt pans. It's just as well we had Carrie, because my mother didn't have a clue how to deal with these strange creatures. Carrie made them into a tasty stew or served them stuffed with breadcrumbs, onion, garlic and herbs, topped with a tomato sauce.

Unfortunately, such treats were enjoyed only once a month if we were lucky. Mrs Clarke also kept us supplied with salt, for which we were very grateful, especially once it was on the ration list.

When it became virtually impossible to buy fresh meat, we were forced to become temporary and unwilling vegetarians. Fortunately, Carrie did things to plain old vegetables that made them exciting and new. From her, I learnt that chopped fresh herbs, such as parsley, basil and mint, make almost anything taste better. Crushed garlic and citrus zest were also new flavours in the Staples kitchen and a positive addition to Mum's plain repertoire. Big salads dressed with olive oil and lemon juice made regular appearances. Carrie taught me that stale bread, cut into cubes, tossed in olive oil then fried till crunchy, takes on a whole new life as croutons, which she served on top of soup or mixed into a salad. It would never have occurred to my mother to do such a thing. The chickens would have enjoyed that stale bread, but they missed out. With rationing, we only gave them what we couldn't eat.

I loved to help Carrie to pick plump, red tomatoes, still warm from the sun, and dig up potatoes, which always had some of the reddish soil still clinging to their white skins. Collecting the eggs from the nesting boxes was one of my jobs each day that I looked forward to. And I loved the familiar sound of our rooster greeting the day each morning.

SALINA PALACE

Mrs Clarke and her husband, Major Nobby Clarke, lived in a large, converted farmhouse in Salina Bay, near the salt pans. It was called Salina Palace.

I asked Mrs Clarke why her house was called a palace. Not everyone in Malta named their house, she explained, but people thought it strange if you didn't. When a house changed hands, you could rename it, so she had chosen to call it Salina Palace. You don't have to be a princess to live in a palace, I thought, as I filed away this information for a time when I might own a house.

Salina Palace—now demolished—was not
a conventional palace by any means!

Nobby was a nickname given to all British men with the surname

Clarke. When I asked Major Clarke about it he said there were several theories for this. Some said the nickname originated because clerks in London used to wear Nobby hats, a type of bowler hat. Another theory suggested that 16th century monks who wrote letters for the illiterate were referred to as "nobby clerks" because they did so much writing that they developed calluses or "nobs" on their fingers.

Nobby's real name was William Edward, and Mrs Clarke always called him Will. Major Clarke, as we called him, was of medium height, lean-framed with short-cropped, salt and pepper hair and unkempt eyebrows pitched at a rakish angle. He was adjutant for the Malta Fortress Squadron, REs, in charge of the RE's Bomb Disposal Section. Major Clarke always had a slightly startled look about him, as you can see from his photograph. Hardly surprising for someone who spent his working day handling unexploded bombs.

Major William Edward (Nobby) Clarke.

Mrs Clarke at the salt pans with the workers.

During the summer holidays, Mrs Clarke invited me and my sisters to spend a few days at her house, to give my mother a break. After breakfast on the first morning, we walked down to the salt pans. The workers were busy harvesting the salt, wearing singlets and shorts, or rolled up trousers. They were paid one shilling a day. The sea water was channelled into shallow squares of equal size, where it was left until the intense sun had evaporated most of the water, leaving the salt behind. It was then raked into piles to dry further before being wheelbarrowed to a shed. After further draining, the salt was cleaned by throwing it through a large sieve which hung from the ceiling. Two men would rock the sieve and all the small pieces would go through. Sometimes girls were employed to crush the larger crystals which remained in the sieve by pushing them through a ceramic ringer. The salt was then packed into hessian bags and sold to various customers, including bakers.[24]

As the lorries arrived to collect the salt, the men loaded the sacks on board. The drivers paid Mrs Clarke in cash, which she stuffed into the pocket of her apron. Back at the house, she counted it into bundles and packed it into an old battered black briefcase. When she called in to see us in Floriana, she always kept the briefcase close by. Once I knew what was inside, I understood why. Mrs Clarke was on her way to the bank, to deposit what looked to me like a small fortune.

The furniture at Maison Notre Dame was standard Army issue. Functional, but fairly drab. Mrs Clarke's house was very different—it was full of antique furniture. The dining room was long and narrow, with a low ceiling and walls covered with tapestries. The gleaming mahogany table could seat 16. The back of each chair was carved with a different coat of arms from one of the Knights of Malta.

While we were staying, the Clarkes hosted a dinner for some senior military men, local dignitaries and their wives. Mrs Clarke showed me how to set the table for a formal dinner and I subsequently taught my mother.

The guests arrived and we sat outside on the terrace in the balmy evening weather, sipping aperitifs. I was in charge of topping up the glasses, while the twins passed round the olives. At 8pm on the dot, we all went inside and sat down in the dining room. The room smelled of the pungent beeswax I had rubbed into the table that morning. Mrs Clarke had made place cards and a master plan, to show each guest where they were sitting. She said they always did that at official dinners, so I made a mental note to tell Mum.

Dinner was a veritable feast. After vegetable soup, we had grilled fish with baked rice and tomato salad. Dessert was thick slices of melon, ripened on the flat roof of Salina Palace and served drizzled with a little sticky port. Apart from the rice and the port, it was all home produce. After dinner, my sisters and I sang a couple of songs and the guests clapped enthusiastically. Major Clarke passed round small glasses of Bajtra, a sticky liqueur made from prickly pears. He let me have some, too, but not my sisters, which made me feel very grown up.

While the house wasn't really a palace, as you can see from the photo, it had been renovated to include modern conveniences, such as a proper bathroom. It still had many of the features of a traditional Maltese farmhouse. The courtyard was spacious with a well and a stone water trough. From the courtyard, an exterior staircase led up to the roof of the ground floor rooms. It had a wall built around it and was called the terrace. From the terrace, you entered the upper room which the Clarkes used as a sitting room for entertaining guests.

On the sheltered terrace, many things were left out to dry, such as bundles of garlic and onions, which were hung on the walls and homemade cheeses, arranged on square flat reed frames. There was also a locked storage room where Dora kept tomatoes preserved in salt, pickled onions and olives in brine. On the roof of the upper room, pumpkins and melons were left to ripen in the sun.

There were several prickly pear trees around the house and one big palm tree at the front. Dora said they were planted long before her time to provide shelter from the strong winds and shade from the sun for the farm animals, such as goats, sheep, horses, donkeys and rabbits. Dora only had two goats, which her housekeeper milked every day. She used some of the milk to make cheese.

Dora said the prickly pear fruit was quite tasty, but I tried one and wasn't impressed. She cut one of the leaves open to show me that they were full of liquid. Dora said the goats wouldn't eat the leaves whole because of all the thorns, but they would eat them if you sliced them up. The prickly pears survived without being watered, which was very important on an island which depended on underground wells.

Like the prickly pear, the carob tree is an evergreen perennial, requiring no care at all, which grows in Malta. Dora picked one of the pods and, after removing the seeds, my sisters and I tasted the pulp. It was very sweet and tasted a bit like chocolate. Dora said she dried the pods and ground them up to make a powder she used instead of cocoa. She gave us a big jar full to take home.

One evening, when we were sitting out on the rooftop terrace having pre-dinner drinks, Mrs Clarke told me the story of her life. Her parents, Giuseppe Baldacchino and Giovanna Calleja, were married in Malta in 1891, in Sliema where I went to school. They lived in a house at Alexandra Gardens, opposite the Stella Maris Church (now the Palace Hotel). Dora was born in 1892 and baptised Maria Dolores Baldacchino, but she was always called Dora.

As a teenager, Dora, who had four younger siblings (one brother and three sisters), was strong-willed. Unmarried Maltese girls weren't allowed to go anywhere without a chaperone and Dora's parents were very strict. She found life in Malta claustrophobic; she wanted to spread her wings and be independent. At the age of 18, she decided to run away to England, having heard a lot about it from the British soldiers stationed on the island. She saved up enough to pay for a one-way ticket on a ship to Southampton and was on her way before her parents realised she was missing.

On arrival in Southampton, Dora travelled 150 miles west by train to Plymouth, where the sister of one of the soldiers she had met in Malta was living. Her name was Claire and she kindly helped Dora to find a room to rent and a job working in a drapery shop called Dingles on Baker Street. Dora settled in quickly and soon had a circle of friends. Not long after her arrival in Devon, she met a charming young man called William Edward Clarke. They married in the nearby village of St Germans in June 1912, when Dora was 20 and Will was 25. Dora was sad not to have any of her family at her wedding, but she was madly in love and Will's family was very supportive.

The newly married couple lived with Will's aunt in Maristow Terrace, Saltash, another village on the outskirts of Plymouth. In 1914, Dora went back to Malta for the birth of her first child, Dolores María Clarke, known as Babs. Her parents were delighted to have their daughter back in the fold and Dora was quickly forgiven for her abscondment. She spent six months with her family, then sailed back to England.

Will joined the Army at the end of 1915 to fight in the First World War. In 1916, the same year that their son Edward was born, Will was sent to fight on the Western Front in France. He left the Army in 1920 after the war had ended. In 1927 Will, Dora and their two children moved to Malta. Dora's father, who was 10 years older than her mother, had died in 1923 at the age of 66. The family business was in dire need of someone to take the reins, so Dora took over the salt pans, assisted by Will.

When he finished school in Malta, Dora's son Edward went to England to train as a veterinarian. When war broke out in 1939, he was working as a vet in Torquay. He wanted to fly, so he applied to join the RAF. Twice he was knocked back because vets were exempt from conscription. On his third attempt, he told them he was a railway porter and got in, earned his wings, going on to become a Squadron Leader. Both the Clarke children got married in England and remained there, so they weren't in Malta during the war, and we never met them.

When the Second World War broke out in 1939, Will, who had been living in Malta with his family for about 12 years, was given an emergency commission in the Royal Engineers Battalion of the Royal Malta Artillery. Following a promotion to Acting Captain, he became adjutant for the Malta Fortress Squadron, which included the bomb disposal sections. By the end of the war, he was a Major. He was always Major Clarke to us.

As a result of the heat and malnutrition, Daphne became terribly thin, and she was always fainting. Mrs Clarke suggested she spend a couple of weeks at her house, as the sea air would do her good. Nowhere in Malta is far from the sea, but she also wanted to try and fatten my sister up. My mother had tried in vain.

When Daphne got back, she said she had hated being away. She missed Joan and didn't like sleeping in a small dark room on her own.

She had never been apart from her twin before and made my mother promise never to send her again.

CHISWICK HOUSE

Chiswick House was a private school for young ladies which opened in 1906 under the joint headship of Miss Ethel Yabsley, a British lady who subsequently became Chief of the Girl Guides in Malta, and Miss Madeleine Sceberras, who came from a distinguished Maltese family.

The Girl Guides is a worldwide movement for girls, similar to the Boy Scouts for boys, which began in Britain in 1909. The Malta Girl Guides, which began in 1918, is the largest Association for girls and young women in Malta, with members joining from as young as 5 years of age. The aim of the movement is to develop self-confidence and life skills.

Chiswick House was attended by the daughters of British Army officers stationed in Malta and a few wealthy locals. The school was in a converted villa on Windsor Terrace in Sliema, one road back from the sea.

My twin sisters and I attended Chiswick House while we lived in Malta, and we were very happy there. It had large airy rooms and a homely atmosphere. We didn't wear uniforms but were expected to dress smartly. There was a strong emphasis on the 3Rs (reading, writing and 'rithmetic) and good manners.

It was a rather grand house, with three marble steps leading up to a small entrance foyer. Inside there were two large classrooms on the right, with a glass panel which could be pushed back, in order to make the space into one large room. This was done when we put on a play or function attended by our families. Straight ahead there was an archway with a column on each side, through which you walked to access the staircase which had a wrought iron balustrade and a wooden handrail. The stationery cupboard was under the stairs. The landing at the top of the stairs was quite large and served as a staff room for the teachers to have their tea break. There were five small classrooms and an office on the first floor.

Juliet Rose Foss took over as Headmistress in 1938, when Ethel Yabsley died. Miss Foss was born in England in 1880, had completed a Bachelor of Arts at Oxford University and was the niece of an Anglican bishop. She was almost 60 when the war started, and she never married. She was tall and thin, with steel grey hair which she sometimes wore plaited like earphones over her ears. She wore pince-nez glasses, perched precariously on the end of her small nose. Ladylike and softly spoken, when she smiled, all the wrinkles and creases in her face disappeared. I liked her, but I was always in awe of her.

Miss Juliette Rose Foss,
Headmistress of Chiswick House School.

With two older brothers, I was what you might call a bit of a tomboy. Rather than play with my younger twin sisters, who kept each other amused, when I wasn't at school I was usually off somewhere with the boys. Miss Foss did her best to turn me into a young lady. I only realised when we were leaving the island that she was very fond of me. On my last day she said: "I'm going to miss you, Margaret. If I had a daughter, I would want her to be like you."

The first year we were in Malta, before the war began, the whole family attended Open Day at Chiswick House. It was a warm day in June and well-attended. My mother wore a floral dress, made by her newly acquired dressmaker, Georgina, and my father was in uniform. They made an attractive couple, and I proudly introduced them to Miss Foss. She was also looking very smart that day, wearing a dark red, crushed velvet dress and a heavy gold choker with a heart locket around her neck. Women always found my father attractive, and I noticed Miss Foss blushing as he turned on the charm.

I was very excited and a bit nervous because I had entered the poetry competition with a long poem by James Elroy Flecker, called "Brumana." I needn't have worried about forgetting the lines, as I can still recite it to this day. It's about England and starts with "Oh shall I never, never be home again! Meadows of England shining in the rain."

In the week leading up to Open Day, Miss Foss would invite all the candidates to her office during the lunch break, one at a time, to give us some coaching and feedback. To get to her tiny office, you had to climb up a narrow spiral staircase which went all the way up the outside of the house from the playground. The walls of her office were covered in books and there was barely enough room for a desk and two chairs. Miss Foss kept her office as neat and tidy as her person. If she shed a tear during the coaching session, you knew you had a winning poem.

As I went up onto the stage, I had butterflies in my tummy, but as soon as I started the poem, my nerves disappeared. As I said the last line, "And dream and dream that I am home again," I glanced at Miss Foss, who was seated in the front row and saw her wipe away a tear. I won first prize and was very pleased with myself. Each year I entered the poetry competition and so did Daphne. One year she came first in her age category with a poem called "Someone," by Walter de la Mare. Another year I recited "The Highwayman" by Alfred Noyes.

Chiswick House was mainly an all-girls school, but we had a few boys under eleven. I think they had to have a sister at the school to get in. One day, when the war was well underway, Miss Foss announced that, in future, a boy in my class called Barry Greenburg was to be called Barry Greensborough. We all thought it rather strange to suddenly change your name. We didn't understand the significance of having a Jewish surname.

My favourite subjects were English, especially reading and poetry, as well as French and Art. Our art teacher was Mr Vincent Apap, a local sculptor who seemed to enjoy coming to the school to teach us once a week. Or maybe he just needed the money. He was about thirty, with mischievous, twinkling brown eyes. Sometimes he wore a jaunty red and yellow striped bow tie. I have always loved painting watercolours of flowers and learnt a lot from him. One day he gave me three paint brushes which were used but still in very good condition. You couldn't buy such things during the war, and I was very grateful.

Madame Fenouil was petite and vivacious, with a small mouth, puckered from years of speaking French. Her steel grey hair was swept up into an elaborate chignon. As well as French, she taught Maths, my least favourite subject. Madame Fenouil was like two different people: I liked her when she was teaching French, but not when she was teaching Maths.

Madame, as we called her, always kept a white lace handkerchief stuffed up the sleeve of her hand-knitted cardigan. The chalk dust would sometimes tickle her nose, sending her into paroxysms of sneezing. She would rummage in her sleeve for the handkerchief and bury her face in it until the sneezing stopped. "Ah mon Dieu, bless me!" she would exclaim.

Before rationing, we brought a packed lunch from home and could buy a snack from the tuckshop at 11am, which was called "elevenses." When food was short, we went without either and were always hungry. One day, a Canadian officer visited the school with a huge fruit cake. He said it was a gift from the children of Canada and we all received a slice. It was delicious, with big pieces of dried fig and whole glacé cherries. I savoured every mouthful and would have given anything for a second slice. No such luck. Treats like that were few and far between.

When the bombing was really bad, while we were living at St Andrews, all the schools in Malta closed. After a week or two, the teachers from Chiswick House started an outdoor school in Colonel Corkery's garden and my sisters and I went there. Eventually, rooms were made available at St George's Barracks and Miss Foss and a handful of teachers ran the school there until it was decided that it was safe enough for us to go back to the house in Windsor Terrace, Sliema.

During the polio epidemic, from November 1942 to February 1943, all the schools in Malta closed for four months. Lessons were delivered by Chiswick House to Army HQ and brought home by my father. It was during the time when we were back at Maison Notre Dame, and I was appointed teacher to my twin sisters. Each morning I set up school in the garden, under the pepper trees. I tried to emulate Miss Foss and my sisters hated me for being so bossy. It was the only way to get them to do any work. We started straight after breakfast and worked until lunchtime. After that it was too hot.

My brothers' school was also closed for four months. During that time, they attended woodworking classes, which the twins and I thought was most unfair.

ST ALOYSIUS COLLEGE

St Aloysius College was built in Birkirkara in 1896 as a seminary for Jesuit priests in their formative years. In 1905, the novices were transferred to Sicily and the building remained vacant for a couple of years. It opened in 1907 as a school for boys. During the Second World War, almost three-quarters of the College was requisitioned by the Medical and Health Department and used as a hospital.

Requisitioning of buildings was common in Malta during the war. The Xara Palace in the old city of Mdina was requisitioned by the RAF and used as billets for airmen. Several schools were turned into hospitals. To replace them, makeshift schools were set up in churches, warehouses and other buildings, but they were still short of space. To address this shortage, children attended school for only half a day, either in the morning or in the afternoon. There was also a shortage of stationery, but everyone shared and somehow we managed.

My brothers both attended St Aloysius for the six years we were in Malta. While Pat was okay with it, Ed hated that school. Corporal punishment was not only permitted in schools in Malta, but encouraged by many parents, especially in schools for boys. The teachers at St Aloysius were mostly Jesuit priests and some of them terrorised the boys with canings and threats. Punishment with a cane, a ruler or a thick, flat, leather strap called a *ferula* was regularly meted out. Five lashes on each hand, which remained red and sore for several hours.[25]

Some of my brothers' friends said that they were used to being hit because their father used a leather belt to discipline them at home. I was shocked when I heard my brothers talking about such things. It didn't happen at Chiswick House and my father never resorted to such methods.

Ed was often picked on or bullied by not only older boys but by the teachers, too. He said that some of them were evil. I never knew what he meant by this, but I didn't like the ghosted look on his face when he said it.

Ed always had an ingenuousness about him that made people, including his older brother, want to protect him. But Pat was in a different class. "If I was there, I'd sort him out," I often heard him saying to Ed.

My father decided it would be good for the boys to take up boxing, so they could defend themselves against bullies. Indoor boxing matches and tournaments were popular among the servicemen stationed on the island. My father found a place in Floriana where the boys could go once a week after school and learn to box. The teacher was a sergeant Dad had met at the bar in the Mess. Knowing how to defend himself helped Ed with the older pupils, but not with the teachers.

He had a beautiful inlaid wooden pencil case my father had made and given to him for his birthday. We had few possessions during the war and Ed treasured that pencil case. He was very artistic and loved drawing.

One day Ed got into trouble for talking. As punishment, his teacher threw the pencil case out of the first-floor window. It landed in the courtyard, where it shattered into small pieces.

"Now go and get it," said Father John.

"Go and get it yourself," replied Ed.

That was Ed's version of the dialogue. He was always inclined to embroider stories, telling us what he wished he had said. In reality, he'd probably said nothing. We always took Ed's stories with a grain of salt.

It wasn't until I reached adulthood that I realised how deeply unhappy Ed had been at school in Malta. While we will never know the full story, it's easy to see, with hindsight, how vulnerable he was. A quiet, sensitive, gentle boy, Ed was a ripe target for bullying and abuse of varying sorts. He was in a constant state of insecurity, and I feel guilty that I was unable to help him. But I was at a different school and just a child.

THE AIR RAID SHELTERS

Between the third and the eighth centuries AD, several underground tunnels called catacombs were excavated as burial places and made into churches by the early Christians. The best known of these catacomb churches are those of St Agatha and St Paul in Rabat. We went there on a school excursion during our first year in Malta.

Whole communities throughout the Middle Ages lived in these caves and some farmhouses beneath Dingli Cliffs were partly composed of caves. The largest cave settlement was Ghar Il-Kbir in Dingli which means The Big Cave.

A single railway line from Valletta to Mdina via Floriana opened in 1883. Unfortunately, the increasing popularity of buses from just after the turn of the century led to its closure in 1931. A tram which linked Valletta with the neighbouring fortified towns known as the Three Cities (Birgu—also known as Vittorioso—Senglea and Cospicua) and also with Birkirkara and Zebbug likewise closed at about that time.

At the start of the war, the British government ordered the dockyard forges to make thousands of picks and shovels. They brought in miners from Wales and other parts of Great Britain to Malta to further excavate the tunnels and catacombs to make them bigger. Some 13 miles of new tunnels were dug out.

During the war, these tunnels were used as air raid shelters, providing protection for thousands of people and underground storage for aviation fuel and other precious commodities. Many people moved in permanently when they lost their homes and had nowhere else to go. Those who could afford it had additional rooms dug out, so a whole family could be together.

Shelters had at least two exits in case one became blocked. Some had benches, deck chairs and folding stools—whatever people could spare from their homes. People installed bunk beds and, as time went on, electric lights. The Maltese always made a little niche in the wall for a small statue of Jesus or Mary and a lighted candle.

During the war, the horse and buggy was not an option for us to get to and from school. It was too dangerous. Instead, my sisters and I ran from shelter to shelter to get from home down to the wharf. I was always the leader, with my two sisters running behind me. We would sprint to a shelter, scuttle down the steps, zip through the shelter (some of them were quite long), clamber up the steps and pop off to the next one.

The shelters provided an ideal breeding ground for mosquitoes and sandflies. You were lucky if you could make it through without picking up any fleas. The air was oppressive. Stale tobacco smoke combined with the sour smell of unwashed bodies, and the stink from the buckets people used as toilets, was overpowering. I tried to breathe through my mouth and run as fast as I could.

As we ran, we often passed people who were digging. Maltese limestone is relatively soft, so they made fast progress. We would give them the thumbs up as we ran past. Once I saw a man carrying some beautiful ceramic floor tiles, so I stopped and asked him what they were for. He took us to the side of the tunnel and showed us a small room he had just finished digging out for his family. Small niches in the walls were filled with personal effects such as bowls, candles and wine bottles. He was going to tile the floor to make it more homely. When I asked why he was going to so much trouble for what was essentially a cave, he told me that his house in Valletta had been flattened by a bomb. This was his home now.

If the ferry wasn't running when we got to the wharf, which was often the case, we got a Maltese water taxi called a *dghajsa*, with two men rowing us across the water. Once on the other side, we walked up the hill to Chiswick House, about half a mile away. Some days the air raid siren would blare out soon after we got to school, so we would head straight to the school shelter and stay there until it was time to go home. Lessons didn't stop and mental arithmetic was one of the teachers' favourite subjects. I hated it.

Coming home, we did it all again, in reverse. It wasn't uncommon to see dead bodies washed up on the beach beside our route. I would try to distract my sisters and run faster, so they wouldn't see them, especially Daphne, who would invariably faint, even if it was a dead goat rather than a person. Almost every day we had to adjust our route to get past the rubble of a newly bombed building.

As I picked my way through piles of stone and bomb craters, wearing clothes which would have fitted a much younger child, my sandals, which I had outgrown, giving me blisters, I daydreamed about another world. A world filled with music, dancing, delicious food and beautiful clothes. A world whose luxuries I sometimes glimpsed when I was reading a book or watching a Hollywood film. A world I kept in my head to enjoy at night when I closed my eyes.

Air raids became a feature of daily life, with the sirens often wailing virtually non-stop, all day and all night. On average we had eight or nine raids a day and the longest went on for more than 12 hours. I spent so many hours in air raid shelters I developed claustrophobia.

THE SEMINARY SHELTER

Directly opposite Maison Notre Dame was a beautiful old building called Casa della Madonna di Manresa. It was built by Jesuit priests in the 18th century and, during our time in Malta, it was used as a seminary.

A disused well under the building was extended by digging passages off to the sides, providing a much deeper air raid shelter than the one in our garden. We used it during the day, when the heaviest raids took place, and occasionally at night.

My father was friends with the senior priest, who gave us a key to the side entrance to the Seminary and said we could use their shelter. We kept the key in a prominent position, hanging on a hook in the kitchen, by the back door. The Seminary shelter wasn't open to the general public, because bibles and other valuable artefacts were stored in the basement, but quite a few of our neighbours had a key. People left a pile of belongings—blankets, pillows and other essentials, such as insect spray, which came in a metal pump and was called Flit— in order to stake out their spot. The bedding smelled mouldy after a while, but it was better than having to take it with us each time.

When the Italians, or "Eyeties," as we called them, first joined the war, their bombing of Malta was rather haphazard. But when the Germans moved planes to Sicily, our lives became hell. Raid after raid meant we spent hours in one shelter or another. The Axis knew that most of the air attacks on their ships were originating from Malta, so they increased the attacks on the island in retaliation and to prevent further damage to their fleet.

To let us know that an air raid was imminent, Handak would run in and out of the house barking. He always knew well before the siren sounded. Then he would go to the top of the bastion and bark at the planes, before rushing back to lead the way down the steps to the Seminary shelter. On many occasions, he almost knocked my mother over, bounding down the stairs three at a time, in his rush to be first.

"That dog will be the death of me," she used to say, laughing. She loved Handak, too.

After the siren came the menacing drone of the approaching planes, followed by the sound of bombs falling and exploding and the earth shaking. On one occasion, two 500-pound bombs landed right on top of the seminary shelter while we were inside. One exploded, but amazingly we came to no harm. Fortunately, many bombs fell into the sea.

During heavy raids, it felt as if the whole island was shaking with the vibrations from an earthquake. Sometimes the few lights we had went out. The Maltese women would start screaming and the babies would wail. Someone would strike a match, while they looked for some candles to light. I would pull my skirt up over my head, as the choking yellow dust made it difficult to breathe. If I close my eyes even now, I can picture myself sitting on a bench in that shelter, surrounded by Maltese neighbours. It's the noise and the smell that come to me most vividly. The overpowering stench of cordite is something I will never forget. You could even taste it. There was also the smell of fear. The women kept up a singsong of the Rosary in Latin, reaching a crescendo as the thuds and tremors edged closer.

We were often joined by several of the Jesuit priests, who would lead the prayers. My favourite was Father Pedro who was in his 20s and came from Chile. Sometimes he would tell us a story about growing up there. As he spoke, his eyes came alive, twinkling like diamonds in the dim light of the shelter. One day, he brought his guitar and played some beautiful ballads.

If we were a bit late getting down into the shelter at night, we would see the sky lit up by flares, which were dropped by enemy aircraft to light up their targets. It was like mid-day as they snowflaked their way through the sky towards the sea or our island. We were surrounded by Army buildings and barracks, which were all enemy targets. Searchlights would criss-cross the sky to find enemy planes. When they found them, we would see the arcing of tracer bullets, trying to bring them down. When the all-clear sounded, we would make our way out of the shelter and go home.

It was impossible to tell what, or who would be hit next. The uncertainty of it, the constant tension, was very wearing on everyone, but especially on my parents.

Nowhere was safe during an air raid.

THE RED FLAG

Auberge de Castille et de Leon was the residence of the Grand Chancellor in the time of the Knights. It was a magnificent building which was completed in 1744. The British used it as a naval signal station. We always called it simply the Castille.

When a daytime raid was heading towards the Grand Harbour and our area of the island, the Castille would raise a red flag. My brothers and I took it in turns to sit up high in the tallest pepper tree at the front of our house, watching for the red flag. So long as one of us sat up in the tree, the rest of the family could continue eating dinner. From the pepper tree, the Castille could just be seen above the house tops, until it got dark. If we saw the red flag, we would tumble down and run to warn the rest of the family that it was time to head to the shelter. The tree was rough, and I always had scratches on my legs from climbing down too quickly.

My father had a telephone at work, but we didn't have one at home—few people did. While local calls were relatively cheap, long distance phone calls were expensive. In today's world of mobile phones and the internet, it's hard to comprehend how poor communication was back then. When Dad was at work and there was a heavy raid in Floriana, he was worried sick that we were all dead. Often, he would rush home, or send Mr Cefai to check that we were okay.

Pat and Ed came up with our own red flag system. When an air raid was over, one of them would hoist a red flag at the top of our pepper tree. By going up onto the roof of a building near the Lascaris Rooms, which was about a mile away as the crow flies, Dad could see our flag and knew we were all okay. It wasn't a proper flag. It was an old red shirt of Pat's taken from the rag bag, but it served its purpose.

After months and months of continuous raids, we grew blasé. The siren no longer made us run. From our back veranda, we could see the Sergeants' Mess just down the hill. Sometimes we would shout out to one of the soldiers there and ask them how many planes were coming. They would shout back "seventy" or "a hundred" or whatever. The more planes, the faster we would run.

One day, we missed seeing the flag on the Castille and the bombing was overhead. We ran to the Seminary, as fast as our legs would carry us. When we got there, we realised we had forgotten to bring the key. Mum sent Ed back to get it, while we tried to flatten ourselves against the wall of the Seminary. A plane dived so low that I could see the pilot with his goggles, black leather helmet and jacket, as he strafed the road right next to us, dropping bombs. As he went past, he turned his head and looked at us cowering beneath him. He dropped a bomb on the NAAFI at the end of the road, just 20 yards away and we were showered with hot shrapnel, stones and rubble.

Daphne fainted with shock and my mother cried, "God help us!"

Daphne and I were on our way home from school. There had been raids all day and lessons at Chiswick House had all been in the shelter. We hadn't eaten anything since breakfast and we were both very hungry. Joan was at home, as she was unwell.

When Daphne and I got to the ferry in Sliema, it wasn't running, so we had to get a *dghajsa*. Fortunately, there was one available. We climbed in and the remaining space soon filled up with Maltese women and children. A Maltese soldier was giving a full account of the morning's bombings to one of the two boatmen.

We had just reached the middle of the harbour when the siren wailed out mournfully. I prayed that we would make it to the other side before the red flag was hoisted. The women began to scream at the boatmen, trying to make them row faster. One woman began to shriek hysterically, throwing herself onto the bottom of the boat and begging the saints to save us. Daphne turned very pale, and I thought she was going to faint, as she usually did in such circumstances. I squeezed her hand and told her it would be all right.

Eventually we arrived at the other side and, as we clambered out of the boat, we heard the loudspeaker blaring out. "Raiders passed. Raiders passed." We breathed a sigh of relief and started to trudge up Great Siege Road, next to Marsamxett Harbour, heading for home.

Suddenly, loud gunfire and whistling bombs made us sprint for a small gap in the bastion, where we huddled with some Maltese workmen. A sailor and two Maltese soldiers joined us. A few minutes later, the sailor said that the raid was over and we could continue our journey home.

The five of us headed up the road, chatting amicably. They were surprised to find English children on the island, as most had been evacuated. We were as brown as berries, but we had fair hair, so they knew we weren't locals. When the soldiers left us to walk down to the submarine base, we continued towards home. It seemed as if the raid was over, but before we had walked 200 yards, I looked up and saw three planes coming at us.

One of them screeched as it dived towards us. In seconds, it was almost above us, firing machine gun bullets along the ground. My father's instruction, if ever we were in such a situation, was to lie flat, but that all went out of my head.

"Run," I shouted to Daphne.

As we ran, hand in hand, a blast lifted my sister and dropped her 10 yards ahead of me in a clump of daisies. It knocked me flat on the ground. When I stood up, the air was full of dust and smoke and at first, I couldn't see Daphne, so I shouted her name. She stuck her head up and started to howl. From a slit-trench close by, a soldier ran towards us, picked up Daphne, who was as light as a feather, and yelled for me to follow him. My heart was pounding. He kindly took us all the way home and my parents were very grateful.

We later learnt that the three servicemen we had met were all killed less than 100 yards from the spot where we had parted ways. So many people I had known had been killed. I decided I had a guardian angel who was keeping an eye on me. Or maybe it was the Staples Luck.

My father wrote in his diary at this time:

One of my workmen was promoted and moved from Floriana to Valletta. I told him to always seek shelter when the red flag was hoisted on the Castille, meaning a raid was imminent on the Grand Harbour area. A few days later, he disobeyed my instructions and was crushed to death under a pile of stones. It was Christmas Eve and I had to tell his wife and give her his week's pay. I set out to his home some miles away with my pay clerk. I was completely at a loss as to what to say to his widow. On the way, my clerk said "You should get the parish priest to go with you." So we went to the church and found Father Hersey and he came with us. The pay was only about a pound or so and the poor woman's breadwinner was gone. All I can say is thank God for Father Hersey. It was the first of many occasions when I was the bearer of terrible news.

Dad was always full of praise for the Catholic priests.

THE BOMB IN THE GARDEN

While the main targets were around the harbours and airports, bombs were dropped indiscriminately, and everything was reduced to rubble. When possible, paths were cleared so people could get through the debris, but many streets became impassable.

Towns and villages in the centre of the island grew overcrowded as refugees, whose homes had been demolished in the raids, were provided with shelter. Many lost everything except the clothes they were wearing. The Government sequestered empty houses and resettled refugees in them. Some moved in with relatives or close friends. Some took in complete strangers whose homes had been destroyed.

Sometimes a bomb dropped and didn't explode on impact. The most common reason for this was that a fuse had failed to arm itself before impact. Sometimes it would detonate after coming to rest. Early in the war, the REs in Malta formed a dedicated Bomb Disposal Unit, to deal with the growing number of unexploded bombs. One of those recruited was Sapper Anthony Mifsud:

> Our commanding officer called us on parade and said, "I am asking for bomb disposal volunteers to step forward." No one moved. Then he walked up the lines, raising his right hand and saying "You, you, take one step forward." He picked a squad of 14, including me. And so the Bomb Disposal Unit was born.

Mrs Clarke's husband was in charge of the unit. It must have been stressful having a husband who spent his time digging up unexploded bombs, but Dora always managed to stay cool. One Friday night in June 1942, while we were in the Seminary shelter, a bomb landed in our garden at Maison Notre Dame. The Staples Luck was again evident because the bomb had missed our shelter and hadn't exploded. Even though we weren't in our shelter that night, but had gone to the seminary instead, we couldn't stop thinking "What if?"

My father contacted Major Clarke, who said he would send a unit to deactivate the bomb which had penetrated the ground, leaving a 25-

foot crater. The edge of the crater just touched the foundations of the house, fortunately without causing any structural damage. The hens in the hen house some five yards away hadn't lost a single feather, which was remarkable, although they did stop laying eggs for several weeks.

The first job of the disposal unit was to find the bomb, which often involved several hours of careful digging. Then they had to figure out why it hadn't detonated when it hit the earth and prevent it from doing so until everyone was safe. The team spent all day and well into the night working on our bomb. It was a Saturday and so there was no school.

My brothers were keen to watch, but my father sent us to spend the day at the Pavilion Officers' Mess.

THE ACCIDENT

Ed was a sleepwalker.

An hour or so after we had all gone to bed, my parents often found him wandering around the house, eyes wide open, but sound asleep. Dad always locked the exterior doors and removed the keys, so he couldn't go outside. They would guide him back to bed and he never remembered anything in the morning.

Pat and Ed shared a bedroom on the first floor, next to the bedroom I shared with my twin sisters. One night, Pat awoke suddenly and saw that Ed's bed was empty. He looked across the room to see Ed standing on the window ledge, ready to dive out of the window!

"What are you doing?" shouted Pat.

And with that, Ed fell out of the window, landing on the concrete driveway, some 15 feet below. Pat ran to get my parents, shouting.

"Dad, come quickly. Ed's fallen out of the window."

The commotion woke me and my sisters. Our bedroom window was open and I could hear a strange noise, like an injured animal. We all ran downstairs to find my brother lying on the drive in a foetal position, unable to move.

Dad rang for an ambulance and Ed was rushed to the military hospital at Mtarfa. He was howling with pain. The doctor in charge told my parents that Ed's spine was broken and he might never walk again.

Next day we all went to visit Ed at the hospital. He was strung up to the ceiling by his ankles which was necessary, the doctor explained, in order to realign the vertebrae while everything healed. Each day the doctor stuck a pin into the soles of Ed's feet, to see if he could feel anything. There was no reaction. The doctor kept reminding my parents that Ed would probably end up in a wheelchair, but he was lucky to be alive. The Staples Luck was mentioned, but Ed said he didn't feel lucky.

One day, about two months after the accident, Ed reacted to the pin being stuck into his foot. We were all there visiting when it happened. The doctor said it was a miracle—the nerves seemed to be reconnecting. My father wiped away tears of happiness and relief. My mother was so choked up, she left the ward to walk around the gardens.

Next day they encased Ed in plaster from his armpits down to his hip.

Altogether Ed spent about 4 months in hospital. The other patients on his ward were all servicemen who had been injured in the war, so there were no other children for him to talk to. He said he really looked forward to my visits. Mum let me make him some toffee. Unfortunately, I burnt it, but Ed said that burnt toffee was his favourite.

He was about 14 years old at the time, an age when boys grow a lot. When he came home from the hospital, he seemed much taller, but very thin. My mother had reorganised the house, so the study became Ed's bedroom, and the outside lavatory was fitted with two metal bars, so he could hoist himself up.

Ed's legs had become very weak from spending several months in bed. He had to learn to walk again. Once he was able to, the doctor, who came weekly to the house to check on his progress, said that Ed had to walk around the perimeter of the garden, three times a day. Tears streamed down his face as he struggled round.

Ed missed many months of school. Whenever I was home, I would keep him company, playing cards, dominos and Scrabble. We had always been close, but now we were closer. Often, I would go with him when he walked around the garden and chat, to take his mind off the excruciating pain.

One day Ed told me that, when he'd fallen out of the window, he had been dreaming that he was at the swimming pool. He and Pat had been taking high diving lessons at the Haywharf Naval Base swimming pool, a ten-minute walk from our house. They both had dreams of competing at the Olympics when the war was over. Ed said he kept wondering what would have happened if he had dived out of the window headfirst, rather than fallen out, when Pat shouted at him.

It gave us both goosebumps to think about it.

There was a putrid smell coming from Ed. Like something had died. The summer heat was making it worse. I mentioned this to my mother and, that evening, as she was sponging Ed down, she put her hand up as far as she could underneath the back of the plaster. When she removed her hand, her fingers were covered in lurid green pus.

Ed went back to the hospital for a few days. A rough piece on the inside of the plaster had been rubbing against his spine when he walked and had made a sizeable hole in his back. Gangrene had set in. No wonder the circuits of the garden had been so painful. The doctor said it was too soon to remove the plaster, so they managed to treat the infection by cutting a window in it.

Ed ended up with a huge scar on his lower back, where the infection had set in. He suffered from chronic pain for the rest of his life and wasn't able to do any more high-diving or contact sports. In later life he told small children that the scar was the result of a shark attack. One of Ed's many tall stories.

My father always got up early and left for work before we had eaten breakfast. If we didn't have school, I would climb into bed with Mum and ask her to tell me one of her stories about growing up in Ireland. She was a great storyteller.

One day, she told me that when my twin sisters were born, she hadn't known in advance that she was carrying twins. Then she told me that the same thing had happened when Ed was born. Ed was a twin and she had delivered two babies. Sadly, the other little boy hadn't made it. This was a story I had never heard before.

Mum said she was only expecting to bring one baby home and that's how it turned out. For the first year of his life, she said, it was impossible to settle Ed at night. She and Dad spent hours walking up and down with him, trying to stop him from crying.

When Ed was 13 months old, I was born. Mum came home from the hospital and, that night, she put me into the cot next to Ed. He slept soundly for the first time ever.

Now I knew why Ed felt he was missing something. I tried hard to make up for his missing twin brother.

Before the accident, the Staples Five had been working on some dance routines to two popular songs by Irving Berlin - "Putting on the Ritz" and "Cheek to Cheek." Ed was very light on his feet and rather fancied himself as the new Fred Astaire. The accident put an end to his dancing days.

WATER AND FUEL

The population of Malta during the war was around 270,000 and today it's almost double that.

The Islands are very densely populated. There are no lakes, rivers, or reservoirs, so water has always been a problem. It rains on average 90 days a year, mostly from November to February. During the summer months, there are long dry spells without a drop of rain. Annual rainfall is only 550 mm and highly variable.

Malta has favourable conditions for the percolation and underground storage of water. The impermeable blue clays provide two water tables between the limestone formations. The principal source for the public supply of water has, for several centuries, been the main sea-level water table. As this only meets about half the island's daily requirements, desalination is the answer for the other half.

The technology behind desalination has a long history in Malta. Under British rule, a plant to distil seawater was built in Sliema to provide drinking water for Tigné Barracks in 1881. It was the world's first commercial desalination plant. The structure was simple but effective: it boiled sea water to separate the water from the salt and other impurities. The British also dug a deep well close to Valletta and installed a motorised pump to bring water up to the surface.

Nowadays, all the tap water in Malta is desalinated sea water. This allows the water authorities to meet the requirements of the farmers who need to irrigate their crops and the growing tourism sector. Malta is also treating 100% of its wastewater before it's used on crops or discharged into the sea. It's the first country in the Mediterranean and only the seventh in Europe to reach this goal.

Heavy bombing during the war broke many of the water pipes which carried water to people's houses. Sometimes when I turned on the tap, no water came out. Other days, when someone had fixed the break, we had water. We shared one bath a week between the seven of us. I hated going in after my brothers and always tried to be first into the clean water.

When I heard Mum running the bath, I went up those stairs like a shot.

Even before the war, most people used horses and buses for transport. For those who did own a car, fuel became scarce as the war progressed. Bicycles became prized possessions and prime targets for theft.

Fortunately, my father had a petrol allocation, which meant he could drive into the countryside to buy a few vegetables from the people who lived there. We always grew vegetables, but with our large family there were never enough. Unfortunately, Dad often came back empty-handed because the farmers, who were trying to grow vegetables commercially, were struggling. Their irrigation pipes had been destroyed by bombs, there was no oil for the pumps, so water had to be transported by hand. One of the farmers told my father he had to guard his crops and chickens at night against theft.

Electricity was in short supply, as there was no coal to produce it, so we had to turn off the fridge. In any case, we had no food to keep in it. The covered market in Valletta took a direct hit in April 1942. The stalls gradually closed anyway, as they had nothing to sell. When meat became scarce and expensive, some people ate their horses and cats.

Instead of electric lights, we used kerosene lamps. When kerosene was rationed, we switched to candles, which in turn became in short supply. We would sometimes put on a show after it got dark, which obliged Pat to play the piano by candlelight. Halfway through, we would often have to run to the shelter. We would finish the show a couple of hours later, or the next day.

MRS PALMER

When we were back at Maison Notre Dame, I often returned to St Andrews Barracks to stay with my best friend, Joyce Palmer, who I first met on the ship coming to Malta.

Accommodation at the barracks consisted of the large four-storey building, where we had lived when we were there, and a dozen or so semi-detached houses. Joyce and her family lived in one of these. She had two brothers. George was younger than Joyce and was a chubby boy before rationing began, though he soon became thin like the rest of us. He was always hungry. I often caught him looking in my overnight bag, to see if I had brought my bread ration with me and could be persuaded to hand it over. Once it disappeared and I'm sure he stole it.

In July 1942, my father asked if we could move back to St Andrews because it was too dangerous to stay in Floriana. We were all packed up and ready to move there on a Saturday morning. I was looking forward to it because we were going to live in a house right next to the Palmers. For some reason the move was delayed until the following Monday. My father wrote:

On that Saturday, the day we should have moved in, the Bosch dive bombed St Andrews and St Georges and struck almost every building. The quarter we were moving to was a semi-detached affair and was utterly destroyed. This was a divine warning to me to stay where we were.

Or maybe it was the Staples Luck. Dad cancelled the move and we stayed in Floriana.

When that devastating raid occurred at St Andrews, Mrs Palmer was in hospital for a few days, having just given birth to her fourth child. Fortunately, her husband and three children were in the air raid shelter that night.

The family were allocated new accommodation, but when Mrs Palmer came home from hospital, she had to bathe her new baby in a large saucepan, as they had nothing much left. Joyce was traumatised for weeks and kept bursting into tears. We decided that nearly being killed was almost as bad as being killed. We went over the various scenarios. What if I had been staying the night and we had all been in her house rather than in the shelter? Talking about it seemed to help.

One day, I woke up to find blood on my nightdress. I couldn't work out where it had come from. Perhaps I had been bitten by something? I was on my way to the laundry, when my mother saw me.

"Whose nightdress is that? Yours or one of the twins?" she enquired.

"It's mine." I said. "I'm sorry. I'll put it in a bucket of water with some salt, to soak. I don't know how it happened."

"Don't worry, it just means you're a woman now," my mother said, as she headed off to the kitchen.

After breakfast, Carrie handed me a pile of reusable sanitary towels she had made by cutting up an old towel.

"Welcome to the club," she said.

I had no idea what was going on, so I went to Joyce's house after school and asked Mrs Palmer. You could talk to her about anything, and I often wished she were my mother. Mrs Palmer told me what she called The Facts of Life. It was a complete revelation to me. She told me that you couldn't get sanitary towels in Malta since the war started, so you had to make your own. When I got home, I told my sisters, so they would be more prepared than I was when their period started. I was cross with Pat, who said he "knew all about it" but hadn't bothered to tell me.

Anything to do with sex was a taboo subject in our house. My mother never said another word on the topic.

THE ARMY STORE

I wasn't as close to Vivienne Wycherley as I was to Joyce Palmer, but I spent more time with her because we both went to Chiswick House school.

Vivienne's mother was a good cook and Vivienne sometimes shared a piece of cake at recess, which we called our "elevenses," because I never had any cake of my own. My favourite was made from stale bread and dried fruit. One day after school, Mrs Wycherley taught me how to make it. She said that the recipe came from a Maltese friend, and it was called Puddina.

Maltese Puddina

10 large slices stale bread
4 oz (125g) mixed dried fruit
1 tablespoon dried mixed peel (optional)
1 egg
1/4 cup sugar
4 teaspoons mixed spice or cinnamon
2 heaped tablespoons softened butter or margarine
2-3 tablespoons sugar, extra

Soak bread in cold water for half an hour. Squeeze bread to expel as much water as possible, then beat with a fork to remove lumps. Mix all ingredients together and spread into a greased shallow baking tin about 8 inches by 10 inches (20 x 30 cm) in size. Bake at 180°C (350°F) for an hour or until nicely browned. Sprinkle liberally with extra sugar, cut into squares and serve warm.

The next day, my brothers were late coming home from school because they had sports. As they walked through the front door, they were hit with the delicious aroma of sugar and cinnamon. Cake-making wasn't on my mother's skill list, so this wasn't something they were used to. The cake disappeared in no time, still warm from the oven. It was the first thing I had ever baked, and my brothers were full of praise. I made it a few times until rationing meant there was no stale bread, let alone dried fruit or other ingredients.

My first attempt at making bread rolls was a disaster. They were so hard, even the chickens wouldn't eat them. We had to soak them in warm water, so they could get their beaks into them. Mum said no more cooking for me. The ingredients were too hard to come by during rationing to permit experimentation.

Vivienne's father was in charge of the Army Store Depot. Apart from military uniforms and civilian clothes donated by the Red Cross, a lot of tinned and dried food was stored there. It was next to their house, encircled by a barbed wire fence and guarded by two big black dogs.

One day after school I went to Vivienne's house to play. Her mother gave us afternoon tea and I couldn't help noticing that they had all sorts of things which we didn't. When I mentioned this to Vivienne, she asked me what I meant. I explained that, in my house, we didn't have any sugar, tinned milk, or anything really. She was shocked when I told her that we often went to bed at night with a gnawing hunger. I also mentioned that my birthday was coming up in September and I would love to have a small party for my friends.

The next time I went to Vivienne's house, her mother handed me a big basket and let me into the storeroom. She said I could take whatever I wanted, which really boiled down to whatever I could carry. I staggered home, my arm almost dropping off and a big smile on my face. I knew my mother would be thrilled. As I left, Vivienne's mother said: "Ask your mother to make a list of anything you need in the way of clothes."

A consignment of Red Cross donations from Maltese expatriates living in the United States had recently arrived. When the boys were all dressed up in their new three-piece suits, Mum said they looked like Mickey Rooney, a famous American child-actor whose films we all loved. The suits were made for a cold climate, so my brothers didn't get much wear out of them, but they were now able to look smart on special occasions.

Two days before my birthday, Vivienne's mother sent a box of food to our house—tinned peaches, tinned cream and biscuits—so I could have a proper celebration. I invited Vivienne, Joyce, three other school friends and my two sisters.

NO NEW CLOTHES

It was impossible to buy new clothes or shoes. Everybody started to look very poor, with children wearing clothes which were far too small for them. There were no raw materials coming into Malta, so people had to make clothes out of whatever they could find.

The slogan was "Make do and Mend." Collars on men's shirts were turned, socks were darned over and over again, trousers were patched and bed sheets were cut down the middle and rejoined, so that the worn-out centres were on the outside. People even made clothes from old curtains.

Silk parachutes were highly prized and used to make wedding dresses and ladies' underwear. When shoes wore out, pieces of cardboard were cut to fit inside, to make them last longer. I had a pair of wooden sandals with rope soles and red, white and blue uppers, made from strips of leather upholstery from a bombed-out car. They weren't very comfortable, but it was better than going barefoot. Coats and jackets were made from RAF blankets, which were highly prized.

With regular kit inspections on the agenda for the junior ranks, my father had to set an example. Mr Cefai made sure his boots held a mirror shine and the brass buttons on his jacket always gleamed. With the scarcity of cleaning materials this became harder. Some of Dad's uniforms had been mended several times.

The Maltese sun was powerful, and it was a disciplinary offence to be inoperative due to a self-inflicted injury such as sunburn. So, apart from checking that the soldiers' rooms were spic and span, and their uniforms were in good order, the Sergeant Major would look for sunburn during kit inspections.

A couple of years after we arrived in Malta, I had grown out of all my dresses, so they had been handed down to my sisters. When the twins were confirmed, there was no one to hand anything down to me, so Mum and I went to see Georgina, the Maltese dressmaker who lived opposite the parade ground. We took a bag of old clothes with us, to see if she could salvage anything to make me a dress for the confirmation.

I thought I looked very smart in my new dress. The blue skirt was made from one of my mother's old dresses and the white top from one of my father's silk handkerchiefs. My mother found a matching blue ribbon to go in my hair. It was too hot for my brothers to wear their Mickey Rooney suits, so they wore their Boy Scout uniforms.

Everyone has a mental picture of their mother. Mine is of her standing in the garden of Maison Notre Dame, where we had a small celebration after the confirmation at the Sarria Catholic church. She had aged so much in a short time. Her dress was several sizes too big and hung off her body like a sack. Her once lustrous hair was pulled back into a shapeless bun. Weekly trips to the hairdresser in Sliema were a thing of the past. My father was standing next to her, and he was also very thin. He wrote in his diary that he had lost eight inches on his waist.

The situation got worse as the months passed. People just did without. Soap was a luxury and toothpaste disappeared. We cleaned our teeth with salt and made shoe polish from soot and wax. Carrie scoured our cooking pans with soil, which was quite effective.

You could make a substitute for most things, but not food. Women started to turn up at our door, begging for food for their children. We had nothing to give them.

The effect of hunger and deprivation took its toll, resulting in frayed tempers. Babies, the weak and the old died and most days we saw a funeral procession on its way to the church.

It was unfeasible to dig graves for the growing number of dead bodies. There were no crematoriums on the island and it's very hard work digging holes in solid rock. Most burials, especially of servicemen, were at sea. Sometimes the bodies were not suitably weighted, and they resurfaced in the harbour some days later. (Cremation became legal in Malta in 2019, but there are to date no crematoriums on the island.)

When we sat down for Christmas lunch on 25 December 1941, to what can only be described as a miserable feast, my mother was so embarrassed she was almost in tears. It was also my twin sisters' tenth birthday.

Buying Christmas and birthday presents was out of the question.

In his Christmas speech, which we listened to on the BBC, King George VI told us all to be strong and of good courage. We gave each other a kiss and a hug and said we hoped Christmas would be better next year. Unfortunately, it would be even worse.

INFECTIONS AND EPIDEMICS

The low number of calories being consumed by the Maltese population was a worry for the health authorities. Starving people run a higher risk of infections. The crowded air raid shelters also contributed to the risk of communicable diseases. And the hot weather in summer always brought more ailments.

During the war, there was a significant rise in bronchitis, pneumonia, typhoid, ariboflavinosis (caused by a vitamin B2 deficiency) and pellagra (caused by a vitamin B3 deficiency). There were several epidemics including typhoid fever, which was said to be caused by farmers using human excrement instead of manure on their fields to try and increase the yield and sewage seeping into the water system due to bomb-damaged pipes. Typhoid proved a real killer.

There were other epidemics, one of which was scabies. Many were affected by this awful skin disease, caused by a lack of subcutaneous fat, which led to weeping boils and terrible itching all over the body. Another epidemic which affected the servicemen was catarrhal jaundice, a virus like hepatitis which made you drowsy, irritable, sick and depressed.

Nobody in our family had typhoid, but skin complaints were a constant problem, caused by our poor diet. My father suffered from eczema around his neck and under his arms, especially in summer. Boils were common. I had an enormous one on my face and wouldn't let anyone touch it. When it burst it left what looked like a beauty spot.

Joan had ringworm on her scalp and was heartbroken when the doctor said she had to have her head shaved. To cover her embarrassment, my mother bought a little organza bonnet. Ointment was applied regularly and, in time, her hair grew back. Having always seen her with somewhat thin, straight hair, we were amazed to see a mass of curls when Joan's hair grew back after the ringworm.

Unfortunately, it reappeared.

Joan cried when my mother said she would have to shave off her new curls. Mr Cefai asked my mother to let him treat the problem and Joan was pleased when he said there was no need to shave her head. He made a concoction of garlic, oil and herbs and applied it daily. Joan was a sensitive child, so he found a quiet spot under the veranda at the back of the house to administer his potion. Lo and behold, the ringworm disappeared.

A few people we knew were very unwell with "Malta fever," nicknamed Malta Dog. The proper name is Undulant Fever or Brucellosis—named after the Scottish pathologist David Bruce, who was stationed in Malta in the late 1800s. He led an investigation into an outbreak of the disease and discovered that it was caused by drinking unpasteurized goat's milk.

By then, the goat man wasn't coming to our house any more with his herd. Dogs could also carry the disease, but Handak was never sick. When we could no longer buy fresh goat's milk, we mixed KLIM milk powder—when we could get it from the NAAFI—with water. The taste wasn't too bad and, in any case, that's all there was.

Brucellosis cases were extremely high in 1945 and 1946, so when the war ended farmers were offered one cow in exchange for 10 goats and the dairy industry gradually took off. Now there are quite a few cattle on the island, the milk is pasteurised and, in 1958, a factory producing cream, yoghurt and cheese opened on Gozo.[26]

In January 1943, schools closed for several months, due to an outbreak of poliomyelitis. There were no vaccinations for this disease back then. Several hundred children, mostly under the age of five, died. Those who caught polio and survived were often disabled for life.

Routine childhood vaccination for polio and other potentially deadly diseases, such as tetanus, whooping cough and diphtheria, didn't start in Britain until after the war. And it is a similar story with antibiotics. While Penicillin was invented in 1928 and production began during the Second World War, it was mainly used by the military for treating battlefield infections and pneumonia.

When I think about all the illnesses which were prevalent in Malta while we were there, I realise we must have had strong genes and strong constitutions. Plus, a certain amount of luck. If you got really sick, there was no guarantee that the hospital could cure you. Even when medication to treat your ailment existed, the chances were that we didn't have it on the island.

We knew people who died of diabetes because they couldn't get insulin. This threat was a constant Sword of Damocles that hung above the whole island.

THE ILLUSTRIOUS BLITZ

Operation Excess was the name given to a series of convoys sent from Gibraltar and Alexandria in January 1941 to destinations in the Mediterranean, including Malta. The island was in desperate need of ammunition, fighter planes, spare parts and aviation fuel. Food and drinking water were running out. It was imperative to get supplies.

One such convoy to Malta was led by the aircraft carrier HMS Illustrious. This ship was the biggest and most modern in the British fleet. She had long been hunted because of the damage she had inflicted on the Axis ships in the region. Illustrious was carrying several fighter planes to Malta, so the enemy was determined to sink her at all costs.

Once Italy joined the war, the Germans were able to move their aircraft to Sicily and use the island as an air base. As the convoy was nearing Malta, German Stukas, which had been lying in wait in Sicily, took off. Wave upon wave of bombers dropped bombs on the convoy.

On 10 January 1941, we knew that something terrible was happening, even before we could see anything. The noise of the explosions could be heard all over the island. The people of Valletta and Floriana crowded onto the bastions, where we had an incredible view.

> The population, disregarding air raid precautions, left the security of the shelters in order to watch the combat from their rooftops. It was an excusable disobedience since the spectacle was completely out of the ordinary... There was enough monotony in the island... Life was extremely dull. Aerial combats in themselves constituted a diversion in the humdrum routine. The fact that the spectacle entailed a certain amount of risk to the watcher added spice to the show.[27]

The noise of the battle grew nearer and nearer until at last we could see what was happening. The shrieking of enemy planes as they dived and dropped their bombs on a ship called Illustrious was deafening. There were many direct hits and several fires started, but she still managed to limp towards Malta. Many other ships from the convoy also made it into the Grand Harbour, bringing their precious cargo. Fortunately, the fighter planes that Illustrious was carrying had taken off just before the attack and were able to come to her aid.

As soon as the convoy was close enough, swarms of Royal Air Force fighter planes took off from Ta Kali airport to go into battle. Tony Cefai was part of a team of volunteers who filled in holes in the runway during raids, so our planes could take off and land. That day they worked tirelessly, hiding in slit trenches then rushing out when it was clear to repair the damage.

Miraculously, even with her rudder and steering equipment badly damaged, the Illustrious did not sink. At 9pm on 11 January 1941 she made it into the Grand Harbour. She was listing badly and fires still burned on board, leaving a trail of smoke behind her. As she arrived, she was attacked by two enemy aircraft carrying torpedoes. Fortunately, the multiple-barrelled guns on the flight deck were still operational and they managed to shoot both planes down. Otherwise, she would no doubt have been sunk.

Malta wasn't the target that day, so instead of hiding in the shelters, we watched an amazing show. A great cheer arose from the crowd as those two planes went down and our Spitfires did their victory rolls.

Well over a hundred of Illustrious' brave crew were killed during the attack and many others died of their injuries later. A call was made for volunteers to help transfer the wounded to hospital and unload the cargo. The Royal Navy Hospital Mtarfa had been on stand-by for several hours, with every surgeon, doctor and nurse waiting to attend to the injured, many of whom were very badly burnt.

It was too dangerous for the uninjured sailors to sleep on board the ships, so they slept in caves which were being used as air raid shelters in Valletta. They were cold and damp, but safe. Maltese people had been sleeping in them for over a year.

My father asked if we would like to put on a Staples Family show at the barracks for the surviving sailors and airmen. We readily agreed. I was shocked when I saw those poor men. To be honest, they weren't men at all. They were young boys, not much older than my brothers. Many had haunted looks in their eyes. My father said they were shell-shocked.

The show was a great success. Afterwards, an American Captain who had worked in Hollywood before the war came up to congratulate us. He said he had an idea for a film about a family like ours that put on shows. He said he would make it after the war ended. We went home dreaming of becoming Hollywood stars.

Five days later, on 16 January 1941, the enemy returned to try and finish off the Illustrious as she lay in the harbour. About a hundred Stukas attacked her in waves, raining bombs on the stricken ship and on the whole of the Grand Harbour and surrounding towns. Fortunately, the Illustrious was moored in French Creek, protected on one side by the sheer rock cliff of Corradino Heights and on the other side by the suburb of Senglea. Several guns were brought from other parts of the island to form a box-barrage around the Illustrious and protect her while she was being repaired. It worked perfectly. Over five hundred people were killed and nine hundred buildings were destroyed in an hour, but the Illustrious survived.[28]

We all cheered when Winston Churchill said, in a broadcast on the BBC, that in their effort to destroy the Illustrious convoy and the Grand Harbour, the enemy had lost 90 planes.

Whenever he could, Dad gave us a full update on what he was allowed to divulge. He said that the enemy was so intent on sinking the Illustrious, they had ignored the heavy losses and kept coming back for more.

Hundreds of Maltese dockers worked on the Illustrious day and night, repairing the damage, until she was ready to sail again. Some near misses exploded in the sea beneath her, causing damage below the water line. Divers went down at night to repair them and were also used to help with pumping out the precious oil from ships which had been sunk, oil that would now be reused.

On 23 January, Illustrious left the Harbour in the dead of night and arrived safely in Alexandria, Egypt, two days later. This ship, which had suffered many direct hits and near misses, had survived, again. Dad said she was one tough lady.

ENSA

The Entertainments National Service Association (ENSA) was formed in 1939 by Basil Dean, a London theatre producer, to provide entertainment for British armed forces during the Second World War. It was part of the NAAFI which, as well as providing sustenance to the men and women of Britain's armed forces, was responsible for their recreation, welfare and morale.

The first big wartime variety concert organised by ENSA was broadcast by the BBC to the Empire and local networks on 17 October 1939, from RAF Hendon in North London, where Adelaide Hall sang, "We're Going to Hang Out the Washing on the Siegfried Line."

ENSA staged over 400 performances between 1939 and 1946

in England and various destinations around the world where British troops were stationed: the Middle East, West Africa, Gibraltar, France and Malta. Some critics said that ENSA stood for Every Night Something Awful. The quality of the shows was indeed patchy, but they were a great morale booster.

It wasn't an easy life for the performers, travelling endlessly and sometimes having to put on a show in an old barn or a derelict farmhouse. They often performed within the sound of gunfire, on a makeshift stage made from planks of wood resting on ammunition boxes. Costume changes were sometimes carried out behind military vehicles.

Many of the British performers, including Gracie Fields, Vera Lynn, Tommy Cooper and Joyce Grenfell, went on to enjoy successful careers in the entertainment industry after the war. Spike Milligan, Peter Sellers and Harry Secombe were seconded from their regiments to join ENSA. They went on to create the highly successful British radio comedy programme called The Goon Show. They might never have crossed paths if it hadn't been for ENSA. Several American and international stars also went on a few tours, including Judy Garland, Marlene Dietrich, Frank Sinatra and Bing Crosby.[29]

During the First World War, the British military authorities decided that a place of amusement and entertainment was urgently needed in Malta, to keep the thousands of convalescing servicemen occupied and out of mischief. These included many Australians and New Zealanders who were casualties from the Battle of Gallipoli.

The Australian Branch of the British Red Cross raised £2,000 for the construction of a simple but elegant building to be erected on a site in Pembroke, between St Andrew's and St Paul's Hospitals. Australia Hall was completed in two years by the Royal Engineers and opened on 22 January 1916 as a recreation centre for some two thousand servicemen who were convalescing at the time in hospitals all over the island. Later, a library, a reading room and a projection room—so the hall could also be used as a cinema—were added.

Australia Hall was managed by the Young Men's Christian Association and the British Red Cross. Between the wars and during the Second World War, it was used for all the visiting ENSA shows, providing a designated theatre, rather than something makeshift for the performances.

The Australian coat-of-arms carved in stone was placed above the main entrance, with a plaque stating: "This building was erected in November 1915 by the Australian Branch of the British Red Cross Society for the benefit of the soldiers of the empire."

When ENSA visited Malta, Mrs Clarke always stayed with us overnight, so we could go to Australia Hall together. We loved their shows and never missed one. Sometimes we went twice.

As we listened to songs such as "There'll Always Be an England" and "We'll Gather Lilacs in the Spring Again," you could have heard a pin drop.

We knew all the wartime songs, such as "Pack up your Troubles in your Old Kit Bag," "It's a Long Way to Tipperary," and "The White Cliffs of Dover." Singing these stirring songs was guaranteed to lift our spirits.

CHRISTINA AND THE WHIZZ BANGS

A British girl called Christina Ratcliffe moved to Malta in the late 1930s to perform as a singer and dancer in a cabaret act at the The Morning Star nightclub on Strait Street, Valletta. She had already found fame as a dancer in the 1935 film *Charing Cross Road*, starring John Mills and June Clyde. When the war started and the nightclub closed down, Christina decided to stay in Malta. She created the Whizz Bangs, a concert party of four men and seven women which toured all over the island, putting on shows for the troops.

When she wasn't performing with the Whizz Bangs, Christina worked as an air traffic controller, known as a "plotter," at the Lascaris War Rooms. She fell in love with an RAF photo-reconnaissance pilot called Adrian Warburton, nicknamed Warby. These "photo-recce" pilots flew planes with the guns removed and replaced with cameras. They were invaluable for keeping the Allies informed of the enemy's shipping movements. If they were attacked, the photo-recce pilots had to try and escape using speed and manoeuvring.

My father knew Christina from the Lascaris Rooms. He and Mum often went to see one of her Whizz Bang shows with the Clarkes. One evening, Dad invited Christina to our house to see our Staples Five show and she brought Warby with her.

We were all completely dazzled by Christina. She was wearing tight white satin trousers, a frilly red and black top and red stiletto shoes, to match her luscious red lips. Her thick blonde hair was curled into the latest bob and her piercing blue eyes were framed by false eyelashes and beautifully arched eyebrows. Of medium height, with a well-toned body, Christina smoked cigarettes through a long, silver and black holder, and walked like a dancer.

Born in Dukinfield, on the outskirts of Manchester, Christina had a soft lilting accent. Like Mum, she had lots of special words in her vocabulary. She always said "loovlay" instead of lovely, called a cup of tea a "brew" and said "owt" instead of anything. Words like bath, grass, dance and glass all had a short vowel, making her sound very different to us.

Warby had sandy-coloured, tousled hair, swept back from a high forehead and he towered over Christina. Born in Middlesbrough, Warby had lost his northern accent by attending a boarding school in Oxford, where he had acquired a fairly posh English accent. Warby had a cheeky grin which lit up his blue eyes and a funny, contagious laugh. The couple were obviously very much in love.

Dad poured some drinks and Pat passed them round, while I passed the olives. As a gift, Christina had brought a bag of old tap-dancing shoes, which she no longer needed. We each found a pair which fitted, and Christina showed us some steps. Ed, who was unable to dance since the accident, looked longingly at a pair which would have fitted him. He never danced again.

Warby had brought a bag of sweets called sherbet lemons that a friend had sent him from England. They had arrived in the mail bag by submarine.

As the grownups sipped their drinks and smoked—apart from Mum, who never touched a cigarette in her life—we counted out the sherbet lemons. Five each. As they chatted about the war, Dad told Warby he was a daredevil, because he was always taking risks on his sorties to take photos. Warby blushed modestly and laughed.

"Flying is a risky business," he said. "The RAF only attracts daredevils."

Our show lasted a couple of hours, including an interval, so within half an hour of our guests' arrival we were underway. Warby and Christina sat very close together, holding hands.

After the show, Christina was full of praise. If the war was still on when we finished school, she said, she would give us all a job with the Whizz Bangs.

"God bless us and save us." said Mum, after they had left. "That girl was poured into those trousers. They left nothing to the imagination. No wonder that fellah can't keep his hands off her."

The Staples Five said nothing. We thought Christina looked stunning.

Mum was always very conservative. Decades later, she was shocked by the advent of bikinis, miniskirts and hot pants.

Christina was a similar size to me and, as I stood next to her in my ugly, childish clothes, I felt very self-conscious. I was developing breasts and should have been wearing a bra, but you couldn't buy them.

I had always wanted an older sister, which is why I loved spending time with Carrie. Christina was in her late-20s, about 15 years older than me. She came round one evening on her own and helped me to style my hair, which I had managed to grow to a shoulder-length bob, in the latest Hollywood fashion. She arrived carrying a bag full of lovely hand-me-down clothes, including two bras. I was thrilled and hung onto Christina's every word. My second big sister.

OTHER PASTIMES

Saturday night dances at the Sliema Club were very popular and my parents often went. Going out at night was risky, but people took the attitude that life goes on. Between air raids, they tried to live their lives as best they could.

The dances, which were rarely cancelled, finished at 11pm, after which the worst air raids tended to occur. This gave everyone time to get home before the sirens started to wail. Sergeant John Mason, who worked cleaning up after the air raids, wrote:

> Most of my work was civil defence, which involved rescue work and first aid ... The bombing wasn't perpetual—they would give you a break and then give you a real hammering. They picked mealtimes and the middle of the night ... I've never seen people like the Maltese for stamina and fortitude ... They would come out after the raids to see if the neighbours were all right and then they would get on with their lives.[30]

Cricket was a popular sport among the servicemen, even during the worst bombing. They played on improvised pitches at various places, including barrack parade grounds and even on the airfields. The Army, Navy and RAF each had a team and there were a few Maltese teams. Sometimes my brothers took part.

The first moving picture with sound was released in 1927, a decade before we moved to Malta. Despite the war, Hollywood was in full swing in the 1940s, churning out hundreds of films each year. We loved going to the cinema, because it took our minds off things, allowing us to escape to another world and forget about our rumbling tummies. It was one of our few pleasures and we went to see almost every film that came to Malta.

The cinemas in Valletta mostly stayed open through the war. They always showed two films, the main one and a B film, so a session took well over three hours, with Pathé News in the middle. *The Wizard of Oz, Gone with the Wind, Casablanca* and the animated Disney films *Dumbo* and *Bambi*. We saw them all. There were also propaganda and morale-boosting films, such as *Winning your Wings* starring James Stewart, and *Victory through Air Power*—the history of aviation—which my brothers enjoyed. The B film was often one with Laurel and Hardy or The Three Stooges, which we all loved.

When the reel broke, as it often did, we stomped our feet in protest, as loudly as we could, until they fixed it.

After seeing Carmen Miranda in *Banana da Terra,* Daphne asked Christina to help her make an outfit with a turban, so she could do a new number in our show, impersonating the gregarious Brazilian singer/dancer. Mrs Clarke found an old sequined red dress she didn't wear anymore, and Christina helped Daphne to turn it into a full-length, slinky dress. Enormous hoop earrings, a few strings of fake pearls, some fake fruit and feathers for the turban and bright red lipstick completed the look. Everyone loved Daphne's impersonation of Carmen Miranda and the outfit was one that the lady herself would have been proud of.

We gleaned lots of new ideas from the ENSA shows and from Christina. Our Staples Five shows improved significantly. We were often asked to put on a performance for a special occasion. We loved dressing up for these performances. It is so much easier to pretend to be someone else when you're in front of an audience. Any nerves you may have disappear immediately.

Mum's waist-length, dark, wavy hair had been cut off in the early 1920s, when short hair became fashionable, so we only ever knew her with short hair. When weekly trips to the hairdresser in Valletta were possible, Mum's hair was always shiny and well-styled. When hairdressers closed, she cut her own hair and used ordinary soap to wash it, as we all did. Luxuries such as shampoo and face creams were unavailable. For a time, my mother cut our hair, too, but she wasn't very good at it, so in due course I took over. I wasn't all that good either, but I did my best. My father got his hair cut at the barracks.

One Saturday afternoon, my sisters and I went to the cinema with Mrs Clarke. During the film, I couldn't stop scratching my head. Afterwards, Mrs Clarke asked discreetly if anyone had checked to see if I had fleas. I told her that wasn't the problem. We had been using carbolic soap to wash our hair and it had given me an itchy scalp. Before rationing, it's what we used to wash Handak, to keep the fleas off. It certainly did that, but it smelled disgusting. The boys didn't seem to mind it, but the four girls in the house—five, with Carrie—hated it.

The next time Mrs Clarke called in, she brought a bag of beauty products, including two big bottles of shampoo made by Schwarzkopf and a jar of face cream for Mum. She said she always had a stockpile, bought on her pre-war shopping trips to London. We were very abstemious with those bottles of shampoo, and we didn't care that they came from Germany. We measured it out by the teaspoonful and made it last for weeks and weeks. For a while, we smelt like lavender instead of like Handak, but when it ran out, we resumed complaining. My father told us that many of the servicemen were bathing in the sea, using a special soap for sea water. This, he said, was surely worse than not having any shampoo.

On Sunday 15 February 1942, the Regent Cinema in Valletta was showing *Northwest Mounted Police*, starring Gary Cooper and Madeleine Carroll. My brothers headed off to see it. A couple of hours later, Mr Cefai rushed into our house in a dreadful state.

"Where are your brothers?" he shouted.

When I told him, he visibly paled and rushed off. The cinema had sustained a direct hit, resulting in many casualties. The ceiling had collapsed onto the audience of teenagers and servicemen who were enjoying a day's leave. I ran after Mr Cefai and stood outside the hospital, watching the injured being taken in for medical aid. One young sailor with a tear-stained, dirty face was helping his shipmate, who looked badly injured. He had carried him all the way from Valletta. I asked if he had seen two teenage boys. He shook his head and said,

"Don't go to the pictures girly, not while this war is on."

We were all relieved when my brothers turned up later, wondering what all the fuss was about. They had changed their minds at the last minute and gone to another cinema.

THE RABBIT

The Governor of Malta, Sir William Dobbie, took over from Governor Bonham-Carter in April 1940. He sent out a leaflet on "Raising Rabbits for Meat," with instructions for taking care of them. I decided to have a go, although I had no plans to eat them. I was looking forward to having lots of new pets to play with.

Cikku, a nickname in Malta for boys called Francis, was one of the construction men who worked for my father. One day he brought me a baby rabbit from his home in Zebbug—which means olives in Maltese—a half hour drive from Floriana into the countryside. She was a dear little white rabbit, and I called her Flopsy. She became very tame and when she was about a year old, I took her back to Cikku's farm to be mated with one of his rabbits. It wasn't a success, but Cikku said we could try again in a few months' time. Flopsy had a very strong character for a rabbit. If Handak got on her nerves she would chase him around the garden and nip him on his bottom, which we all thought was hilarious.

Once Cikku invited me to spend a weekend with his family. He was in his twenties, single and living with his parents and two sisters. His sister Bernie had an English fiancé called Brian and Cikku wanted me to meet him. My father drove me there after breakfast one Saturday. It was late spring and there was a riot of colour from the wildflowers which adorned the sides of the road—dwarf irises, jonquils and anemones.

After coffee with Cikku and his family, my father headed home, saying he would be back on Sunday afternoon to pick me up. Bernie showed me the guest room, which was on the third floor, at the top of the house. It contained a terrifying array of stuffed animals and birds, preserved in fixed poses, beneath glass domes. Cikku's older brother was an amateur taxidermist. I didn't look forward to sharing a bedroom with all these dead animals. On the other hand, I had my own tiny bathroom with a lime green bath and basin and mosaic tiles on the walls.

Cikku's mother's face was arranged into a permanent smile, contrasting with her husband, who never smiled. He had a face which was well-baked and wrinkled from the Maltese sun. The mother didn't speak any English, so we communicated by smiling at each other. As the sun was going down, we sat on the rooftop veranda sipping Ruggata, a sweet drink made from almonds, sugar, vanilla and cloves. It's a non-alcoholic, home-made concoction, which the Maltese drank in summer, diluted with cold water. We all made polite conversation for half an hour, then went inside for dinner. Cikku's mother served a delicious casserole which was full of meat, something we ate very rarely in our house. I found out later it was rabbit. Brian, the British fiancé, joined us just as we were sitting down. Short in stature, with heavily-Brylcreemed hair, he walked with a swagger and was, to use one of Mum's expressions, very full of himself. I didn't like him, but Bernie was clearly besotted. After dinner, we played cards and I'm pretty sure he cheated.

We all helped to clean up, then I climbed the stairs to my room, put on my pyjamas and got into bed. Even though it was dark, I knew all the dead animals and birds were looking at me with their beady eyes. Despite being the object of their stares, eventually I managed to fall asleep.

In the middle of the night, I awoke suddenly. The moon was shining in, and the curtains were flapping in the breeze from the half-open window, like the wings of a trapped bird. I was terrified. I turned on the light and read my book until it was time to get up.

THE DEMISE OF THE RABBIT

The dining room at Maison Notre Dame was windowless and lined with dark wood panelling. With a round table and seven high-backed chairs, also in dark timber, it was rather sombre. The room wasn't big enough to fit any other furniture or more people. If we had visitors, which didn't happen very often, we would eat early, and the adults would eat later. When we had guests, Mum used the Wedgwood floral dinner service which had been a wedding present. She had added to the original 8-piece setting over the years, buying a few additional pieces in Darlington, whenever she had some spare cash.

My father always made a point of being home for dinner. It was a formal occasion, and we took it in turns to say grace. He was strict about table manners and would send us out if we misbehaved. I can only remember being sent out once, but my brother Pat was regularly banished to the kitchen to eat his meal with Carrie. She was only a couple of years older than Pat, very pretty and well-endowed. Pat had a crush on her and much preferred the company in the kitchen. I didn't miss much and noticed that Carrie would blush whenever she saw Pat.

With just a small bowl of soup from the Victory Kitchens and a slice of bread, dinner was usually over in less than ten minutes. Afterwards, my father would bring us up to date on what was happening in the war, no doubt leaving out anything which was secret. We would listen to the BBC news on the wireless and discuss things afterwards. On Sundays, there was a music show we loved, with a band leader called Nat Allen and a singer called Anne Shelton. We invariably knew the songs and would sing along.

One evening, instead of the usual Victory Kitchen soup, we were eating a particularly delicious stew of meat in a tomato sauce with mashed potatoes. My father had acquired a small allotment at the back of the Pietà cemetery. His first crop of potatoes filled two big sacks and he was very pleased with himself. Mr Cefai helped him to look after the allotment, so my father gave him half the potatoes, to take home to his family.

It was the first time we had eaten meat for over a month, and we were all enjoying it.

Suddenly Pat said, "Did you give your rabbit any water today, Mags? It's been really hot."

"Finish your meal," said my mother.

"No, I had better do it now," I said, as I rushed out into the garden. "She'll be thirsty."

I ran outside to find the door to Flopsy's cage wide open. She was nowhere to be seen.

Distraught, I came back into the dining room shouting.

"She's gone, she's gone. What's happened to my rabbit?"

"Sit down and finish your meal," said my mother. "You probably didn't close the door properly when you fed her this morning and she must have escaped. We'll help you to find her after dinner. She'll be somewhere in the garden."

I sat down and picked up my knife and fork. I put a piece of meat into my mouth and started to chew. It tasted like chicken and was delicious. As I looked up, I saw Pat smirking at Ed and twitching his nose, like a rabbit. My brothers started to laugh, and I knew what had happened.

Tears sprang to my eyes as I ran from the room. I felt like a cannibal and have never eaten rabbit since.

RABBITS AND CATS

Quite a few cats went missing at that time, including Timmy. I spent hours calling for her around Floriana, in the places where she liked to hunt for mice, but to no avail. I knew that you couldn't tell the difference between a skinned cat and a skinned rabbit, unless the tail was left on. Timmy was very friendly and would have been easy for someone to catch. I tried not to think about it.

A few weeks later, Cikku called in to see my parents and stayed for a beer. He told us that one of his neighbours was selling skinned rats to the Army Mess. When people are starving, he said, they don't ask what they're eating. My mother said she had been offered them at the market one day, but she would sooner starve than eat rats.

Cikku offered to bring me another baby rabbit, but I said no thank you. He also told us that his sister Bernie had discovered that her British fiancé Brian had a wife and family in England.

He was ever after referred to as The Rubbish Man.

THE BOY SCOUTS

Scouting is a worldwide youth movement to support young boys in their physical, mental and spiritual development. The Scout Association of Malta was founded in 1908, just a year after it was founded in Britain by a military man, Lord Baden-Powell. The Association encouraged its members to have interests, hobbies and aims in life. They worked on character and leadership development, citizenship training and personal fitness by way of challenging, enjoyable and interesting activities which taught the boys both skills and values.

My brothers joined the Scout group for British boys, called the Cavaliers, soon after we arrived in Malta. The group met at the Scout Association's Central Headquarters, which was only about 300 yards away from Maison Notre Dame in Floriana. My father got very involved with the scouts' activities and was on the Scout Association Committee.

During the war, the Boy Scouts in Malta supported the Allied forces in many ways. All able-bodied men were fighting the enemy, so teenage boys like my two brothers were invaluable in taking on all sorts of jobs. Whenever anyone important visited the island, Pat and Ed were called on to be part of a Boy Scouts Guard of Honour.

Boy Scouts were employed as coast-watchers, messengers and administrative staff at the hospitals. Older boys like Ed and Pat, who were 15 and 16 at the height of the war, worked after school as telephone operators at the dockyard. They were also employed when convoys were unloaded, checking everything off the manifest and making sure nothing was stolen. Anyone caught stealing during unloading in the ports was given 32 days' imprisonment.

The Scout Headquarters in Floriana was destroyed by German bombers on 7 April 1942. My father wrote in his diary that achievement badges were "blown to high heaven."

Major Sam Staples and Father Hersey at the Scout Hall, after it was bombed in 1942.

Ed searches for anything worth salvaging at the Scout Hall after the bombing.

Not long after the bombing, several Scouts appeared wearing dozens of badges they couldn't possibly have earned legitimately. My father interrogated my brothers. They said they weren't involved in the scam, although they had been offered some of the badges. Just as well. My father would have come down on them like a ton of bricks if they had been involved. He was a stickler about honesty. The Scout Secretary, Father Hersey, made the culprits hand over the ill-gotten badges and the matter was resolved.

Father Bernard Hersey OFM (Order of the Friars Minor—a branch of the Franciscans) was the son of a British serviceman married to a Maltese woman. He was trained as a teacher and heavily involved in both football and scouting. His role as Secretary of the Scout Association was a paid post.

Pat was keen to get a badge as a Rover Scout. He went on a 24-hour lone march, but he was very underweight due to rationing and hadn't the stamina to complete the return journey. Dad had to go and collect him.

Lieutenant Cook, the Army photographer at the time, was always known as Cookie. After the Scout HQ was destroyed, he was looking for interesting subjects to photograph. Dad arranged for Pat, Ed and some other Scouts to be at the Scout Hall one Saturday afternoon. Cookie took a series of photographs of the boys looking for anything which could be salvaged from the rubble. They were published in J A Mizzi's *Scouting in Malta*. One photo showed Pat holding up a big bass drum. It had lost its skin in the bombing and was just a wooden hoop. The photograph had the caption "Goodbye to all that." The aim was to boost morale and show what an amazing job the Boy Scouts were doing in Malta during very difficult times.

My father was on the Executive Committee and drew up the plans for the new Scout Headquarters.

Plans for rebuilding the headquarters were discussed by the Executive Committee in June 1944, when the war in Europe was not yet over. Four different proposals were set out by Major H W Staples of the Royal Engineers. The first was to rebuild on the old foundations, using much of the old building material to save on expenditure. The cost was estimated at £1,225. A second plan, similar to the first, envisaged an improvement in the sanitary conditions, estimated at £1,335. The third proposal also contemplated building on the old foundations, but with the layout reversed so the main foyer would be at the front of the building, opposite the main drive, with the stage at the far end of the hall and as wide as the hall itself. Total expenditure £1,527. The fourth and final design which was unanimously approved was an extension of the third plan, with two extra dressing rooms at the far end of the hall on either side of the stage, which could also serve as offices, estimated at £1,750. Major Staples said that plan 4 would increase the opportunities of letting the hall for special occasions at a higher rate, thus recovering the added expenditure.[31]

When the war ended, the high demand for materials and labour pushed up the cost of rebuilding. Labourers worked for the contractor who paid the highest wages.

When work began on the new Scout HQ in 1945, the Association was told that the estimated cost had already risen. The contractors asked for an advance of £2,000, which the Association paid using £1,000 from its funds and another £1,000 borrowed from the bank. By February 1946, costs for building materials in Malta had risen steeply. Fortunately, in the meantime, the Scout Association had received £2,000 as its share of the war damage fund of £30 million contributed by the British government for the reconstruction of buildings which had been destroyed by bombing. Unfortunately, this amount would not go nearly as far as it would have done before the war.

The demand for building materials continued to rise, pushing the original quote of £1,750 up to £4,000. The chairman of the building committee, Colonel Vella, refused to pay any more to the contractors until he was assured that the work was being carried out according to specifications. An investigating team was brought in from the Royal Engineers. Their report said that the work had been carried out in a slipshod manner. Resolving these issues was quite a saga and, by the time the building was complete, the estimated cost had more than doubled.

The final cost of the building, which was officially opened on 1 September 1948, three years after we left Malta, was £4,735.[32]

THE BATMAN

Before soldiers had motorised transport, an officer's batman was in charge of his "bat-horse," the name given to a horse that carried his kit during a military campaign. This is where the name batman originated.

My father's batman, Tony Cefai, was a member of the Malta Auxiliary Corps. A good batman took pride in his boss's appearance and my father always looked impeccable. In a hot climate, with lots of changes and official functions, it was a time-consuming job.

While washing and ironing my father's uniforms was one of Tony's main tasks, he also collected the mail, acted as chauffeur—especially for my mother, who didn't drive—and ran errands. Tony was Dad's indispensable right-hand man. By having an assistant to take on all the time-consuming, administrative tasks, my father was able to concentrate on his work.

Tony lived with his mother and three younger sisters, Josephine, Geata and Lily, in a small two-storied house at 5 Granaries Square, just around the corner from the Sarria Church in Floriana, where we went to Mass. He was 27 when we arrived in Malta and still single. His sister, Geata, worked as personal maid to the governor's wife at San Anton's Palace. She met all the VIPs who visited Malta because they always stayed with the governor. She had met the British Prime Minister Winston Churchill on several occasions and said he was very nice and always left her a generous tip.

Tony's sister Josephine worked as a nurse at King George V Hospital in Floriana, which is now renamed as Sir Paul Boffa Hospital. It was built in 1922 as a memorial to men of the Merchant Navy who died in the First World War. Before the war, most babies were delivered at home, but in 1939 a midwifery ward opened at the hospital. During air raids, Josephine and the other nurses would take all the new babies into the basement of the hospital. The mothers stayed in their rooms and sheltered under their beds. When the hospital was severely damaged, on 7 April 1942, all the patients and nursing staff were moved to other hospitals. Josephine loved babies. She got married towards the end of the war and had five children.

With a big house and five young children, my mother was always busy. Tony often helped her with a few chores, especially when Carrie took time off to visit her family in the countryside. When we still had chickens, Tony brought scraps from the Sergeants Mess, and I remember him sitting in the kitchen, peeling potatoes for our evening meal. He was like a member of the family.

The Staples sisters in Malta circa 1942.
Margaret (13), Daphne and Joan (11).

Having left school at 13 and worked his way up to a senior position in the Royal Engineers, my father believed that education was the key to getting on in life. He often reminded us that the man who thinks he knows it all is a complete fool. He studied or read for an hour or two each evening before bed. His motto was "Knowledge is Power."

This was a lesson he would share with Tony, too. Dad encouraged Tony to go to night school and paid for his classes. By the end of the war, Tony had secured a government job as a Civil Foreman, responsible for coordinating and supervising civil building works. He had his own desk with his name on a little stand on the front. He was very proud of himself, and my father was very proud of him.

When my father was sleeping at the barracks, rather than at Maison Notre Dame, Tony slept in a room nearby. Once asleep, my father would sleep soundly for seven hours. Even loud noises wouldn't wake him. Whenever there was a raid, Tony would shake him vigorously until he was awake, then they would head to the shelter together.

I must thank Tony Cefai for his complete loyalty to me. My life would have been lost several times, but for him. But he knows what I think of him.[33]

THE ARTISTS

My father was checking progress on the construction of the Lascaris War Rooms, when he noticed a young Maltese man who was painting the doors of a toilet block. He was doing a very professional job, surprisingly so considering the less than vaunted venue for his work. Having trained as a painter in his teens, before he joined the Royal Engineers, my father knew a good painter when he saw one.

"You're doing a great job," said my father, "What do you normally do?"

"I'm an artist," replied the young man.

"What sort of things do you usually paint?" enquired my father.

"I mostly paint portraits of people, but there's no money for commissions at the moment and I need to put food on the table. That's why I am doing this. I can't even buy any canvas."

The young man was in his twenties and his name was Emanuel Vincent Cremona. In Malta, they always shortened Emanuel Vincent to Emvin. My father realised that his talents were being wasted and arranged for him to get a job at the Manoel Theatre.

The Manoel Theatre was named after the Grand Master of the Order of the Knights Hospitaller, Antonio Manoel de Vilhena, who commissioned and paid for its construction in 1731. It is said to be Europe's third oldest working theatre. Located in Old Theatre Street in Valletta, it seats 623 people in an oval auditorium with three tiers of carved wooden boxes which are elaborately decorated with gold leaf and a pale blue *trompe-l'oeil* ceiling that resembles a round cupola. It's an architectural masterpiece.

During the Second World War, the theatre, which had fallen into disrepair, provided temporary accommodation for people who had lost their homes in air raids. Occasionally, they showed a film there for the servicemen.

Following the destruction of the Royal Opera House by a direct hit in April 1942, the government decided to restore the Manoel Theatre to its former glory. My father knew the people in charge of this project. They were looking for local artisans to carry out the intricate work, which would take many years.

The following month, Emvin Cremona started work at the Manoel Theatre. To thank my father for getting him the job, he said he wanted to paint a portrait of someone in our family. Dad said the twins were too young to sit still, so he chose me. I was about 14 at the time and went to Mr Cremona's studio in Valletta once a week for eight half-hour sittings. Canvas was unobtainable, so he painted my portrait on plywood, showing me holding a bunch of pink peonies. Fortunately, he only needed the flowers for the first session. It was easier posing without them (see my portrait inside the front cover).

Emvin, who said he was too young to be called Mr Cremona, had short black hair, lightly oiled and swept back from a high forehead, large brown eyes, a neatly trimmed moustache and beard and generous lips. To protect his clothes, he wore an off-white cotton coat, splattered with paint and a colourful cravat around his neck.

His studio was quite small, accessed by a narrow staircase. The walls were covered with portraits and sketches and there were no windows, but a circular skylight in the ceiling flooded the studio with light. Set upon an easel was a half-finished portrait of a lovely young girl on her wedding day, dressed in a pale champagne-coloured, full-length, silk gown, a strand of shimmering pearls around her neck and flowers in her hair. Her face was in three-quarters profile and she was reclining on a *chaise longue*, one dainty pale pink satin slipper peeping out from the hem of her gown.

The author Linda Peek with Marco Cremona
(well-known artist Emvin Cremona's son)
at Gallery Cremona, Rabat, Malta, 2017.

Each time I came to the studio, Emvin had made more progress on that work until one day it was finished and a week later it had gone. While I have always loved painting still-life, especially flowers, I have never had the aptitude or patience to paint people. I felt I knew the girl in the wedding dress based on his painting alone and was in complete awe of Emvin's skills.

Another half-finished portrait was of a beautiful woman with chestnut curls, high cheekbones and blue, almost violet eyes. She was wearing a low-cut dress, with a fine gold chain around her alabaster neck. I thought she looked very sad and Emvin confirmed that indeed, she had recently lost a small son to polio.

While he worked, we chatted and I got to know him quite well. He had been studying painting in Rome at the Regia Accademia di Belle Arti for two years when Italy entered the war in June 1940. It was a wonderful school, he said, but hard work. He had spent hours and hours honing his technique. He had just managed to catch the very last boat from Italy to Malta before Italy joined the war, by the skin of his teeth. He wasn't married, but showed me a photograph of his fiancée, Lilian Gatt. They planned to marry as soon as the war was over.

I told him that art was my favourite subject at school, followed by poetry. He asked if I had seen the work of a famous Italian artist called

Caravaggio at St John's Co-Cathedral in Valletta. When I said I had read about it, but hadn't seen it yet, he offered to take me.

Dad dropped me off at St John's one Saturday morning. Emvin was waiting for me, wearing black trousers, a black open-neck shirt and a maroon, silk cravat. He knew Valletta like the back of his hand and gave me a running commentary.

St John's Co-Cathedral was built by the Order of St John between 1573 and 1578 as their headquarters. The cathedral's dome dominates Valletta's skyline and inside there are nine chapels. The most famous artist who worked on the cathedral was Michelangelo Merisi (1571-1610), known as Caravaggio, and the cathedral is home to some of his precious works.

Caravaggio arrived in Malta in 1607, having fled Rome because he was wanted for murder. He was already a renowned artist and when he arrived in Malta he was feted and admitted to the Order of St John. In return for this honour, he agreed to paint *The Beheading of St John the Baptist*, a work over 10 feet high and more than 15 feet across. Considered one of his masterpieces, it is the largest painting Caravaggio ever made and the only one he signed. Emvin spent half an hour discussing the finer details of the work. I was mesmerised. Then we went to see another of Caravaggio's famous works, *St Jerome*, which was also in the cathedral.

Afterwards we went for a walk around the narrow, cobbled streets of Valletta. Some of the most beautiful parts of the city were hidden away from the main streets and I had never been to them before. As we walked, Emvin told me what had happened to Caravaggio. It was a good story and he really brought it alive. The artist's freedom from justice only lasted a year. When he was caught, he was imprisoned in Fort St Angelo in the middle of the Grand Harbour. He later escaped to Sicily, where he painted several works before heading back towards Rome in hope of a papal pardon for a murder he had committed there in his youth. On his way, he died, likely of malarial fever, at the age of 38.

Valletta is one of the smallest capital cities in the world, but some of the streets are like roller coasters. We did a lot of walking, up and down the hills. It was sad to see how much had been damaged by bombs, but there were still a lot of beautiful buildings to admire.

Emvin had brought a picnic of bread and cheese, olives and figs, which we ate, sitting on a park bench, for lunch. When people shared food with you during the war, you felt really privileged. We were all on short rations.

As it was getting dark, Emvin dropped me home. He said that next time we went on an excursion he would show me the Mosta Church, which had the third largest Christian dome in Europe. I gave him a kiss on each cheek to thank him for such a wonderful day. He gave a little smile and blushed, almost matching the colour of his cravat.

One day, while I was sitting for my portrait, a sculptor who rented a nearby studio popped in. As he was chatting to Emvin, he kept looking at my hands. Before he left, he asked if he could use them as a model for a statue of St Theresa, he had been commissioned to make for the Parish Church of St Mary's in Attard, a name that means the village of roses. St Theresa was the name of my confirmation saint, so I was delighted to agree.

The sculptor, whose name was Marco Montebello, explained that all the famous Renaissance paintings show women with fingers shaped like little legs—fatter at the top and tapering down to pointed fingertips. Such fingers were rare, and he had been searching for some time to find an example on which to base his statue.

Mr Montebello insisted on asking for my father's permission to use my hands for the statue. Dad agreed and the following week he made a plaster mould. I had to hold my hands as if I were clutching a crucifix to my chest.

When the statue was unveiled some months later, we were all there to watch. From that moment on, I felt I had a special relationship with St Theresa and often called on her to protect me and my family from the bombs.

On 16 December 1943, Emvin invited my family to the opening of an exhibition of his paintings at the British Council. By the time we left, every painting had a sticker on it, meaning someone had bought it. We had no idea that Emvin Cremona would go on to become one of the most famous Maltese artists of the 20th Century, but we weren't surprised when he did and felt very proud to count him amongst our friends.

Statue of Saint Theresa with Margaret's hands in St Mary's parish church, Attard, Malta by well-known sculptor, Marco Montebello.

MORALE BOOSTERS

The Italians decided to destroy another convoy on 26 July 1941. There were six ships in the convoy bringing desperately needed supplies to Malta and they had just entered the harbour. Just before dawn, an Italian ship brought eighteen small motor launches, nicknamed "pigs," to a point nine miles north of the Island. These boats had a torpedo head in the bow. They were usually manned by two men who would try to escape as soon as the torpedo was set on course to enter the harbour and blow up one of our ships.

The pigs (we kids loved the name) were too small to be picked up by radar, but a Maltese gunner stationed at Fort St Elmo heard their engines, spotted them and raised the alarm. We loved it when Dad told us these stories after dinner. The pigs were picked off, he said, one by one, by the coastal gunners. The last four were finished off by aircraft.

On 9 April 1942, the Rotunda Church at Mosta sustained a direct hit during Mass. The bomb came straight through the dome and landed inside the church but didn't explode. There were about 300 people in the church at the time and, miraculously, nobody was injured.

The Governor, Sir William Dobbie, spoke most evenings on the Rediffusion to encourage everyone to believe that God was on our side against the evil forces of the enemy. Despite not being Catholic, he made a great impression on the Maltese people and helped to boost morale. Churchill also spoke regularly in an attempt to lift our spirits.

The war had lasted far longer than anyone thought it would.

On 15 April 1942, King George VI awarded the George Cross to the Island of Malta with the following citation: "To honour her brave people, I award the George Cross to the island fortress of Malta, to bear witness to a heroism that will long be famous in history." Instituted in September 1940, this medal was the highest British award for bravery that could be made to civilians and ranks. It was equal to the Victoria Cross.

The people of Malta were very proud to receive this award and it certainly helped to boost morale, but it didn't solve the problem of imminent starvation. My father said he saw some graffiti on a wall in Valletta which said, "Bread not medals."

THE THREAT OF INVASION: OPERATION HERKULES

As if the bombs and starvation weren't enough, we were also living with the threat of an invasion hanging over the island. This worry in the back of our minds was made manifest when, in January 1942, a leaflet was handed out which said, "What to do in an Invasion." It was not hugely helpful, basically recommending that we take cover and stay off the streets.

Several members of the German High Command—especially Field Marshal Kesselring—were in favour of an invasion, as was the

Italian dictator Mussolini. While Malta was in British hands, they said, they could never beat the Allies in Africa.

In February 1942, Hitler agreed with the proposal to invade Malta with German and Italian paratroopers and the operation was given a name: Operation Herkules. The Allies heard about the plan and were very worried that it would go ahead. By late April everything was ready, but Hitler hesitated to give the go-ahead. General Rommel, who was running the North African campaign, said that he needed the resources that would have to be committed to an invasion of Malta.

Another factor which contributed to Hitler's hesitation was that he hadn't forgotten the invasion of Crete by German paratroopers in April 1941, which was another Kesselring initiative. The Germans had lost 150 transport aircraft and many paratroopers during that operation, which had been a costly exercise. Hitler's compromise with Kesselring was to postpone the invasion of Malta until August. Fortunately for us, the circumstances had changed by then, including the campaign against the Russians on the Eastern Front, and the invasion was cancelled, but nobody knew this at the time.[34]

Instead of invading, Hitler sent the Luftwaffe and the Italian air force to pound Malta relentlessly with bombs. A sustained aerial attack, combined with an effective sea blockade, would do the trick, he thought, and bring the island to its knees.[35] Perhaps we were on our knees, but we were still alive and kicking. The land invasion is what would really have signalled our end. Perhaps there was a degree of luck involved in Hitler deciding not to invade, though if you ask most Maltese, they would say it was divine intervention.

Nevertheless, the ongoing siege of the island meant that almost no supplies were reaching us. A convoy sent in February was beaten back in the Mediterranean and the March convoy was largely destroyed in the Grand Harbour during unloading. Only about a fifth of the goods made it. My father said that the one ship which got through was full of beer and cigarettes. Not much use when we were starving. He said the April and May convoys were both cancelled because, until Malta had more air power, it was considered too risky.

The first Spitfire planes arrived in Malta in 1942 in the March convoy. They were faster than the enemy's Stuka bombers and in time made a big difference to the defence of the island. However, many were destroyed by the enemy as they sat on the tarmac in Malta, quite literally the mechanical equivalent of sitting ducks. The RAF learnt the hard way to try and ensure they were up in the air when the enemy was attacking.

It wasn't easy. The planes were often waiting to be serviced or needed spare parts, which were in very short supply. Sometimes there were about 60 pilots available, but only a handful of serviceable planes. Where possible, the technicians cannibalised damaged planes, removing parts which could be used to repair others.

While some of the pilots had fought in the Battle of Britain, others were very inexperienced. Add to this poor living conditions, lack of food, non-stop raids and runways full of holes—making them very difficult to navigate, especially in the dark—and you get an idea of what they were up against.

There was a lot of camaraderie and bonding, but these men were risking their lives every day and they were exhausted. There was no transport for them to get from their billets in Mdina to the airports, so once they had walked there, they stayed there all day, playing cards and drinking whisky.

As Warby had said to my father, the RAF attracted daredevils. One such daredevil was George "Screwball" Beurling. Born in Quebec, he joined the RAF after being rejected by the Royal Canadian Air Force in 1940. In his first week in Malta, flying a Hurricane, he shot down nine enemy bombers. Four months later, he was the island's leading fighter pilot, with 29 kills to his credit. Beurling earned his nickname, Screwball, because he often broke formation to attack every enemy aircraft in sight. He survived the war but was killed in a crash when taking off from Rome in 1948. Many of the RAF pilots were described by their colleagues as mad. One Leading Aircraftman Hendry "lay down on the tarmac at Luqa airport and took photos whilst Jerry bombed the place."[36]

RAF tours were cut from six to three months, after which time the pilots were usually burnt out. Those in desperate need of rest were sent to St Paul's Bay in the north of the island for a few days. It was rarely bombed, and they could swim in the sea.

Despite a strong body of opinion that Malta was indefensible, Churchill insisted that the island was vital to his war plans and must be held at all costs. He was encouraged in this view by Governor William Dobbie and Admiral Andrew Browne Cunningham, Commander-in-Chief of the Mediterranean.

In April 1942, Churchill asked US President Roosevelt if he could borrow the American aircraft carrier USS Wasp—which could carry more than 50 Spitfires—to take some to Malta. Churchill wrote:

> There are now in Sicily about 400 German and 200 Italian bombers. Malta can now muster only 20-30 serviceable fighters.

Roosevelt agreed and, in May 1942, the USS Wasp and HMS Eagle between them delivered 61 Spitfires to Malta, in what was called Operation Bowery.[37]

Even with this new delivery, Malta was nowhere near being on an even footing with the enemy in the air. We were almost out of aircraft fuel and ammunition, and we desperately needed food and medicines. With almost 24-hour bombing, day after day, had an invasion occurred, surrender would have been practically inevitable.

OUR LOWEST EBB

We were existing on the meagre ration of soup from the Victory Kitchens and the bread ration, which had been cut to half a slice per person per day. My father said that even the soldiers were on half rations. The government made all the farmers hand over their crops, so they could be evenly distributed and to avoid any of it being sold on the black market.

Lord John Gort—nicknamed Tiger Gort—replaced Sir William Dobbie as Governor of Malta in May 1942. It was said that Dobbie was suffering from ill health; some thought that he had lost his grip.[38] The new governor tried to set a good example by eating the same rations as the Maltese people and getting around on a bicycle.

Physical Training Parades were cancelled because they were making the men too hungry. All the coal had been used up, so the electricity stations had shut down. Our fridge had been turned off for months. For lighting we used hurricane lamps which burnt kerosene—if we could find any kerosene. Everything was running out.

Nicknamed the Magic Carpet Service, the submarines brought in urgent medication, mail and some food supplies. But this was just a drop in the ocean. My father said we needed twenty thousand tons of food a month to feed the island's population. The submarines were always submerged in the harbour at night, so the enemy bombers couldn't see them. Despite that precaution, the base at Manoel Island suffered heavy losses due to bombing in 1942.

A few of the sickest women and children—both Maltese and British—were evacuated to Cairo one night in two bomber planes. They had underlying health issues which, combined with malnutrition, meant they would have died if they had stayed. My father said they were so unwell they could hardly stand, but they made it to Egypt and hopefully recovered.

For miles around the Grand Harbour, all you could see was devastation. It was like a graveyard of half-sunken wrecks, debris, thick black oil and decomposing bodies. Mutilated body parts and dead goats bobbed up and down in the murky, smelly seawater. Afternoons spent swimming in the crystal-clear sea were distant memories.

It was summer again and the Axis forces had held Malta hostage for more than two years, trying to bomb us into submission. My father said we had endured a greater tonnage of bombs than England had during the Blitz of London. When bombing didn't make us surrender, the enemy tried to starve us out.

There was no food in our house. Three days in a row, the Victory Kitchens had nothing left by the time I got to the front of the queue. Dad asked Mr Cefai to dig over the Jerusalem artichoke and the potato patches one more time, to see if we had missed a few, hiding under the surface. He found a small handful of artichokes, one potato and one carrot, which Carrie made into a watery soup. I will never forget what it's like to feel so hungry that it's impossible to focus on anything else. First, your body eats your fat, but we didn't have any. Then you get a painful gnawing feeling, as if your stomach is trying to eat your insides. Daphne kept fainting. My mother cried, not because she was hungry, but because she couldn't feed her children.

The people of Malta believed that only the Almighty could save them. Prayers were chanted incessantly in the shelters, to God, the saints and especially to Mary, mother of Jesus and patron saint of Malta. She had saved them before during sieges and they believed she would do so again.

Morale on the island was at its lowest ebb. It was expected that Germany would invade, and Malta would surrender within a matter of three to four weeks. My father had heard stories of the first days after surrender to the enemy. The looting, the beatings, the rape of women of all ages.

It's when I discovered that gun hidden in the linen cupboard.

OPERATION PEDESTAL AND THE END OF THE SIEGE

If fortune or divine intervention had staved off an invasion of Malta, it also brought us relief, just when death by starvation seemed imminent.

On 15 August 1942, the feast day of the Assumption of Our Lady, the remains of a convoy of ships named Operation Pedestal limped into the Grand Harbour bringing 23,000 tons of general cargo—mostly food—and 5.5 tons of military stores, including aviation fuel and kerosene. This was enough to keep us going for two months.

Having learnt their lesson with previous convoys, each of the items was spread among the numerous vessels, to avoid losing all of one item if a ship went down.

Everyone had heard of the imminent arrival of this convoy of food and there were thousands of people lining the bastions, watching, waiting and hoping. We knew that, if this convoy didn't get through, we were doomed. The whole island was starving.

Like earlier convoys, Operation Pedestal had been attacked many times on its way and several ships, including the aircraft carrier HMS

Eagle, had been sunk with heavy casualties. There was genuine fear that the same thing would happen again, and the remaining ships would be sunk before our eyes. As we watched, enemy planes came again and again to bomb the convoy, but with little success. My father wrote:

> Our boys on the Ack-Ack guns deserve the highest praise as day after day and week after week they send their shells heavenward. Today they brought down 40 enemy planes, which brings the total this month to over a hundred.

He also wrote at this time that there was a shortage of pilots and gunners, due to heavy casualties. This meant that the men had to work double shifts and survive on very little sleep. Those in charge turned a blind eye to the level of alcohol being consumed. With the continual bombing, it was the only way some of the men could keep going.

When the ships finally docked, there was great jubilation from the bastions. We all waved Union Jacks and Maltese flags. Many were in tears. The sailors on board the ships waved back and returned our cheers.

Operation Pedestal was renamed the Convoy of Santa Maria by the Maltese people because it arrived on Saint Mary's day. *The Times of Malta* reported the convoy's arrival under the headline "Merchant Navy defies Axis blockade. Ships came through living hell."

After the disastrous earlier experiences, when newly arrived vessels were attacked and sunk in the harbour, Operation Ceres was immediately set in motion. This was a well-planned, around the clock off-load, using soldiers, dockers and civilians to transfer the precious cargo into bombproof caves on the island. Men from all walks of life headed to the quay to help. Crates were passed from hand to hand, and within six hours the ships were unloaded and out to sea again. My brothers were part of the Boy Scout team, helping to check off all the items on the manifests.

The convoy unloaded enough supplies to last the island for two months. The next day my mother was able to buy enough food to put a proper meal on the table for the first time in over two weeks. There were even a few leftovers to give to Handak.

Operation Pedestal was the turning point. It was as if the enemy knew that nothing they could do to the island of Malta would break the people's spirit. Our little island refused to die.

The raids continued for a time, but with less ferocity. In September 1942, there were only 60 air raids on Malta, compared with 180 in July. There was a further episode of serious bombing in October, but eventually the Axis realised they had lost the battle to neutralise Malta. By November 1942, as the Axis diverted their forces to the Battle of Tunisia, attacks on Malta were rapidly reduced, effectively ending the siege. It had lasted two and a half years.[39]

If Operation Pedestal had failed to get through, the island would have been forced to surrender, giving the Axis a free run for their convoys to sail unimpeded through the Mediterranean to North Africa. The British Eighth Army would most likely have been defeated on the Alamein Line.

Without Malta, Britain could easily have lost the war.[40]

THE KING'S VISIT

About a year after awarding the George Cross to Malta, King George VI decided to visit the island. He wanted to personally pay tribute to the Maltese people and the servicemen, both Maltese and British, who had defended the island by land, sea and air during the siege.

His highly secret visit to North Africa and Malta began on the morning of Saturday, 12 June 1943, when he landed in Algeria. That evening, over dinner with Admiral Sir Andrew Cunningham, Naval Commander-in-Chief in the Mediterranean, the King broached the subject of his visit to Malta. It had been agreed to in principle by the British Prime Minister, Winston Churchill, but needed to be signed off locally, for security reasons. The Admiral was impressed by George VI's arguments and needed little persuasion.

At 8:15 am on Sunday 20 June 1943, King George VI, dressed in naval whites, arrived in Malta on HMS Aurora, commanded by Rear Admiral William Agnew. The visit had been kept so secret that local officials in Malta didn't hear about it until three hours beforehand.

My father was closely involved in planning the 14-hour visit, so he knew all about it. Just before he left home at dawn that morning, he told us the big secret he had been keeping for just over a week.

After an early breakfast, we walked into Valletta, just over a mile away. We joined a throng of thousands of people from all over the Island who were heading in the same direction, towards the centre of town. When we got there, we saw that many people were climbing up onto the ruined buildings to get a better view. Mum wouldn't allow that, so we stood by the side of the road.

The bells of all the churches filled the air. The excitement was palpable. The police outriders arrived, indicating that the King was approaching. Great cheers and applause broke out. He was in an open-top car, and we were in the front row with a fantastic view. People threw flowers and shouted, "God save the King."

Afterwards, we walked home for a late lunch. At 6pm, Mr Cefai came in my father's car to take Pat to Verdala Palace, where he was to take part in a musical performance that night. My father and Pat didn't get home until nearly midnight, but we were all still up, waiting eagerly for them to fill us in on the day's activities.

King George's first port of call that morning had been to the Grandmaster's Palace, where he had a meeting with the governor, Lord John Gort. The King stepped out onto the Palace balcony and received a rousing ovation from the crowds in the square below.

Then he went to the Naval Dockyard. Many of the military buildings had been flattened by bombs, so he was shown around the Lascaris War Rooms, housed in a complex of tunnels. This would be the command centre from which the Allies would mastermind the invasion of Sicily and then the Italian mainland. When my father was introduced to the King as the officer in charge of work on the Lascaris Rooms, he was full of praise.

King George then went to the district of Senglea, where he walked through the narrow streets, shook hands with some of the people and saw all the ruined buildings. My father walked a few paces ahead of the monarch and his entourage. He said that the King was clearly moved by the terrible destruction and the obvious affection and warmth shown by the ragged population. A few weeks later, we watched the Pathé News coverage of the visit at the cinema and were able to pick my father out.

The governor, Lord Gort, hosted lunch at his summer residence, Verdala Palace. Located near the town of Siggiewi, in the Buskett Gardens—one of the few wooded areas on the island—the Palace was built in 1586 by one of the Grand Masters, Cardinal Verdala. Built on an elevated tableland above a valley, it has panoramic views. With an embattled turret on each of its four corners, it looks more like a mediaeval castle than a palace.

Inside there are two floors, but the corner turrets are about five storeys high. The entire palace is surrounded by a ditch, like an empty moat. Although the turrets and moat give the palace the appearance of a fort, it was never intended to withstand any attack. Like all the other palaces in Malta, the interior is very ornate, with frescoes on some of the ceilings.

Fourteen guests, including the King, sat down to lunch. As you can see from the original table plan, it was a star-studded occasion.[41] Going around the table from the top left, in an anti-clockwise direction:

- Chief Justice of Malta, Sir George Borg
- Sir Alex Hardinge, Private Secretary to the King
- His Grace the Archbishop of Malta, Mauro Caruana
- His Majesty King George VI
- His Excellency the Governor of Malta, Lord John Gort
- Air Chief Marshal Sir Arthur Tedder, Head of Allied Air Forces in the Mediterranean
- His Lordship the Bishop of Gozo, Mikiel Gonzi
- Captain Arthur Wellesley Clarke, Royal Navy, Chief of Staff to Governor Gort
- Air Vice Marshal Sir Keith Park, RAF Commander in Malta
- Lieutenant Governor Sir David Campbell, Deputy Governor of Malta
- Admiral of the Fleet Sir Andrew Cunningham, Commander, Mediterranean Fleet

- Rt Hon Harold Macmillan, British Representative in the Mediterranean, based in North Africa
- Vice Admiral Arthur John Power, Second in Command, Mediterranean Fleet
- Major General Walter Hayes Oxley, Head of the Army in Malta

My father and his small team of organisers watched the lunch dishes go past as they sat in a small room off the palace kitchen, eating ham sandwiches washed down with lemonade. The King's party started with Lobster Royal, then tucked into Chicken Paprika with steamed vegetables, followed by a light citrus dessert which the chef had named Soufflé Verdala. Dad managed to stick one of the menu cards in his pocket, after the guests had left the table, as a souvenir.

After lunch, the King knighted one of the guests, a New Zealander called Air Marshal Keith Park, who had been overseeing the air defence of the island. His clever tactics had changed the way Malta was defended. He ordered the Spitfire pilots to attack the bombers when they were coming towards the island, rather than waiting for them to arrive and drop bombs on the island. An offensive rather than defensive approach.[42]

The King then retired to one of the palace bedrooms for a rest. An hour later, the party set off for him to inspect the main aerodromes. At 7pm, there was a formal dinner back at the Palace, followed by half an hour of musical entertainment. Pat sang two songs and said he wasn't a bit nervous. We didn't believe him. Again, my father wasn't a guest at the dinner—there were only 20—but he was in the background, making sure everything went smoothly. The King stood up and said a few words, describing the visit as "The real gem of my tour."

King George left Malta at 10pm on HMS Aurora. It was the first time a British sovereign had visited Malta since 1911 and was a great morale booster for everyone on the island.

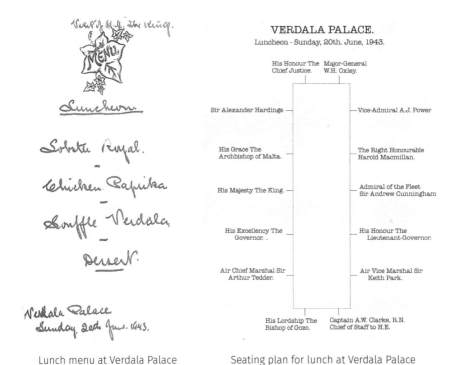

VERDALA PALACE.

Luncheon - Sunday, 20th. June, 1943.

His Honour The Major-General
Chief Justice. W.H. Oxley.

Sir Alexander Hardinge — — Vice-Admiral A.J. Power

His Grace The The Right Honourable
Archbishop of Malta. Harold Macmillan.

His Majesty The King. — Admiral of the Fleet
Sir Andrew Cunningham

His Excellency The His Honour The
Governor. Lieutenant-Governor.

Air Chief Marshal Sir Air Vice Marshal Sir
Arthur Tedder. Keith Park.

His Lordship The Captain A.W. Clarke, R.N.
Bishop of Gozo. Chief of Staff to H.E.

Lunch menu at Verdala Palace   Seating plan for lunch at Verdala Palace
for King Geoge VI's visit.   for the King's visit.

THE LASCARIS WAR ROOMS AND OPERATION HUSKY

In the early part of 1943, Malta was a hive of activity and Dad said he was "in the thick of it," supervising the finishing touches to his "baby," the Lascaris War Rooms.

Located underground, at the southern end of Valletta, these rooms consisted of several enlarged tunnels, some 150 feet below the Upper Barrakka Gardens. The rooms, named after Grandmaster Giovanni Paolo Lascaris, were accessed by a long flight of steps near the Auberge Castille.

In 1939, the original tunnels were turned into an air raid shelter. As the enemy continued to bomb military installations on the island, it became clear that they needed somewhere safer, preferably underground. As Garrison Engineer, Dad supervised all the technical drawings and subsequent work on this major, top-secret project to expand the air raid shelter and turn it into Allied Headquarters. He had a team of three Assistant Garrison Engineers and several junior engineers working for him. Excavation work began in 1940, but the project wasn't completed until early 1943.

There was no natural light and ventilation was provided through pipes salvaged from sunken ships. There were three main operation rooms for the Army, the Navy and the RAF, and several smaller rooms. Working in this command centre during the war were one Fighter Controller, numerous plotters, wireless operators, telephone switchboard operators, coders and decoders. The job of the Fighter Controller was a very stressful one. He had to give the Allied pilots a tactical picture of what was going on around them and guide them towards the best position to shoot down the enemy.

At the height of the war, there were more than fifty female civilian plotters working at Lascaris. Several were Maltese and some were as young as fourteen. Women like Christina Ratcliffe, who worked for the RAF as a plotter, sat in front of a large map on a table measuring 8 x 15 feet. They wore headphones to hear details of enemy aircraft locations coming in from radar stations and observers along the coast. They plotted their positions on the map, moving the planes to their most recent location. Sometimes they flew below the radar when it was hoped they would be spotted by observers. Christina worked her way up until she was in charge of the whole team.

The Allied military started to use each room as soon as it was finished. The Lascaris War Rooms became the command centre for the Allied invasion of Sicily, code-named Operation Husky, which took place on 10 July 1943. The aim was to drive Italy out of the war and secure the Mediterranean against Axis attacks.

The invasion was conceived by the best military minds. British General Montgomery moved from Egypt to Malta on 3 July, where he was joined a few days later by British General Alexander and American General Eisenhower, so crucial was this operation to the course of the war.

Troops landed in Sicily at 3am on 10 July and the enemy surrendered just over a month later.

THE END OF THE SIEGE

The 3,343rd raid on Malta since the siege began on 11 June 1940 took place on 20 July 1943.

It was the last.

With the fall of Sicily to the Allies in August 1943, Malta became the command centre for the Allied invasion of the Italian mainland. Thousands of troops arrived, as well as ships bringing food and other commodities. They mostly got through without incident.

The war was going well for the Allies, and it was hoped that Italy would soon capitulate.

On 8 September each year, Malta celebrates Victory Day with a public holiday. It marks the end of two sieges they have survived: the Great Siege of Malta by the Ottoman Empire in 1565 and the Siege of Valletta by the French Blockade in 1800.

On Victory Day 1943, we were all gathered on the quay to celebrate this national holiday. There were bands playing and people in traditional dress dancing. Several Royal Navy warships were lit up for the occasion, their searchlights trained onto the Statue of the Madonna.

Suddenly the captain on board the largest ship announced that Italy had surrendered. This was translated into Maltese by the Senglea Parish priest, who had been invited on board.

The huge crowd erupted in frenzied shouts of happiness and joy, laughing, crying, kissing and hugging one another. The Italians, who had tried so hard to destroy us and who had caused so much suffering, had surrendered. The church bells of the city and surrounding towns and villages started ringing and the air raid sirens joined in with the all-clear sound. The brass bands on the quay played the Maltese people's favourite hymn to the Virgin Mary. They believed she had saved them. It gives me goosebumps to think of that moment in my life.

A month later, Mussolini was ousted, and Italy joined the Allies against Germany.

Our war ended on 8 September 1943, when the Italians surrendered, and my father wrote:

That this 120 square miles with 300,000 souls held out against the worst the Axis powers could do is remarkable. It was a close-run thing, achieved through skill and perseverance.

Despite 15,000 tons of bombs, 1,581 civilian deaths, many injuries and near starvation, the Maltese people had refused to surrender.[43]

Malta's limestone proved to be a formidable construction material that withstood much of the bombing. Nonetheless, more than ten thousand buildings were destroyed or extensively damaged. Many beautiful buildings, such as the Opera House, were gone. Others had crumbling corners and pock marks from bullets. Badges of honour worn proudly by this brave little island.

Maison Notre Dame was still standing, which was quite amazing, considering the number of bombs which had fallen on Floriana. My mother had invited the priest to bless Maison Notre Dame when we first moved in. We often remembered this and thanked God that she had.

OUR LAST YEAR IN MALTA

Our last year or so on the island was easier in most respects, but many things were still rationed or impossible to buy. Rationing in Malta was affected by rationing in Britain, because most items were shipped in from there.

Everyone was weak and undernourished. Tuberculosis, dysentery and polio were common. One in three babies died. Food was still rationed and even when we could buy more, we had problems digesting it because our stomachs had shrunk. We went to a Christmas party in December 1943 at St Andrews, and we were all sick afterwards from eating too much rich food.

As soon as the bombings eased off, people moved back to their homes to clean up and rebuild. The streets in Valletta were cleared of rubble. Cars and buses were able to go about their business. The Black Out order was lifted, and life started to get back to normal.

Although in some ways it had never stopped, life picked up where it had left off, with a swing. Valletta became alive again and the cafés and cinemas were full. Shops and businesses resumed their normal activities. Church bells rang as couples who had been waiting for months, if not years, tied the knot. We were all just glad to be alive.

Walking the streets of Valletta, all you could see were bombed-out buildings, remnants of homes, shops and businesses. There were also a huge number of military installations to be rebuilt. My father was kept busy supervising the work.

The bombed site of the Opera House was cleared of rubble, but rebuilding was repeatedly postponed, in favour of reconstruction projects that were deemed to be more pressing.

Warby left Malta in October 1943. In 1944, he was stationed at RAF Mount Farm in Oxfordshire, England. He managed to pop back and see Christina whenever he could. When the war was over, they planned to marry and live somewhere warm and sunny. Maybe Malta. Maybe the south of France.

In April 1944, Warby went missing in an American aircraft during an operation over Germany. He failed to meet at the rendezvous and was never seen again. Christina, who was in the Lascaris War Rooms when he fell off the radar, was beside herself with grief. When she called in to see us, she tried to put on a brave face.

"Of course, he's all right," she said with false cheerfulness "He's gone missing before. He'll just walk in that door like he always does." She never lost hope that he would turn up.[44]

Young men started to take notice of me in 1944, the year I turned 15. Some invited me out, but I wasn't interested. I attended a couple of dances with Christina, who was now on her own. It was still hard to buy clothes, so, as my surrogate older sister, she always lent me a dress and curled my hair in the latest style. The Victory Roll was very popular. Lots of men invited Christina out, too, but she wasn't interested either. She would always be Warby's girl.

Over the course of 1944, hundreds of patients were moved from military hospitals in Malta to hospital ships which took them back to England. Some of the military hospitals closed, including the one at St Andrews, which had undergone heavy bombing during the siege.

Dad heard on the grapevine that his posting was coming to an end. He made enquiries regarding the quarantine paperwork required for shipping Handak back to England.

From our back veranda, which was about 40 feet above the ground, with amazing views across the harbour, you could also see anyone walking up the road towards our house. On school days, Handak would sit there, watching and waiting for us to come home. As soon as he saw us trudging up the hill, he would run up and down, barking with excitement. He was always happy to see us.

One day, Handak lost his footing and fell. We ran to the bottom of the bastion where he lay whimpering. He couldn't walk and we realised he had broken his back. Dad rang a friend who had worked as a vet before the war, and he came immediately with an injection.

I stroked his long silky ears as he slipped away. He was a loyal friend and we had been through so much together.

THE MALTA CONFERENCE

We had been in Malta for six years and, if it hadn't been for the war, Dad said, we would have left three years earlier.

The Malta Conference was set up to plan the final assault on Germany. It took place at Montgomery House in Floriana from 30 January to 3 February 1945 and was a high-level event attended by US President Roosevelt, British Prime Minister Churchill and several other military bigwigs. The aim was to present a united front against Stalin at the Yalta Conference, which took place a few days later in Crimea.

Dad was very busy during the Conference, but as soon as it was over and all the VIPs had left the island, he got his marching orders. My mother supervised the packing of our belongings, while we said goodbye to all our friends.

LEAVING MALTA

In the 1920s, flights carrying paying passengers had become more common, with the introduction of the multi-engine Lawson C2, which was specially built to carry passengers. Planes were not pressurised, which meant they had to fly at a low altitude and make more frequent stops. Flying was dangerous and expensive, but it was still quite popular amongst the wealthy. Air sickness was common and many planes had a nurse on board to look after the passengers. Despite this, the number of passengers gradually grew and the aviation business was well on its way to becoming an important part of the global economy.

Then came the Second World War, and progress in commercial aviation slowed right down. It didn't take off again until the mid-1940s. When we left Malta, a few days after the Malta Conference ended, it was still the norm for British military families to travel by sea.

Mr Cefai and his sisters and the Clarkes waved from the wharf as we sailed out of the harbour. They had become part of our family and we were going to miss them. I couldn't help thinking how much had happened since we arrived six years ago. So many people had died defending that tiny island. We were lucky to have survived.

I was leaving, but I would never forget. Malta had become a part of me.

Our ship sailed in a convoy because the war hadn't ended. In his last comment on Malta, my father wrote:

Apart from a few scares and destroyers whipping around like terriers after prey, we reached Glasgow safe and sound.

That concludes my story of Malta. But if you want to know what happened to us after we left the island, please read on.

PART 3

AFTER MALTA

THE FAMILY SPLITS UP

We sailed out of the Grand Harbour on 12 February 1945 and arrived in Glasgow on 16 March. My father stayed in England, working with the Royal Engineers. Conscription didn't end until 1960, so both my brothers were called up. They chose to follow my father and become Sappers in the Royal Engineers.

Mum, my sisters and I sailed directly to Belfast and from there we travelled south by train to Limerick. We stayed for almost a year with Mum's sister Kitty, who was living in the house in James Street where Mum had grown up. Kitty's husband, Paddy Dalton, had been hit by a car and killed when he was on his bicycle in 1937, leaving Kitty a widow after only five years of marriage. Her unmarried sister, Annie, lived next door where the Brosnahans used to live. Kitty and Annie were the only two of Mum's siblings who stayed in Ireland, although she did have several Brosnahan cousins living in and around Limerick.

There were two reasons for spending a year in Ireland. Firstly, we were all seriously undernourished and rationing after the war wasn't as bad in Ireland as it was in England. Secondly, we had nowhere else to live. My father had plans to buy a house, but he didn't want to rush into it.

The house in James Street had been modernised since the time when Mum was growing up, but it was still very small, especially compared with Maison Notre Dame. There were only two bedrooms, so Mum shared one with her sister Kitty and my sisters and I shared the other one. We attended the Presentation Convent School in Limerick where we all had to study Gaelic.

I don't have very fond memories of our time in Limerick. I missed Dad, my brothers and my friends in Malta and I didn't like the school. I felt as if we were marking time, waiting for Dad to say we could move back to England. Ed and I corresponded weekly and remained close.

On 7 May 1945, the Germans surrendered and the war in Europe finally came to an end. The Japanese, who had joined the war in 1941, surrendered on 2 September 1945.

The following April Dad bought 59 Alexandra Avenue, a small, terraced house in Gillingham, which was always known in the family as 59. It was just a few miles from the RE headquarters in Chatham. Mum, my sisters and I moved back from Ireland to live there in May 1946.

Sam in Gillingham Kent, 1946.   Hilda Mary in Gillingham Kent, 1946.

Our furniture had been in storage for nearly ten years. When it was delivered to 59 by Binns it was like Christmas. I had forgotten the lovely carved wooden pieces from Hong Kong. With only three bedrooms, it wasn't a big house and it's just as well that Pat had been posted overseas. Mum and Dad had one bedroom, my sisters and I shared another, and Ed had the third bedroom, which was only just big enough for a single bed. My favourite chest of drawers, with a Chinese story carved into it, ended up in our bedroom.

After Malta, my father held various teaching positions at Royal Engineers Schools of Military Engineering in England and in Africa. We didn't accompany him when he was working overseas.

Staples Five as teenagers
in Gillingham Kent, 1946.

In 1948 he was posted to the Mackinnon Road Depot, about 60 miles from Mombasa in Kenya, in the middle of the African bush. The project was to build a large complex of warehouses, to centralise the storage of thousands of tons of munitions, left over from the war. These valuable assets were dotted around the Middle East, Africa and the Mediterranean and they wanted them all in one place. Conditions at the depot were very basic. Dad slept in a tent and said it wasn't unusual to wake up and find a rat or two sharing his accommodation.

DAD LEAVES THE ROYAL ENGINEERS

In 1949, when he got back from Kenya, Dad said it was time to leave the REs. He was too old to be sleeping in tents and his eyesight had deteriorated:

> I had foolishly walked about in Hong Kong and Malta without dark glasses and given little thought to the fact that I had only one pair of eyes.[45]

He soon got a job as Clerk of Works at the Royal Engineers Kitchener Barracks in Chatham, where he had worked before, this time in a civilian capacity.

Margaret Staples singing in Gillingham 1946.

Sam and Margaret in Gillingham Kent, 1946.

As the Second World War came to a close in 1945, so did the government's rationing programme, although it didn't all happen at once. Sweets were taken off the ration list in April 1949, although sugar was still rationed. This caused a mad rush on sweet shops by people like my brother Ed, who loved them. Rationing for sweets then had to be reintroduced in August and remained in force until

1953. Food production and food imports took a decade to get back to normal, made worse by frequent strikes by dock workers.

As a Christmas treat that year Dad took the whole family to see *A Streetcar Named Desire* which was on at the Aldwych Theatre in London. Dad remembered meeting the charming playwright, Tennessee Williams, well over a decade earlier in Hong Kong, long before he became well-known.

I completed a secretarial course and got a job with Marconi Electronics at Rochester Airport in Maidstone Road as a Pitman shorthand-typist. I continued with singing lessons and sang in a semi-professional capacity with paid gigs, often backed by the Reginald Simpson orchestra. My repertoire included songs such as "O Danny Boy" and "My Love is Only for You."

On 31 July 1946, the American film *The Bells of St Mary*, premiered at the Majestic Theatre in Rochester, the city next to Chatham, starring Ingrid Bergman and Bing Crosby. The organisers were looking for a singer who looked like Bergman to dress up as a nun and sing before the film began. I was 17, about 12 years younger, but bore an uncanny resemblance to the Swedish star, so I got the job.

Programme of preview of the Bells of St Mary's in Rochester, Kent.

Margaret dressed as a nun.

Fashion had stalled during the war when most people were in uniform, and leisurewear was dictated by rationing. After the war, it took off again. The New Look for women was all the rage in the late 1940s and early 1950s, with rounded shoulders, a cinched waist and a full, A-line skirt.

With my first few pay packets from Marconi's I bought myself a new wardrobe and threw out all the clothes from my early teenage years, which I had long since grown out of. It felt good to be working and earning my own money.

MEETING KEN

At the end of 1947, I was at a New Year's Eve party at the Central Hotel in Gillingham, with my parents and sisters, when I met the love of my life, Ken Hutchinson. He was tall, dark and handsome (a cliché yes, but a lovely one in reality), and I was pleased when he asked me to dance for a second time. My friends all said he looked like the Hollywood star Gregory Peck. Before the song ended, the music suddenly stopped, and they started the countdown to midnight.

Before I knew it, Ken was giving me a long, lingering kiss on the mouth. My father, who was close enough to see, was shocked and asked my mother who I was kissing. Mum came to my rescue and said, "Oh, him? She's known him for ages."

William Kenneth Kirkwood Hutchinson, known as Ken, was born on 10 July 1920 in Stafford. He had a sister and two brothers and left school when he was 14, with no formal training. Ken joined the RAF at the start of the Second World War and soon became a gunnery instructor. Many summers spent at Hill House, a dairy farm in County Durham, in the very north of England, where his father had grown up, had provided lots of opportunities for shooting rabbits, pheasants and wild ducks. Ken had 20:20 vision and was an excellent shot. After the war, he took up horticulture, working in his father's market garden nursery.

Whenever he was home during the three years that Ken and I were courting, as they called it back then, and Ken rang the doorbell at 59, Pat would sing a well-known English ballad called "To Be a Farmer's Boy," accompanying himself on the piano. This was to make fun of Ken's agricultural background. The more I shouted at Pat to stop, the louder he sang. Fortunately, Ken had no musical background whatsoever and never noticed.

When the war ended, the Allies became the occupying forces. British and American Army bases were set up all over West Germany, while the Soviet Union occupied East Germany. In September 1950, I celebrated my 21st birthday with a party at the Central Hotel. A week or two later, Dad was offered a civilian job as Garrison Engineer at the Army base in Bad Fallingbostel, Germany. The plan was that my sisters and I would move there with my parents after Christmas.

Margaret's 21st birthday, Gillingham, 23 September 1950.

Ken was sure that if I moved to Germany, I would meet someone else. He begged me to marry him and stay in England. I had just turned 21 and "come of age," earning the right to vote and I knew I had met the man I wanted to spend the rest of my life with. However, my parents needed some convincing that this was a good idea. Women's rights were minimal at that time and our lives were pretty much controlled by men. My father and Ken discussed the matter, man to man. Dad told Ken that he would have to keep me in the manner to which I was accustomed. By this he meant that I would never have to go out to work and would always have domestic help in the house. Ken promised to do this, and they shook hands.

MARRIED LIFE

On 13 January 1951, just before my parents and sisters left for Germany, I became Mrs Hutchinson.

Margaret and Ken on their wedding day,
13 January 1951.

We spent the first few years of married life living at 59 and my two girls, Linda and Diana, were born there in 1952 and 1954. It was a bit of a squash in that small, three-bedroom house, but Ed lived with us. On Fridays, Ed and I would go and see a film. Ken wasn't a movie addict, so he babysat. When we saw *The Titanic* in 1953, we remembered my mother's story about someone she knew who had lost their life on that fateful journey, which made it all the more real. On Saturdays, Ken and I went dancing at The Central Hotel. Ed would babysit. He wasn't able to dance since he broke his back.

When we were out walking, Ken would stop and stroke every cat and dog we passed. It was one of his endearing traits which had confirmed in my mind that he was the one. It was inevitable that, soon after we married, a stray black and white puppy would join our household. We called him Paddy and we have had dogs ever since. In our family, a house is not a home without a dog.

My mother-in-law, Jessie Kirkwood Berrie Hutchinson, née Bain, was born in Falkirk, just outside Edinburgh in Scotland. My father-in-law, William Kidd Hutchinson, met her when he was in charge of the gardens at Battle Abbey, a partially ruined Benedictine abbey in Sussex which had been turned into a stately home by Sir Augustus Weber, a baronet. At the time, Jessie was running the dairy.

When we first met, Ken asked me if I could cook and I said no. He thought I was being modest. Having grown up with strict rationing my cooking skills were almost non-existent. In the early years of our marriage, I grew sick of hearing Ken waxing lyrical about his mother, a brilliant cook, who could make the butter into the shape of swans, for afternoon tea. "If you want butter shaped into swans, you'd better go back," I would say, teasingly. Fortunately, Jessie took me under her wing and taught me a few basic recipes, so we wouldn't starve. Not the swans, but more practical things.

At Sunday Mass at St Mary's in Gillingham, I met a girl my age called Mary Huntley, who lived near us. She went out with Ed a couple of times, but nothing came of it. We saw quite a lot of each other, and I asked her to be Linda's godmother. As her godfather, my brother Pat spoiled Linda for the first few years of her life, bringing exotic presents when he was stationed in Hong Kong, such as a life-size walkie-talkie doll. After Malta, Pat didn't live at home again. We only saw him a couple of times a year, but when he arrived, he was like a breath of fresh air, with his contagious laughter and sense of fun. The Staples Five all laughed at the same stupid things, and I missed Pat when he wasn't there. Then in 1958, when Linda was six, he got married and had his own family to spoil.

Mary Huntley married and gave birth to three sons. Her brother was badly burnt during the war, when the ship he was serving on was bombed. He died a few years after the war ended, leaving three sons. For some reason, his wife was unable to cope, so Mary adopted her three nephews, making hers a family with six boys.

In the 1960s, Mary and her family took advantage of an assisted passage scheme to emigrate to Australia as "Ten Pound Poms." This scheme allowed British people to pay only £10 per person for the sea passage, a fraction of the real cost. Poms is the nickname Australians use for British people. It stands for "Prisoner of Her Majesty" and dates back to the convict era when many people who ended up in Australia were sent there as convicts. Mary and her husband headed off with their six strapping lads to start a new life. They were just what the Australian government, which was trying to increase the post-war population, was looking for. We stayed in touch, writing every Christmas time.

King George VI died in 1952 of lung cancer. Like his father and grandfather, he had been a heavy smoker. His eldest daughter, Elizabeth, became Queen. When she visited the nearby city of Rochester in 1954, I joined thousands of people waving enthusiastically as the cavalcade drove through the High Street, pushing two-year-old Linda in her pram.

My generation grew up in a cloud of cigarette smoke. It was everywhere: in the home, in the cinemas, in the air raid shelters. Doctors even smoked in hospitals when they were doing their rounds. The staff room at Chiswick House was always smoky during the teachers' tea break. The smoke would waft down the stairs and into the classrooms. Pretty much the only place where people didn't smoke was in church. My mother never smoked, but my father did, and both my brothers took it up after the war. I smoked for about 20 years from the age of 20. Ken and I both gave up in our early 40s when we understood the risks.

Nobody wore sunglasses or sunscreen, taking another big risk we were unaware of. We had a lot to learn.

A poor diet and lack of dental care in Malta caught up with me in my mid-twenties. After two pregnancies, my upper teeth were in a sorry state. The dentist said dentures were the best solution. The cost of crowns, something he mentioned as a possibility, was way beyond our means. Nowadays, extracting a tooth is the last resort, but back then it was common practice to pull them all out and many people had dentures. My siblings had similar dental issues, apart from Daphne who ended up living in America, where regular check-ups and preventative dentistry were both well-established some years before they were in England.

Antibiotics had been used during the war on soldiers, for fighting wound infection and pneumonia, but they were not available to the general public. General practitioners started to prescribe them soon after we got back to England, so I had the benefit of Penicillin, if I needed it, during my pregnancies and when my children were young.

In 1953, Edmund Hillary made it to the top of Mount Everest. My father was impressed, but remained adamant that man would never walk on the moon.

Rationing in Britain finally ended at midnight on 4 July 1954, bringing to an end 14 years of restrictions.

Ken built a house on his father's nursery in Rainham, working at weekends and after work until it was complete. We moved there from Gillingham in 1958. Following the Maltese tradition of always giving a house a name, I called it Floriana. In accordance with Ken's promise to my father, I had stopped working at Marconi's when I got married and we employed a cleaner to come in once a week.

Ken's father virtually retired when he turned 70 in 1958. Despite the fact that Ken was now running the business, his parents weren't very generous and paid him a low wage. Every Christmas they gave us a turkey, but my mother-in-law's frugal Scottish background didn't allow her to be more generous and give Ken a share of the profits.

When we moved to Rainham, Ed stayed at 59, but he often came over to babysit. We bought our first black and white television to keep him happy. One night while we were out, Ed went to check on Linda and Diana, who were about six and three years old at the time. Diana's bed was empty. Ed searched the house from top to bottom. Diana, or Dee Dee as we called her, was eventually found, standing on the windowsill. Ed had to look behind the curtains to find her. Her eyes were wide open, but she was sound asleep. Fortunately, it was a single-storey bungalow, so if she had fallen out of the window, she didn't have far to fall. Nonetheless, it gave Ed a fright.

Ed with nieces Linda and Diana circa 1959.

Our son David was born in 1960, a couple of years after we moved to Rainham. By that time Linda was eight and Diana was almost six. The sleepwalking genes were not the only ones to be passed down the line. I gave up professional singing when Linda was about three, but the singing and performing genes were also evident in my children. Linda and Diana and a couple of their friends put on shows in our garden, to raise money for a local charity which bought coal for the elderly to heat their houses during winter. They invited all the neighbours and local shopkeepers, charged them to get in, and dragged all our chairs outside for them to sit comfortably during the performance. An old wind-up gramophone player was also dragged out into the garden. It provided much amusement for the audience as Linda's friend, Brenda Grant, who was in charge of winding it up as well as helping the performers to change their outfits, struggled to do both tasks. As the performers sang along to the likes of Gracie Fields, the songs got slower and slower and then suddenly sped up again. The audience struggled to keep straight faces. My one vinyl record, which I had recorded before I got married, was badly scratched by the time the children had finished with it. Fortunately, it has since been digitised.

When she was about 10, Linda started working on Saturday mornings in the farm shop, where we sold all the produce, to earn a bit of pocket money. Ken's father, who was in his mid-70s, sat in the corner of the shop and appeared to be dozing. In fact, Grandpa was watching her like a hawk. The tomatoes were weighed to order and the adding up was done in your head, quite a challenge for a 10-year-old. "You put one too many in that last pound of tomatoes," he would say. "If you do that every time, you'll put us out of business."

Weekly cooking classes were compulsory at Linda's school from the age of 11, and she loved it. As she gradually took over more of the cooking at home, I was able to spend more time gardening, which was always my passion. I taught her to make Mrs Clarke's wartime Spag Bol, but with minced beef instead of tinned corned beef.

BAD FALLINGBOSTEL

Mum's happiest years were those she spent in Bad Fallingbostel. She and Dad led a much quieter life. After the tumult of the war years, she finally found the peace she sought, her children happily settled, food on the table and her darling Sam by her side. Dad took up painting and fly fishing. He liked to socialise with men who had been through similar experiences in the war. Men who understood. They often invited friends round to play Bridge, or other card games such as Cribbage or Whist.

Twice a year, Mum and Dad drove from Germany to England and stayed with us. One of their trips always coincided with the Ideal Home Exhibition in London and we would all go together. Dad loved the 1955 film *The Happy Wanderer* and sang the theme song at the top of his voice all around my house. We knew all the words by the time they went back to Germany.

My parents travelled extensively in Germany, Italy, Denmark and the Balkans. Every trip was planned down to the last detail and recorded in his diary. They often drove from Fallingbostel into the Harz Mountains and stayed at the glamorous Harzburger Hof. As I write it is now closed and awaiting demolition.

Dad was due to retire at the end of 1963, after 12 years in Fallingbostel. The plan was to move back to England, sell 59, and build a bungalow in the adjoining town of Rainham, where I lived. He drew up the plans and everything was ready to go. Pat was asked to go to the Ideal Home Exhibition and look into central heating options. After retirement, they were planning a long road trip around the United States, visiting Daphne in Scottsbluff, Nebraska and Joan in Denver, Colorado.

In May 1963, a few months before his 63rd birthday, my father died of a massive heart attack. The stress of Malta and smoking no doubt contributed to his early death. I cried buckets.

The whole family was devastated. My mother returned alone to England and moved into 59 with Ed. She begged Joan to come back from America, which she did.

WHITE GABLE AND MERESBOROUGH NURSERY

Ken lost both his parents in the first half of 1965. In order to divide the inheritance between the four siblings, the nursery had to be sold. We were saddened when Floriana and the greenhouses were bulldozed by the new owners, to build an ugly housing estate. With Ken's share of the proceeds, we bought land in a small hamlet outside Rainham called Meresborough.

We moved to Meresborough in 1966 and lived there in a caravan for 18 months, while Ken built a huge greenhouse and a house for us to live in, which we called White Gable. Ed drew up the plans and Ken did all the work, apart from the wiring and the plumbing. He was a true handyman and would take on any practical task.

Meresborough Nursery was a successful business and I enjoyed creating a garden around the house, with all my favourite plants and flowers. I have always loved gardening and flowers and attended art classes until I was well into my 80s.

As my mother slowly lost her eyesight, she became more dependent on Joan. Mum spent her free time at church, at the Irish Club, or visiting family. She never learnt to drive and relied on Joan or Ed to take her anywhere. The three of them would attend Mass in Gillingham every Sunday, then come over to see us at Meresborough Nursery and have coffee, before driving home to 59 for a late lunch. She loved the singer Tom Jones and was thrilled when we took her to see him in London in the 1970s.

Mum died peacefully in 1980, at the age of 86.

I didn't do any paid work after I got married but, for nearly 40 years, I was a volunteer for the Samaritans (Lifeline), working at a call centre, providing crisis support and suicide prevention for people in need.

Ken was an active member of Rotary, and I joined Inner Wheel, a group which was originally founded for the wives of Rotarians. I was President and later Area Chairperson of Inner Wheel and always involved in their activities. Ken and I especially enjoyed putting on cabaret shows to raise money for charity. Ken had trouble singing in tune, although he had perfect pitch when whistling, but he could dance. With my encouragement, he learnt to dress up and make a fool of himself with the rest of the team. We had a lot of fun putting on those shows.

A group of Rotarians came over from Germany to visit our club. We put on a show for them, and they had such a good time, they were almost rolling in the aisles. Our wartime enemies were now our friends. Forgive and forget. Blame it all on Hitler.

I taught our three children my repertoire of songs and how to sing in harmony. Travelling anywhere by car, we always followed the Staples tradition—singing made the journey pass much more quickly. The Staples' performing genes again became evident when Diana said she wanted a guitar for her 13th birthday. It wasn't long before she and

Linda, who was 15 at the time, were doing paid gigs at weekends as The Kirkwood Sisters.

My children make fun of my tendency to hoard food, but I can't help it. My pantry is always full to overflowing, with several tins, jars, or packets of all the staples. Habits of our youth are hard to break. At least I have never had to keep it padlocked.

TRAVEL AND RETIREMENT

Linda stopped performing with Diana when she turned 19, joined the Foreign Office and moved to London. Her first overseas posting was Geneva, where she met her future husband, Matthew Peek, an Australian diplomat.

Over the next 35 years Matthew worked his way up the diplomatic ladder, with overseas postings to Israel, Malaysia, South Africa, Chile, France and Denmark—the last three postings as Ambassador. In between these exotic overseas destinations, they had stints back home, in Canberra, Australia, where their three children were born.

In 1978, while they were posted to Israel, I joined them for a holiday in Tel Aviv. Ken was too busy running the nursery to join me. I loved visiting all the places mentioned in the Bible, such as Jerusalem, Bethlehem, the Red Sea, the Dead Sea and Jericho. It was more than 30 years since the Second World War had ended, but a routine flyover of Israeli fighter planes made me dive for cover under the nearest table. I felt stupid, but it was an automatic reaction to a sound I hadn't heard in decades.

When Linda and Matthew were living in Kuala Lumpur, Malaysia, I flew over and spent a couple of weeks with them and their three children, James, Catherine and David. Walking through the Chinese wet markets took me straight back to Hong Kong in the 1930s.

Approaching retirement, Ken allowed himself a bit more leisure time. In 1990, we both made it to Australia. It had always been my dream to visit Canberra, which at that time had been my daughter's home for 15 years, but this was our one and only trip Down Under. With so many parks and gardens Canberra was a lovely garden city.

When we visited Sydney Ken said: "You could grow grass on a tennis ball in this climate. If I'd come here in my youth, I would never have gone back." Then in 1995 we went to visit Linda and Matthew when they were posted to Santiago in Chile.

Our son David joined the RAF and when he left in 2002, he decided to emigrate to Canada with his family and we went to visit them. Over the years I also visited Daphne in America a couple of times.

When Linda and Matthew were stationed in Paris, followed by Copenhagen, we visited often—it was lovely to have them so close to England. With one daughter in Australia (or wherever she happened to be) and a son in Canada, we were able to travel to interesting places to see them. Of course, we missed having them close by, but you can't have it both ways.

Fortunately—or should I say thank goodness—Diana stayed in England, so we had one of our three children living in the same country. She went on to become a professional singer as Diana Kirkwood and travelled extensively. When she was performing on cruise ships in the Mediterranean, she was allowed to take a guest with her, and Ken and I both took advantage of that perk. Diana's son, James Beeny, has inherited the musical genes. He and his partner Gina Georgio are talented stage musical producers and songwriters.

Linda and Matthew's three children have all married and between them produced our six great-grandchildren. We missed all the weddings and births, and I really felt the distance between Australia and England. Photos don't make up for living close by and holding those little bundles of joy in your arms.

When he reached his 80s Ken started to slow down and decided to rent out the business to his long-time worker, Peter Luxton. We were still living in the bungalow on the nursery, so every morning Ken would wander along to see what was going on and chat to customers. He had taught himself welding and become quite an expert. All the local farmers would bring things for him to fix, broken axles and the like. I called them "Thanks very much Ken jobs," because no money ever changed hands. But when the cherries or apples were in season, they would bring us a box.

Ken was nine years older than me. In 2005, he suffered a stroke which left him paralysed on one side, unable to speak or walk, and in a wheelchair. While unable to join in the conversations, he understood everything, laughed in all the right places and occasionally managed to say one word, which was invariably a swear word. Ken died in 2010, aged 90. We were just a few months short of celebrating our 60th wedding anniversary. I cried buckets once again.

MY BROTHER PAT

Pat followed in his father's footsteps, joined the REs straight after the war and made it his career. He served in many places and one of his early postings was Hong Kong. The entire Staples family loved Chinese food, or "chow" as we called it and, over the years, many family celebrations have taken place in Chinese restaurants.

In 1957, Pat was posted to the Emblem Barracks in Antwerp, Belgium, where he met and married the love of his life, a Belgian national, Mariette Jaumin, who was working for the Army. Not long after their marriage, Pat was posted to Tripoli in Libya and it was there, in 1959, that their son Shaun was born. Shaun has two sons, and they are the only ones to carry on the Staples surname.

During a posting back home to Chatham, their daughter Sally was born in 1962. A stint in Barton Stacey, Hampshire was next, then he continued to follow in his father's footsteps with a three-year posting to Malta. Pat renewed his friendship with Tony Cefai, who had married Helena and had a daughter, Marlene. The Cefai family remain close friends.

Pat loved meeting new people, trying to speak different languages and experiencing different cultures. He was gregarious, kind and generous and wherever he went, he made close friends.

From Malta, he was posted to Sennelager in Germany and from there to Wisbech near Cambridge. After three years at the Army Apprentice College in Chepstow, he went on his final posting to AFCENT (Allied Forces Central Europe) in Holland, where he made new friends of all the nationalities in NATO and was promoted to

Lieutenant Colonel.

This posting saw him through to retirement, something he was dreading, as he loved his life in the Army. The thought of becoming a civilian worried Pat, but aged 55 years, he was snapped up by The Guide Dogs for the Blind Association, as Manager of Installations. He worked in Windsor, travelling extensively to check up on Guide Dogs centres all over the country. During a trip to Forfar in Scotland, he died in his sleep in February 1985, aged just 57.

The whole family was in shock when Pat died. He was so young and we were devastated. Pat had often said that he wouldn't live to a ripe old age, always adding that he had had a great life. The cause of death was hardening of the arteries. Like my father, Pat smoked all his life and paid the price.

Staples Five without Pat, but with his son Shaun in 1992. Back row: Joan, Shaun and Daphne; front row: Ed and Margaret.

MY BROTHER ED

When I married Ken, my parents moved to Germany with my sisters and Pat was overseas with the REs. Ed, who had also joined the REs, was working at the nearby Brompton Barracks so he stayed at 59 and lived with Ken and me. He was like a second father to our children.

When Linda was four and a half and started school, Ed, who was about 28 at the time and very handsome, used to take her there, perched on the handlebars of his bicycle. By today's standards, it was very unsafe, but she loved it. He fell in love with her teacher but was too shy to ask her out. When Linda brought her schoolbooks home at the end of the first year, Ed discovered that she had written in her diary, "I love Miss Shaw and so does my Uncle Ed." He was mortified.

When he left the Army in the 1960s, Ed continued to work in London for the Ministry of Public Works as a draughtsman, but in a civilian capacity. His section was responsible for the maintenance of historic monuments, such as Buckingham Palace and Windsor Castle. He never married and continued living at 59, joined by my mother—when my father died in Germany—and Joan, when she moved back from America.

Ed the draughtsman circa 1955.

Ed loved his nine to five job. He often complained that colleagues were promoted over him, but he never wanted to be in the limelight, or to be in charge. He caught the same train each day from Gillingham to London. His friends would save a seat for him and they played cards during the one-hour journey to the city.

Every Saturday, Sunday and public holiday, Ed would drive to our house at the nursery, where we sold tomatoes, cut flowers and plants and stay for two or three hours. He never joined us for lunch, saying he had eaten a late cooked breakfast. He taught our three children to play card games, including a popular three-hander called Sergeant Major. On the rare occasion that they managed to beat him, he said they were "jammy."

Ed was always a movie buff. In the early days of my marriage, when he was living with us in Gillingham, I went with him. But after we moved to Rainham and subsequently to Meresborough, I was too busy. When they were old enough, Ed took my children to the cinema. They went to see all the films starring Jerry Lewis, Norman Wisdom, Hayley Mills and Cliff Richard. Ed loved a good Western and often went on his own to see John Wayne or Clint Eastwood. And he never missed a James Bond movie. When VHS home video players took off in the 1980s, Ed was in his element. It's probably just as well he didn't live to see streaming because he would have been an incurable binger!

Ed wasn't very practical and his efforts to help often turned into disaster. On one occasion, Ken had put our car up on a ramp and was carefully scraping rust off the bottom of the fuel tank. When he went to serve a customer, Ed picked up a screwdriver and decided to help. Unfortunately, in his enthusiasm, he put the screwdriver right through the tank. Ken was a patient man, but Ed often pushed him to his limits. He loved to give Ken's customers horticultural advice, although he hadn't a clue what he was talking about. If it was possible to trip over something or knock something over, Ed managed to do so. He was our very own Mr Bean—a popular British comic character created by Rowan Atkinson in the 1990s.

Ed was a gentle man, more at ease with children than with adults. At family gatherings, he sat with the children and never drank alcohol. Sensitive and somewhat introverted, today you would probably say that he was on the spectrum. While he enjoyed good health, Ed was plagued by chronic psoriasis, especially in hot weather. Stress made it worse.

He had 11 nieces and nephews: five in England (my children and Pat's) and Daphne's six in America. He loved taking them to London or Canterbury for the day. He knew both places like the back of his hand. Ed was a terrible driver, taking no notice of other drivers and careening off the road or into another lane without indicating. It's a miracle the children survived. The introduction of compulsory seatbelts in 1983 made me worry a little less.

Ed with five of the six Winner children and Hilda Mary, Scottsbluff, Nebraska 1968. From left to right: Ed, Jim, Anne, Mary, Tom, Nana Staples, Bob. Paul was born two years later.

With a bag of sweets in one pocket and a pack of cards in the other, Uncle Ed loved showing magic tricks to children and telling them tall stories. They were suitably impressed when he told them that his office was supervising renovations at Buckingham Palace and he had seen the Queen's toilet. When writing out a cheque, he always said, "I could put several zeros on there, if I wanted to."

When Ed's nieces and nephews married and had children of their own, he became their favourite uncle, too. His nieces and nephews had by this time seen through his tall stories. Now he had a new audience of small people to entertain. Every child should have an Uncle Ed.

In his 50s, Ed joined the Gillingham Male Voice Choir where he sang as a tenor. Over the years they travelled to various destinations in Europe to perform.

I suspect Ed's lack of relationships as an adult was linked to his experiences at school as a child. When he was in his early 60s, my old friend Mary Huntley came to visit us from Australia. She had settled in Melbourne and her six boys were grown up and married. Recently widowed, Mary stayed with us for a couple of weeks. When Ed called in, the spark was rekindled and there was romance in the air. Taking her life in her hands—although I don't think anyone warned her, preferring instead to cross our fingers—Mary headed off with Ed for a short holiday, with him driving.

When they returned, they sat very close to each other on the couch, starry-eyed and holding hands. There was talk of marriage, but Mary wouldn't move back to England and Ed wouldn't move to Australia. So that was the end of that. Mary went back to Australia.

Soon after he retired at the age of 65, Ed was diagnosed with tunnel vision and lost his driving licence. I told him that if he came to my house at the nursery by taxi, I would drop him home, but I wasn't going to take him both ways. He stopped coming, except on Sundays, when Joan wasn't working and could drive him over.

Apart from the choir, Ed led a lonely life during his last few years, watching videos and eating peanuts and sweets. In terms of what he liked to eat, he never grew up: bacon and eggs, sweets and chocolates, roast meats with lots of gravy, white bread and butter, ice cream, anything sweet and nothing green. All the things they couldn't get in Malta during the war.

Ed died in December 2001, at the age of 72, of a pulmonary embolism. Always very careful with money, he left more than enough to pay for all the taxis that he never ordered.

My daughter Diana dealt with the funeral directors. They asked her for some of Ed's clothes, so they could dress him for his final journey. She chose his favourite grey trousers and sky-blue jacket that his choir wore for performances.

Diana put a bag of his favourite sherbet lemons in one of the pockets. Wherever Ed was going, we knew he would need them.

I missed him terribly.

MY SISTER DAPHNE

Daphne was 13 when we left Malta. Having studied ballet with Princess Poutiatine for almost six years, she had just begun dancing *en pointe,* and was looking forward to a recital solo. Instead, she finished school in Limerick, then studied secretarial business training in Gillingham with her two sisters.

In January 1951, Daphne and Joan moved with my parents to Bad Fallingbostel in Germany. Daphne worked as a personal assistant for a British officer and Joan had a secretarial position in a nearby office.

The twins had always done everything together, so when Joan decided to go back to England to train as a nurse, Daphne went too. In the second week of training at Lambeth Hospital in London Daphne was assigned to work in an operating theatre. Her job was to assist the surgeon and anaesthetist, then clean up the theatre afterwards, ready for the next operation. When the surgeon amputated the patient's leg and handed it to Daphne, she promptly fainted. That was the end of her nursing career. She decided she wasn't cut out for it and headed back to Germany, leaving Joan to finish her training.

Back in Germany, Daphne met her future husband, First Lieutenant Francis (Frank) L Winner of the United States Army. After a whirlwind romance, they married in 1955 and moved to the United States. The first stop was Omaha, Nebraska, where Frank studied law and Daphne got work with the Columban Fathers; then to the cowboy country of Western Nebraska, where the Winners brought up six children: Anne, James, Robert, Mary, Thomas and Paul. They were married for 48 years until Frank's death in 2003.

Daphne lived out her Catholic love of those in need, visiting the sick and the poor, bringing food and clothing, running errands, alleviating loneliness and taking strangers under her wing. Every immigrant wife had a friend in Daphne, who understood the adjustment needed and loved meeting people from other countries and hearing different languages. She delivered Meals on Wheels for years and, when they returned to Omaha in retirement, Daphne and Frank were hospice volunteers.

Daphne's wedding, Fallingbostel 1955. Back row from left to right: Pat, Auntie Molly, Margaret, Frank Winner, Daphne, Joan, HIlda Mary and Sam. Front row: Ed and Linda. Sam was 55 but looks older. The war had taken its toll.

Linda aged 3 as Daphne's bridesmaid.

Music also remained a lifelong joy. Daphne sang louder and more beautifully than anyone at Mass and, until she was well into her fifties, was frequently asked to sing at weddings and funerals. When all her children were at school, she took a part-time job as activities director for a senior centre, which involved a lot of musical fun. Daphne was an enthusiastic member of the Panhandle Oratorio Society as a soprano in the 1960s and 1970s.

She died peacefully aged 87 in 2019.

MY SISTER JOAN

A few days after Ken and I married in January 1951, my parents and the twins moved to Germany. Like me, both my sisters had completed a secretarial course and they soon found jobs.

The National Health Service was founded in Britain in 1948, not long after the war ended. One of Joan's friends back in England wrote telling her that Lambeth Hospital in London was offering nursing courses. Joan, who had always wanted to be a nurse, decided to go back to London and enrol in nursing. She managed to talk Daphne into going with her. When her twin dropped out of the course after less than a month and went back to Germany, Joan was not really surprised. Daphne clearly wasn't cut out for a career in nursing.

On completion of her training, Joan became a State Registered Nurse. She continued to work at Lambeth Hospital and added to her qualifications by studying midwifery. The night shifts were exhausting, so after a couple of years she decided to try private nursing, which was well-paid with better hours. Joan was soon hired as a live-in nurse and carer for Lady Almina Carnarvon in Bristol. Lady Almina was first married to the Earl of Carnavon, whose home, Highclere Castle in Hampshire, was used in the TV series *Downton Abbey*. Lady Almina ran a hospital in the castle during the First World War and this was incorporated into the TV series. After her husband died, Lady Almina remarried and moved to the Isle of Wight. When her second husband died, she moved to Somerset and from there to Bristol, where she died in 1969, aged 93.

In September 1961, at the age of 30, Joan moved to the United States, to be near her twin. Daphne had been living in Scottsbluff, Nebraska, since her marriage some seven years earlier. Joan stayed with Daphne and worked as a doctor's receptionist. Daphne's children loved having Aunt Noan, as they called her, living with them, but Joan was keen to get back to nursing. In order to work as a nurse in the United States, she was required to upgrade her British qualifications. Joan moved to Denver and enrolled in a course to achieve this.

My father died less than two years after Joan had moved to America. At my mother's request she moved back to England. I am pretty sure she ended up regretting that decision. Mum would have been fine without her, living with Ed and not far from me and my family.

Joan lived at 59 for the rest of her life with Mum and Ed. After Mum died in 1980, she lived with Ed for the next 21 years.

In the early 1980s Joan went to Romania to work for three months as a volunteer in one of the overcrowded orphanages. Under the communist regime of Nicolae Ceausescu, abortion and contraception were forbidden. He believed that population growth would lead to economic growth. Families grew and many children ended up in orphanages because their parents couldn't afford to feed them. Conditions in orphanages declined after 1982, as a result of Ceausescu's decision to use all available money to repay foreign debt.

Joan returned to England with horror stories. The orphanage where she had been working had no heating and very little food. The smaller children spent 24 hours a day in cots. Some of them were four or five years old and unable to walk or talk. Others were between one and two years of age and couldn't even sit up. Due to malnutrition, lack of exercise and human interaction, delayed cognitive development was common.

Women who worked at the orphanage with Joan had no training and often abused the children. Due to the abuse children received from staff, older children learned to mistreat the younger ones. There weren't enough clothes available, so some children spent the day naked. Nappies were also unavailable, which meant that children were often left sitting in their own faeces and urine. They all had their heads shaved, making it difficult to tell one from another.

Joan was shocked and traumatised by the conditions. She spent her time in Romania trying, in vain, to make changes.

Back in England, she worked as a District Nurse, visiting people in their homes. She had a couple of boyfriends, but never married. She travelled a fair bit, visiting Linda and Matthew in Israel, Malaysia, Chile and Paris and Daphne in America.

Joan was kind and generous and her nieces and nephews loved her dearly. She dreamed of owning her own house and bought crockery and other household items to take there. She kept all these things, packed in boxes, on the landing, at the top of the stairs at 59. Unfortunately, the terms of my parents' will meant that while she could live at 59 with Ed, she couldn't sell it and use the money. Joan couldn't afford to buy her own house and Ed didn't want to move.

She died in 2004, just three years after Ed.

- On 15 April 1942, King George VI awarded the George Cross to the Island of Malta with the following citation: "To honour her brave people I award the George Cross to the island fortress of Malta, to bear witness to a heroism that will long be famous in history."
- On 23 April 1943 the scouts of Malta were awarded the Bronze Cross—the highest decoration for gallantry of the Boy Scouts Association of the British Commonwealth and Empire—in recognition of their courage, heroic endurance and devotion to duty in the war for freedom. The bravery of the scouts during the frequent air raids, became a byword among the Maltese population.

Medals awarded to Major H. W. Staples RE (113841) (Sam) from L to R: 1939-1945 Star; Africa Star, Defence Medal (UK); War Medal and MiD (oakleaf); Long Service and Good Conduct.

- On 6 April 1944, Sam was Mentioned in Despatches (MiD): "The King has been graciously pleased to approve that the following be Mentioned in recognition of gallant and distinguished services in Malta: Corps of Royal Engineers. Captain H. W. Staples (113841)" MiD describes a member of the armed forces whose name appears in an official report written by a superior officer and sent to the high command, in which their gallant or meritorious action in the face of the enemy is described. They are not awarded a medal for their actions but wear an oak leaf on the ribbon of the appropriate campaign medal. By the time he left the Army, Sam had been awarded five medals. You can see the oak leaf on the fourth medal from the left.

- When Sam left the Army in 1949, a letter from the War Office said, "I am commanded by the Army Council to express to you their thanks for the valuable services which you have rendered in the service of your country at a time of great national urgency."
- Margaret received an informal medal from Chiswick House for never missing a day of school during the heavy bombing.
- In 1980, Valletta was declared a UNESCO World Heritage Site in recognition of its unique history and architecture.

My first trip back to Malta was an emotional rollercoaster. As the plane landed, all the memories came flooding back. I was transported to my childhood in a flash and cried bitterly.

Since then, I have returned on several occasions, with various members of my family. Tony Cefai was always there to meet us at the airport. He married Helen on 29 April 1956, when he was 43 and she was 33. They had one daughter, Marlene, who was born in 1959. Tony retired in 1972 as a Civil Foreman, having started work with the British Army in 1926 when he was 14 years old. He died in 1981, three years after Helen.

The Second World War left Malta economically and physically devastated. In 1943, before the cessation of hostilities, a firm of consultants called Harrison and Hubbard were commissioned to prepare a reconstruction plan for Valletta and its surroundings. This included the reconstruction of bomb-damaged street blocks and slum areas, the opening-up of a broad new boulevard through Floriana, a new bus terminus at City Gate, a broad access road to Valletta, and the opening-up of new squares and arcades.

In 1947, the British government gave £30 million to help with the rebuild.

There was heavy migration from Malta after the Second World War until the early 1980s. Between 1946 and the late 1970s, over 140,000 people left Malta on the assisted passage scheme, with many of them migrating to Australia. Despite this, the population has grown since the war to over half a million.

It was fun to revisit all our old haunts and admire the work which had been carried out on the damaged buildings. Every place I visited provoked a chain of memories. Each time I went back to Malta, a bit more work had been completed, but it took several decades. Malta was granted independence in 1964 but the British maintained a presence there until 1979. When they left there was still a lot of work to be done.

Dragonara Palace became Malta's first casino in 1964. We went there one evening to try and make our fortunes. No such luck.

I felt very proud when I visited the Scout Hall my father had designed, after the old one was flattened by a bomb in 1942. And Dad's "baby," the Lascaris War Rooms, which were used by the British until independence in 1979, mostly by NATO during the Cold War. They closed down in 2005 but were acquired by the Malta Heritage Trust and Fondazzjoni Wirt Artna in 2009 and are once again open to the public. Restoration began soon after acquisition and it is now complete and a popular tourist destination.

Dora and Will (Nobby) Clarke were my parents' friends rather than mine and, sadly, after my father died, we lost touch.

The Opera House in Valletta was decimated by a direct hit on 7 April 1942. A debate ensued on whether it should be rebuilt or whether the site should be used for something else. At one point, it became a parking lot. An open-air theatre was officially opened on the site in 2013.[46]

The Is-Suq tal-Belt food market in Valletta, built in the 19th century, also suffered heavy damage during the war. In 2018, it was fully renovated and modernised to become a state-of-the-art culinary destination.

Australia House, where we saw all the ENSA shows, has fallen into disrepair and is no longer used. There is talk of a restoration plan.

I went back to Chiswick House with Daphne in 2003. It has grown tremendously and is no longer located in Windsor Terrace. The old house was demolished in the 1990s for a high-rise development. After a tour of the school, we gave a talk to the pupils about our school days more than half a century ago, in the middle of a war. They asked lots of questions. I regret not having kept in touch with Miss Foss who apparently returned to England after the war.

Emvin Cremona became one of Malta's best-known artists. The volume of religious work he produced was quite incredible. He was asked to finish the ceiling of the church of St Joseph in Msida, after the artist Inglott suddenly died, because they had similar styles. He then went on to paint the ceilings of the Ghaxaq, Floriana and Hamrun parish churches. Various works, too numerous to mention, are located in other churches in Malta. Emvin designed all the Maltese postage stamps from 1957 to 1970: 62 sets of stamps comprising more than 170 original and first-day cover designs.[47]

He married Lilian in 1948 and they had four children. His son Marco followed in his footsteps and became an artist, painting in oils and watercolours, as well as producing ceramics and sculptures. Emvin died in 1987, aged 68. The portrait he painted of me the year I turned 15 is a treasured family possession. It will be handed down the female line, to my eldest daughter, then her daughter, and so on. My daughter Linda visited Marco in 2017 at his Galleria Cremona in Rabat.

Marco Montebello was also very successful and went on to become a prolific and well-known sculptor. The statue of St Theresa with my hands is still in the Attard parish church. When I go to Malta, I always call in to say hello to her.

I have kept in touch with Joyce Palmer and Vivienne Wycherley. We live in different parts of England, so we don't see each other very often, but we always write to each other at Christmas.

When I went back to Malta in the early 1980s, I looked up Christina Ratcliffe, who was still living in her flat in Floriana. She invited Ken and me to call in one evening for a drink. She told us that she had been awarded a British Empire Medal for her war efforts. When we talked about Warby, her eyes glistened, as she fought back tears.

After the war, she discovered that Warby was married to a woman called Eileen Mitchell, known as Betty. When they married, he was 21 and she was 27, a divorcee with a nine-year-old daughter and they had only known each other a few weeks. Not only had Warby not told Christina that he was already married, but he hadn't told his parents or the RAF, either. After he disappeared, Mrs Warburton appeared and said that she was his widow and beneficiary to his will. She said that they were separated and had never lived together, but divorce papers had never been served.

To Christina, Warby would always be that cheeky 26-year-old daredevil she had last seen in 1944. She said that she hadn't given up hope that he would turn up one day. She waited for him in Malta until her death in 1988, aged 74.

In 2002, some 14 years later, Warby's remains and those of his aircraft were found in a small village in Bavaria, west of Munich.[48]

Every time I went back to Malta, I tried to find Carrie, who had been like a sister to me when I was growing up. Unfortunately, her surname, Galea, is one of the most common surnames on the island. And, as a woman, she had probably married and taken her husband's name. I got a taxi to take me to her old house, but it had been pulled down and none of the neighbours were able to help.

Malta today is buzzing with tourists. The old city of Mdina, which I had only visited once or twice when we were living in Malta, is truly beautiful. We were too busy during the war, hiding in the shelters, to do much sightseeing. When the little tourist shops all close in Mdina at night, the shopkeepers bring everything inside and close the doors, leaving no trace of the modern world. The city at night looks much the way it did in the time of the Knights.

No wonder the film industry loves Malta. Apart from all the old buildings, the sun shines almost every day. On several occasions we passed a camera crew, busy filming a scene for some blockbuster or other. Mdina is beautifully lit and there are some excellent restaurants. The cuisine in Malta has really taken off and on my last visit we enjoyed some superb meals all over the island.

Growing up in Malta during the war was an experience I will never forget but, as you have seen, it wasn't easy. Indeed, I have often said that Hitler stole my childhood. Those six years had a huge impact on me and shaped the person I have become.

The people of the island were so welcoming that I put down roots. I hope you have enjoyed my story and that it inspires you to visit my second home. You won't be disappointed.

AFTERWORD

The first time I went to Malta was in 2017, about a year before my mother Margaret died. She asked me to have one last try to find Carrie Galea. She gave me a letter to give to her if I found her, with several family photographs that she wanted her to have. Since my mother's last visit in the late 1990s, the Internet had become a part of our lives. So I did some research before I left Australia and found a few leads to follow up when I got to Malta.

We only spent a week on the island, which is not very long when there is so much to see and do. While I was there, I felt an affinity with Malta and its people. A warm feeling of connection and belonging. I made many enquiries about Carrie, without success. Then, on the last day, one of my Maltese contacts rang to say he had found a woman about my age who was probably Carrie's daughter.

We spoke on the phone and arranged to meet in Floriana for coffee. As an attractive woman in her sixties, with silver-grey hair, walked towards me, I knew that I had found the right person. Her name was Carrie, like her mother, and we both fought back tears as we embraced. We went up to the counter to order coffee and an ice cream for the little granddaughter Carrie had brought with her. Then we sat down and chatted as if we had known each other all our lives.

Carrie's mother had passed away some 10 years earlier of cancer, leaving a husband, five children and several grandchildren. She said that her mother had often talked about her British "sister," Margaret, who had a lovely singing voice and with whom she had spent many hours in the air raid shelter, chatting, knitting, telling stories, laughing and crying. Then she told me something I didn't know: that my mother had taught Carrie to read and write. Listening to the stories my mother read to Ed had provided Carrie with a wide vocabulary and a love of books. After the war she went back to school and trained as a primary school teacher. Her teachers were amazed at how many books she had read. Carrie never let on that she had in fact listened to them being read by my mother.

Carrie told me where her mother was buried and I went there to lay a bunch of flowers on her grave, from her "sister" Margaret. I gave Carrie the letter from my mother and she promised to write to her and tell her all about her long-lost Maltese sister. My mother was thrilled when the letter arrived some weeks later, with photos of Carrie and her family.

By searching on Google, I discovered that Maison Notre Dame had been turned into office space for The Malta Foundation for the Wellbeing of Society. The foundation was set up in 2014 to encourage vulnerable young people to improve their lives through education and training. Sam, my grandfather, would have approved of such a worthy cause.

I sent an email to the Foundation saying that my mother had lived in the house during the war, and I would love to have a look around. When I arrived with my husband Matthew, they were happy to let us wander around unsupervised. It was surreal, walking through a house I had heard so much about, seeing my mother's bedroom and the window that Ed had fallen out of. Apart from office lighting and desks, very little had changed. All the dark wood panelling was still in the dining room and study and the old-fashioned kitchen was still very basic. The only mod cons seemed to be a kettle, a microwave and a fridge. I closed my eyes and tried to imagine my Uncle Pat playing the piano, but the house was devoid of the vitality that had made it home to the Staples family. I didn't manage to go into the air raid shelter but was told that it was used for storing the gardener's tools.

After losing her beloved Ken in 2010, my mother moved to Tunbridge Wells, to be closer to my sister, Diana. She died there in August 2018, a month before her 89th birthday. I flew to England from Australia and after the funeral my sister and I sorted through my mother's photographs and papers. There were so many half-written stories about Malta, it was clear that she wanted to share her experiences. As she hadn't written a book, it was clearly my job to do so. It took me five years to stop procrastinating and start writing.

I remember my grandfather, Sam Staples. Little snippets from my childhood. His loud singing, which filled our house whenever he and Nana visited from Germany. His enthusiastic, contagious zest for life. Him sitting on a stool in the kitchen at our house in Rainham while my mother applied a stinky potion to his bald head. He had read somewhere that chicken manure would make his hair grow back. It didn't work. The time he tried to tutor me in maths and lost his patience. I told him I preferred Uncle Ed.

Margaret, Tunbridge Wells, 2016 aged 87.

Margaret aged 88 with Linda, Tunbridge Wells, 2017.

But Grandpa Staples died when I was 11, so I didn't have time to get to know him well. It's only through research for this book that I have achieved this. His diary has been invaluable in writing this memoir, in understanding who he was as a young man, before he became my grandfather.

When he died, Nana came to stay with us in Rainham for a few weeks. Fifty-nine had been rented out and she had to wait for the tenants to move out. Each morning I would climb into bed with her and she would tell me stories about growing up in Ireland. I loved them, especially the one about Nelly Phelan almost chewing her fingers off. Kids love gory stories.

Many of my mother's stories were in my head; others were on a cassette and in letters. I have filled out her stories with a lot of research and a little imagination. I have had countless conversations with my sister Diana and brother David, to make sure our memories tallied.

It's been fun chasing small shards of knowledge to track down some of the characters in this story with whom we had lost touch. Surprises cropped up often. You wouldn't think there were two Major Nobby Clarkes in Malta during the war, both with a wife called Dora, but there were.

I had no idea what Dora was short for and I didn't know Major Clarke's first name, only his nickname, Nobby. I spent a lot of time trying to track down the descendants of the wrong Major Nobby Clarke with a wife called Dora. She was British and my mother had always said that Mrs Clarke was "Maltese, married to a British officer." It seemed a strange mistake to make.

Clarke or Clark is a very common surname and, in England at that time, almost all male Clarkes were nicknamed Nobby, especially in the military. Eventually I tracked down a descendant of the right couple and am now in touch with Dave Clarke. It's nice to think that his grandmother Dora and mine, Hilda Mary, were best friends and helped each other during those tough times in Malta.

From Dave I learnt that his grandparents Dora and Will—his family never called him Nobby—went back to England in 1946, after the war. They settled in Golders Green in London, not far from where their daughter Babs lived with her family. By this time Will was over sixty, had left the REs and decided to retire. Will died in 1971 at the age of 84 and Dora died a decade later in 1981, at the age of 89.

The Salina Salt Pans fell into disrepair after the Clarkes left Malta and were abandoned altogether in the 1980s. In 2011, a multi-million-dollar project for the regeneration of the area was approved by the Maltese planning authority. The walls surrounding the salt pans were rebuilt, the pans cleaned and the commercial production of salt resumed. The surrounding marshland was also cleaned, bird-watching posts installed, and a visitor's centre built.[49]

James Holland's book *Fortress Malta: An Island Under Siege* provided invaluable background reading. I also have the little handbook which was given to my grandfather Sam and all military personnel when they were posted to Malta in the 1930s. It doesn't have the date of publication, but there's a photo of Governor Charles Bonham-Carter at the beginning. He was Governor from 1936-1940 and Sam arrived in January 1939, so it was probably printed in about 1937 or 1938.

My mother always said that Miss Foss was called Joan Rose Foss. After some research I discovered that her first name was Juliet not Joan. She was one of 13 children and her youngest sibling, some 30 years her junior, was Hubert James Foss, an English pianist and composer and the first Musical Editor for Oxford University Press. I discovered that she had sailed back to England in July 1947 and died at the Bernard Sunley Care Home in Woking in 1974 at the age of 94.

My two uncles Pat and Ed were both in the Boy Scouts of Malta, so I contacted them to see if they had any further information. Reuben Lanfranco, Mario Ellul and Edward Carola have all been very helpful. Not only were they able to send details of my grandfather's involvement in rebuilding the Scout's HQ after it was gutted by bombs, but they sent me photos.

Marlene Bell, Tony Cefai's daughter, has also been very helpful, as has Bernie Mizzi, the current principal of Chiswick House School, who was able to describe the interior of the house on Windsor Terrace, where the school was housed when my mother attended. It was demolished some time ago to make way for a high-rise building.

As I write, it's been more than five years since my mother Margaret left us. I miss her voice, her sense of humour and her love. I can't listen to a recording of "O Mio Bambino Caro" by Puccini, or "O Danny Boy," without tears pricking my eyes. She sang them both so beautifully.

Apart from a beautiful singing voice, my mother had a lovely speaking voice. I am glad that I got her to make some recordings, singing the songs we all loved and reading some stories, so that my children and their children can enjoy them.

When I told my mother I was going to marry an Australian she said, "I'll never see you again." I told her not to be so dramatic, but we did spend many years living a very long way from each other. In the early days of my marriage, we wrote literally hundreds of blue airmail letters to each other, in a time before emails and Skype. I still have them in a box somewhere.

Thank goodness for today's much-improved communications. I miss our daily video calls when my mother would invariably greet me in French, enquiring after my health: "Bonjour ma petite, comment allez-vous?" Madame Fenouil would have been proud.

I like to think that if she were here with us today Margaret would be pleased that her story has been told.

ACKNOWLEDGEMENTS

Writing a book is a huge undertaking and you can't do it alone.

I would like to thank my editor Noah Charney for his excellent work on my draft and Urška Charney for the layout and the maps.

Thanks also go to Amanda Hollingsworth for recording and editing the audio version and to Bryony Hill, Michael Brissenden and Remar Sutton for their positive critiques.

I am grateful to Sam Staples' half cousin Bill Kennington who lovingly typed out Sam's hand-written diary some years ago.

Dave Clarke, grandson of Dora, was able to fill in the gaps in Dora's life and send me some photos.

The Boy Scouts of Malta, especially Mario Ellul, have been very helpful, providing information and photographs from their archives. Bernie Mizzi, Principal of Chiswick House, was able to describe the villa on Windsor Terrace, now demolished, which housed the school before it moved to new premises. Tony Cefai's daughter, Marlene Bell, supplied information about her father and some photos.

I would also like to thank my husband Matthew Peek, sons James and David Peek, daughter Catherine Peek and friends Marilyn Warner, Julia Roberts, Claudia Botti and Michelle Clark. Their assistance with reading and rereading the stories and making suggestions and comments has been invaluable.

In colourising the original photograph and designing the front and back covers, as well as editing all the other photographs in the book, James Peek has made a big contribution, with great patience.

This has been a family effort.

ENDNOTES

1   Staples, Herbert William 1900-1963, personal diary, unpublished. Please note that all personal diary quotes come from this same source and will therefore not be cited individually.
2   Ibid.
3   Ibid.
4   Johnson, Nicholas, *Tobacco in the Trenches*, https://www.pointshistory.com/post/world-war-i-part-5-tobacco-in-the-trenches
5   Staples, Herbert William 1900-1963
6   https://www.rootsireland.ie/limerick-genealogy/limerick-history
7   https://www.theirishstory.com/2013/05/16/ireland-and-the-great-flu-epidemic-of-1918/
8   Staples, Herbert William 1900-1963
9   http://ssmaritime.com/PO-Narkunda-1920.htm
10 https://famoushotels.org/news/sarkies-1st-asian-hotel-chain
11 Gatt Rutter, Joseph, *Illustrated Guide to Malta and Gozo* (University Press Oxford, 9th edition), Introduction.
12 https://www.rbth.com/history/334877-paul-russia-maltese-knights-order
13 Gatt Rutter, Joseph, p. 55
14 Ibid., p.44
15 https://www.naafi.co.uk/history
16 https://poutiatineandtheartofballet.wordpress.com/princess-natalie-poutiatine/
17 Malta at War vol 1, *Volunteers for Home Defence*, issue 9, p.243
18 *The Times of Malta*, 10 June 2016
19 Macintyre, Ben, *SAS Rogue Heroes* (Penguin 2017), p. 93
20 https://maltagc70.wordpress.com/2020/10/01/1-october-1940-malta-under-blackout
21 Staples, Herbert William 1900-1963
22 Gatt Rutter, Joseph, pp 25-26
23 Staples, Herbert William 1900-1963
24 Dingli, Pauline, *Salt Pans in Malta* (SKS 2019), p. 157
25 Guillaumier, John, *The Times of Malta*, 12 February 2018
26 https://vassallohistory.wordpress.com/street-vendors/a-malta-dairy-history/
27 De Domenico, *An Island Beleaguered*, Gov Muscat, 1946
28 Holland, James, *Fortress Malta: An Island Under Siege* (Phoenix 2003), pp. 86-100
29 http://www.arthurlloyd.co.uk/DruryLane/ENSA/ENSA.htm

30 Mason Sgt John, *Images of War, The Real Story of World War II*, The Imperial War Museum, part 13, p. 351

31 Archive of the Scout Association of Malta, Logbook of the Association, Vol. II

32 Ibid.

33 Staples, Herbert William 1900-1963

34 Holland, James, p. 263

35 Bonello, Michael & Caruana, Richard J, *Malta George Cross*, p.16; Deiulis, Nick, *Malta: World War II's most intriguing "What if?"* October 2021

36 Bradford, Ernie, *Siege: Malta 1940-1943* (Hamish Hamilton 1985), p. 97

37 Churchill, Winston, *The Second World War, Vol IV, The Hinge of Fate* (Cassell 1951), pp. 268-269

38 Holland, James, p. 299

39 Hastings, Max, *Operation Pedestal: The Fleet That Battled to Malta, 1942* (Collins 2021)

40 *Images of War, The Real Story of World War II*, The Imperial War Museum, part 13, p.348

41 National Archives of Malta

42 Holland, James, p. 339

43 Independent.com.au, *The World War II Siege of Malta in Numbers*, 31 May 2020

44 Holland, James, pp. 433-434

45 Staples, Herbert William 1900-1963

46 *The Times of Malta*, 25 April 2022

47 *The Times of Malta*, 27 May 2019

48 *The Oxford Mail*, 30 November 2002

49 *The Times of Malta*, 19 February 2011

Use the QR code or the link to see all the photographs from the book and to listen to Margaret Staples singing "Oh Danny Boy" in 1946.

https://woodlandspublishing.au/malta-a-childhood-under-siege/

www.ingramcontent.com/pod-product-compliance
Ingram Content Group UK Ltd.
Pitfield, Milton Keynes, MK11 3LW, UK
UKHW031326150125
4121UKWH00022B/159